God's Men of Color

Books by Albert S. Foley, S.J.

GOD'S MEN OF COLOR

THE COLORED CATHOLIC PRIESTS
OF THE UNITED STATES 1854-1954

With a Foreword by His Excellency Richard J. Cushing

ARCHBISHOP OF BOSTON

By ALBERT S. FOLEY, S.J., Ph.D.

SPRING HILL COLLEGE

FARRAR, STRAUS & CO. · NEW YORK

Imprimi Potest:
  DANIEL H. CONWAY, S.J.
  Praep. Prov. Missour.
  Dec. 15, 1953

Nihil Obstat:
  RT. REV. THOMAS J. RILEY, Ph.D.
  Censor Librorum

Imprimatur:
  ✠ MOST REV. RICHARD J. CUSHING, D.D.
  Archbishop of Boston
  November 3, 1954

© Copyright 1955 by Albert S. Foley
All rights reserved, including the
right to reproduce this book in
any form.

Library of Congress catalog card number: 55-6683

First printing, 1955

Manufactured in the United States of America
American Book–Stratford Press, Inc., New York

Foreword

To devise means of recruiting the native clergy has always been an essential element in the missionary program of the Catholic Church. No group of human beings, whether they be distinguished by race or by nationality, can ever become firmly integrated into the body of the faithful unless they raise up their own priests to minister to their spiritual needs, and their own religious brothers and sisters to carry on the works of Catholic action. Missionaries who establish the Church in virgin territory serve only a passing need. If they are truly zealous they will look for vocations not in the land which they have left behind them but among the souls to whom they bring the blessings of Christ's Redemption.

Father Foley's book presents a somewhat surprising record of the development of vocations among the colored people of the United States. Let us admit that, in numbers, God's Men of Color have not been in proportion to the millions of their race who have claimed the ministrations of the Church. More important to note, however, is the fact that for the past one hundred years they have actually been represented in both the religious and the diocesan clergy of the Catholic Church in the United States, and that in the course of years their number has slowly but steadily increased. This is the reason why we can hope for the eventual conversion to the Church of the Negro population of the great nation which has labored so mightily and so effectively to restore the Negro to his rightful position of human dignity.

Some one once asked me what is the policy of the Catholic Church in relation to the admission of colored students to our ecclesiastical seminaries. My answer was brief and simple: there is no need to ask the question. Let colored students apply, as do any others. If they measure up to our standards, they will be accepted. If they are rejected, it will be for the same reasons that any others are rejected. As I reflect upon this incident in the light of Father Foley's book, I find

v

reason to hope that in the not too distant future there will be nothing unusual about the presence of colored students in our seminaries and in the novitiates of our congregations of religious men and women. There is no reason why young colored people should consider themselves excluded from the priesthood and the religious life. Indeed there is every reason why they should aspire to be priests and religious and why all the resources of the Catholic Church should concentrate on counteracting the prejudice which has discriminated against colored people in the past. I know that I echo the sentiments of every one in authority in the Catholic Church when I say that our seminaries and our ecclesiastical houses of study are open to every one who can serve the interests of the Church, and that considerations of color carry no weight in determining the fitness of those whom God has blessed with the beginnings of a religious vocation.

Perhaps the best thing I could say about Father Foley's book is that I hope that no similar book will ever be written again. "God's Men of Color" represents the account of a struggle against obstacles that never should have arisen. Each chapter of this book relates the achievement by heroic souls of a goal that should have been possible without the disappointments and heartaches which they have unfortunately experienced. "God's Men of Color" will deservedly attract a wide circle of readers, and I am sure that every one who looks through its pages will thank God, as I do, that the Church has been blessed by the priestly ministry of those who are here grouped together by reason of the accidental circumstances of their racial origin. I am certain, however, that the ideals of the priesthood contemplate no division along the lines of color among those who share in its dignity and its supernatural privileges. The priesthood was instituted by Christ our Lord for all men. Individual priests must represent all groups of men; they must not be selected according to arbitrary standards imposed by human prejudice and preference. It is not for us to question why God has decreed differences of color among those whom He has called to membership in His Church. It is our sacred responsibility to welcome into the Church every one who is brought to its doors by the light of faith, and to recognize as candidates for the priesthood all whom God's grace will endow with its human prerequisites.

These, I know, are Father Foley's thoughts as he presents this inspiring book as a contribution to the religious history of the past one hundred years. During all my years as a priest and a bishop the cause of the missions has been closest to my heart. I thank God that I can look into the future to the time when there will be no problem of color in the Catholic Church in the United States. One hundred years from now some one will perhaps write a book not about God's Men of Color, but about God's Men as a truly Catholic Church has called them to the priesthood from every segment of human society. Only then will our missionary endeavors among the colored people of the United States have achieved definite success. Only then can we be certain that the group to which God's Men of Color belong will never again be excluded from the Mystical Body of Christ by human selfishness and intolerance.

✠ Richard J. Cushing,
Archbishop of Boston

Acknowledgment

A word of acknowledgment is certainly and gratefully due to those whose generous co-operation has made possible the compiling of this volume of life sketches of colored American Catholic priests.

To the living priests who co-operated in this undertaking I herewith express my appreciation. Though most of them were reluctant to have any publicity for themselves and their work, they yielded to my cajolings when it was pointed out to them that the story of their careers would help to stimulate vocations, to dispel misunderstandings, and to encourage more church authorities to accept them as integral parts of the Catholic system in America.

For access to archival data on the deceased colored priests, I am grateful to Very Reverend Father William C. Bauer, S.V.D., provincial of the Southern Province of the Society of the Divine Word, to Very Reverend Father Francis H. McGlynn, C.S. Sp., provincial of the Holy Ghost Fathers, and to Very Reverend Father Thomas J. McNamara, S.S.J., Superior General of the Josephite Fathers. Very Reverend Peter Harrington, S.M.A., provincial of the Society of the African Missions, also aided by making available data concerning their efforts at developing the colored priesthood through their house of studies in Tenafly, New Jersey.

I am also indebted to others who started out on similar projects or who have written about individual colored priests. Among these I would like to cite especially Sister Mary Ellen O'Hanlon, O.P., Ph.D., formerly of Rosary College and now of St. Clara's Convent, Sinsinawa, Wisconsin. She had started independently on a somewhat allied plan for a study of Negro priests when we became aware of our parallel labors. She graciously bowed out of the field but has assisted with research, encouragement, and proofreading.

A special word of appreciation is due to Father Leo C. Brown, S.J., director of the Institute of Social Order, St. Louis University. It was while on duty under Father Brown as a staff member of the Institute of Social Order that the present writer was given the encouragement and assistance to research, assemble and write the centenary story of the colored priesthood in the United States.

A final note of thanks goes to Austin Park, S.J., of Spring Hill College, for his valuable aid in wrestling with the meticulosities of the index.

Spring Hill, Alabama
December 1954

Table of Contents

God's Men of Color

CHAPTER I

Pioneer Priest and Prelate

BISHOP JAMES AUGUSTINE HEALY, D.D.

1830-1900

In a pioneer's loghouse on a Georgia plantation, seven miles up the Ocmulgee River from Macon, was born on April 6, 1830, of an Irish father and a mulatto mother, James Augustine Healy, destined to be the first colored priest of the United States, and the first to hold the office of bishop in the country.[1]

His father, Michael Morris Healy, had come to Jones County in 1818, in quest of land and wealth. In the land lotteries of 1823 he had won almost 1,300 acres. He had built up in subsequent years a thriving plantation on the east bank of the Ocmulgee River, at the point where Jones, Monroe, and Bibb counties converge.

In 1829 he had taken to himself, most probably as his common-law wife, a sixteen-year-old slave girl—bright, intelligent, industrious Mary Elisa, purchased in all likelihood from rich Sam Griswold of Clinton who owned her sister Nancy.

His "trusty woman Elisa," as he calls her in his last will, bore ten children for Michael Healy. He loved her devotedly. But by the iron statutes of Georgia, she could not be emancipated save through a special act of the legislature. By the same laws, all her children were born absolute and perpetual slaves. Yet three of these children, born in serf-dom, were to be raised to the dignity of the priesthood—a remarkable achievement for any single family, but especially for a colored one of those days of slavery.

---

[1] A full biography of Bishop Healy has been published under the title, *Bishop Healy: Beloved Outcaste* (Farrar, Straus and Young, New York, 1954), by Albert S. Foley, S.J.

Michael Healy was justly proud of his children, the first three of whom were boys. To circumvent the harsh oppressive law code on slaves in Georgia, he took James up North in 1837 to place him in a Quaker school in Flushing, Long Island. During the next few years, his two other brothers, Hugh and Patrick, were also sent up to join him. His sister Martha enrolled in the Quaker's school for girls in Flushing also. In the early 1840's, James pursued his further studies in the Franklin Park Quaker school of Burlington, New Jersey.

In 1844 a chance meeting between Michael Healy and Bishop John Fitzpatrick of Boston changed the course of James's life. On a boat plying up the Atlantic coast, the old pioneer encountered the young vigorous bishop. Finding him sympathetic, he unfolded to the prelate his strange story. The result was that the bishop persuaded Michael Healy to send his four boys to the newly founded Holy Cross College in Worcester, Massachusetts, and his oldest daughter, Martha, to the Notre Dame Sisters' school in Boston. The bishop personally arranged for Martha to stay at his own sister's home.

At Holy Cross, James and his brothers soon became Catholics. They were instructed in the faith by the Jesuit missionaries who conducted the college. Together with the sons of the recent famous convert, Orestes Brownson, they were baptized on November 14, 1844. In the deeply religious atmosphere of the college, James grew to love the faith and the Church that were his as the birthright of a part-Irish lad. For five years James outdistanced even the brilliant Brownson boys in college work that deepened and broadened his mind. His still extant college writings, diaries, speeches, poems, and essays show too how these years sowed within his soul the desire to dedicate his life to God in the priesthood.

James Healy graduated with first honors in the first class to complete the course at Holy Cross in 1849. Soon afterwards he applied for admission to the Sulpician Seminary in Montreal. In September, 1849, he journeyed thither to pursue his studies for the priesthood.

Before the year was out, the death of his parents in Georgia (his mother in May, his father in August, 1850) posed a serious threat to his vocation. His next oldest brother, Hugh, assumed responsibility for the younger children. A New York businessman, John Manning, who had been named trustee and executor of the estate by Michael Healy, agreed to manage the financial affairs of the family.

Difficulties also arose from other quarters, threatening his chances for the priesthood. The time for his reception of minor orders approached in 1850. James was excluded from the ordination class because he could not produce the necessary documents to prove his parents' marriage and his freedom from the impediment of illegitimacy. On appeal to Bishop Fitzpatrick, a dispensation from the impediment was subsequently granted. James received minor orders the following year.

Prompted by the ambition to become a seminary or college professor, James decided, after receiving the subdiaconate on June 5, 1852, to transfer to the more famous Sulpician Seminary in Paris. As a student in the famed French institution, James continued to make a brilliant record. By 1854 he was ready for ordination to the priesthood. This he received in the Cathedral of Notre Dame on the island in the Seine, June 10, 1854, Archbishop Sibour officiating at the ceremony.

Father Healy planned a few more years of sacred studies in Europe before returning to the States. A family crisis brought on by the sudden death of his brother Hugh obliged him to cut short his studies and return to Boston soon after his ordination.

There he was incardinated into the diocese by Bishop Fitzpatrick who all along had regarded James as his special protégé. Meanwhile, two of his other brothers, Patrick and Sherwood, had also begun their studies for the priesthood, Patrick as a Jesuit in Frederick, Maryland, and Sherwood in the footsteps of James, first at Montreal and then in Paris.

Back in Boston, Father James Healy's first assignment made him assistant to Father George Haskins at the House of the Angel Guardian, a home for orphan boys, and in the North End Church of St. John on Moon Street nearby.

Father Healy courageously threw himself into the turbulent apostolate of the cholera-ridden slums. He endeared himself to the Irish immigrants in their tenement warrens by his administration of the Sacraments to the victims of the cholera epidemics that were then decimating the slum population of Boston, along with the other killers of the poor—typhoid, pneumonia, and tuberculosis.

It was this brave apostolate in the face of dangerous contagion and death that dispersed the opposition which Father James had feared. Even up to the time of his ordination, he had not known whether he would be able to function effectively as a priest in Boston. He learned that the story of his Georgia background had become widely known along the church grapevines in Boston. For a while he had thought of "taking refuge" in a religious order and burying his talents as a seminary professor. He even wrote of himself as a "poor outcast who was afraid to show his face in Boston."

His first months of ministry dispelled all his fears. Under the strong and determined patronage of Bishop Fitzpatrick, Father Healy boldly launched his career as a priest of God. Men accepted him as such when they came under the spell of his personal holiness. They respected him for his dauntless zeal. They were stirred by his outflowing sacred eloquence. They came to recognize him as a true priest all the way to his sacred finger clasp. He had come unto his own, and his own received him well.

Father Healy's proven competence and his ready acceptance by the parishioners paved the way for his first promotion before the year was out. Bishop Fitzpatrick transferred him to the Cathedral staff, appointed him assistant in the church, and designated him as his personal secretary. Relying upon his accurate knowledge of canon law and church procedure, he authorized Father James to undertake the establishment of the first chancery office in the diocese. In June, 1855, the bishop officially appointed him chancellor and deputized him to handle most of the routine business of the diocese, the bishop's account books, his official correspondence with other bishops, with the sixty-one priests of the diocese, with the many seminarians in American and foreign seminaries, and with the religious orders of men and women working in the diocese.

It was a sizable task for a young priest. Father James endeared himself to Bishop John by thus relieving him of the major part of the maddening meticulosities of his office. The two ecclesiastics became fast friends and constant companions. Bishop John pressed Father

James into the limelight. He chose him as his favorite preacher in the Cathedral, his master of ceremonies for all of the big occasions there and throughout the diocese, and his companion on his vacations up and down the coast.

Even more of the administrative burdens fell to Father Healy's lot when doctors ordered Bishop John to give up all labor and retire for a year's rest in 1857. Father John Williams was appointed nominal vicar-general, but practically all of the diocese's official business was transacted by the bishop's secretary and chancellor.

Father James was fully equal to the task. Still in his vigorous twenties, the young priest had a facile pen, a vigorous and incisive mind, and a dignity of bearing somewhat out of proportion to his rather diminutive stature. His steady eyes, strong cleft chin, and broad brow commanded respect, even of those tempted to remark on the swarthiness of his coloring or the bushiness of his massive head of hair.

By 1860, when his brother, Father Sherwood Healy, joined him in Boston, Father James Healy was acknowledged as one of the foremost Catholic clergymen of the city and diocese. In 1862 Bishop Fitzpatrick appointed him rector of the Cathedral in addition to his other work. He remained in this post (save for a half-year vacation in Europe to restore his health) until the death of Bishop Fitzpatrick in 1866.

Under Bishop Williams, successor of Fitzpatrick, Father James Healy was designated as pastor of the Church of St. James on Albany Street in the South End, the largest parish in Boston. His achievements in that position added to his renown. For nine years he guided the destinies of the large congregation with zeal and competence. He built the large basilica-type church that stands today on Harrison Street, a monument to his resourcefulness and impeccable taste. He ruled the Irish congregation by the persuasiveness of his eloquence and the sincerity of his holiness.

In the wider arena of civic life, Father Healy became the bishop's deputy for the social apostolate. He played a decisive role in the development of the Home for Destitute Catholic Children, an institution that still harbors the homeless child. He took a personal interest in the establishment of the House of the Good Shepherd, perceiving the need for rehabilitating girls who were victims of the disorganized life of the slums. He was also active in promoting and financing the St. Ann's Foundling Home, which grew out of the children's ward of Carney Hospital when that occupied the old Howe Mansion in South Boston.

Active also in the organization of the first Catholic Union of Boston, Father Healy worked closely in conjunction with the leaders of that militant group to secure redress for the disfranchised immigrants who were victimized by the slanted laws of the Commonwealth. Boys ensnared by the law for petty delinquencies, poor folks sent to the state institutions on Boston Harbor's Long Island and elsewhere, orphans assigned by the court to non-Catholic families, even to farmers far out in the western states, and sick persons immured behind hospital walls that excluded priests and church ministrations, were all objects of Father Healy's solicitude. He annually appeared before the boards of directors of the public institutions, pleading that the Church be allowed to minister to these distressed souls. His persistence finally won out when, in 1875, the first breaches were made in the Puritan strongholds and religious services were allowed in the public institutions.

Father Healy achieved fame as a feature orator for the big occasions in church life in Boston. He spoke at dedications and special assemblies, such as that of the first great Catholic Festival in the Boston Music Hall in 1874. There he held an audience of three thousand spellbound by his graphic description of the development of Catholicism in New England.

His eloquence was put to good use also in nullifying the efforts of non-Catholic partisans to levy a ruinous series of taxes on Catholic churches and institutions in 1874. Appearing before the special committee that held public hearings in the State House, Father Healy championed the immunity of the Church from these proposed taxes with telling logic and persuasive appeals. He vindicated the right of the Church to be considered a public benefactor by reason of the social welfare works which it undertook, thus saving the state hundreds of thousand of dollars each year. He won a deferment of the spiteful legislation, and it ultimately died a natural death.

In 1874, when the bishoprics of both Portland and Hartford became vacant at the same time, Father Healy's name was proposed publicly as a likely candidate for one or other of them. In February, 1875, Rome announced that he had been selected to succeed Bishop Bacon of Portland. Father Healy accepted the honor, moved to the "palace" in Portland the next month, and was consecrated as bishop of the see on June 2, 1875, in the new Cathedral in that city, the first Catholic bishop to be so elevated to the episcopacy in the state of Maine.

The achievements and personality of Bishop Healy are still vividly remembered in the church lore of Portland. For twenty-five years he capably guided the destinies of the sprawling diocese. He found only ten permanent church buildings in Maine when he arrived, the other two dozen parishes having but made-over Protestant churches, old halls, or temporary structures. A similar condition prevailed in New Hampshire, where there were only twenty-one parishes and eleven missions. Under Bishop Healy's guidance, the diocese grew so rapidly that it had to be divided in 1885, the see of Manchester, embracing all of New Hampshire, being cut off with thirty-seven parishes and mission stations and about 45,000 Catholics.

The church in Maine itself prospered to the extent of adding about sixty churches, sixty-eight mission stations, eighteen more schools, and an equal number of convents and welfare institutions, all built during Bishop Healy's term of office. The Catholic population of the state had more than doubled, numbering more than 96,000 by the end of his career.

Beyond these externals of his episcopate, Bishop Healy is still remembered as "the children's bishop." The church lore of Portland still tells how, when the winter's snow was on the ground and the gay children were sporting about Munjoy Hill on their sleds, Bishop Healy was often seen out on the promenade in his horse-drawn sleigh. His coming was the signal for still more happiness for the youngsters. At his invitation, they would hitch their sleds to the rear of his sleigh. He would then drive around the park and up and down the hills, holding the reins and clucking the horse, with a train of happy children riding the sleds behind him. For those who had no sleds, the bishop reserved the privilege of riding with him in the sleigh.

In the summers, the streets around the Cathedral were often the scene of Bishop Healy's strolls. His school children crowded about him as he walked down the street, vying with one another for the privilege of holding one of his fingers, clutching at his coattails to keep near him. He often had candy for them and a few cookies from the Cathedral kitchen.

The orphans were his special care. He was a regular visitor at their St. Elizabeth's Home on High Street. He had personally founded the home and was its main benefactor. He was often seen in the back-yard playground, keeping the lonely children company, holding the youngest in his arms, and acting as father to them all. For their enjoyment in summertime, he purchased half of Little Diamond Island in Casco Bay and built a vacation home for them. He himself dwelt in a little cottage at the edge of the property, spending many a happy summer day in the midst of these outcast children.

To the other poor, Bishop Healy was also a benign patriarch. They remember him a half-century after his death as a friendly prelate whose activity bore more resemblance to that of a busy parish priest than to that of an aloof bishop. He came to know most of his Cathedral parishioners by name. They brought to him their complaints and woes. Many of the faithful were recent Irish immigrants who worked along the docks as longshoremen, or in the small industries and shops of the port city as day laborers, toiling from seven to seven every day for nine dollars a week.

It is still in the vivid folklore of the poor in the neighborhood that Bishop Healy often paid the overdue taxes of the poor, took care of doctor bills for the sick, and hurried to the aid of widows in their distress. They still picture him as riding through their neighborhoods on his spirited horse with his saddlebags filled with provisions for the destitute poor.

Unlike his predecessor, Bishop Bacon, and his successor, Cardinal O'Connell, Bishop Healy personally administered the Sacraments to "his parishioners" in the Cathedral parish. He took his regular turn saying Mass both there and in the many mission chapels in the environs. He often hastened out to give the last Sacraments to the dying or to bring Communion to the sick.

In the context of the close spiritual relationships that Bishop Healy established between himself and the parishioners of the Cathedral, some of the most revealing stories of his career in Portland are still recounted even to the present day. The good church folk gossiped about his color and his ancestry, especially when his sister, Sister Mary Magdalen of the Congregation of Notre Dame in Montreal, came to visit him from Villa Barlow in Vermont or from Montreal.

After one of these occasions, Bishop Healy happened to be hearing confessions in the Cathedral on a Saturday afternoon, as was his custom when more pressing church business did not engage him. A young lady in her late teens entered the confessional. She was more than half finished her telling of her sins before she realized that it was the bishop to whom she was confessing. She paused. Bishop Healy tried to induce her to continue, assuring her that nothing she said ever could be repeated outside. Still she refused. "I can't tell you the rest of my sins," she said.

The bishop was all patience and kindness, but he urged her to complete her confession.

"But it's something I said against the bishop," she finally admitted, almost at the point of tears.

"Well, now, my child," he asked in a fatherly tone, "what did you say against the bishop?"

"I said that the bishop was as black as the devil!" the distraught girl blurted out, not knowing what to expect for penance.

"Oh, my child," the bishop said, "don't say the bishop is as black as the devil. You can say he's as black as coal, or as black as the ace of spades, but don't say he's as black as the *devil!*" The girl left the confessional later, chastened in the restrained fire of the bishop's charity.

Another time a young lad rattled through his sins hurriedly on a Saturday afternoon. He finished his litany of peccadillos by adding, ". . . and I called the bishop a nigger!"

The bishop drew aside the curtain and said to the thunder-struck, wide-eyed boy, "Well, son, is there anything wrong with being a Negro? Take a good look at your bishop. Is there anything wrong with being a Negro?" The boy could only gulp in chagrin and shake his head.

The people knew that he was a colored man, but they revered and loved him as a holy bishop. One of the older parishioners told me that she remembered how the parish folks would gather outside the Cathedral after Mass on Sunday and would start off their gossip sessions by remarking, "Glurry be to God, the bishop is a Negro!" But then they would go on to comment how wonderful his sermons were, how rich and melodious his voice as he sang High Mass, how cute were the "bishop's boys"—the altar boys he garbed like miniature monsignori to add to the pageantry of his pontifical Masses.

Among the Sisters who taught in the school and worked in the institutions that Bishop Healy built, he was also a legend of paternal gentleness. The registers of his five thousand letters are full of evidence that Bishop Healy was a cherished and respected friend of the many sisterhoods that were in Portland in his time.

The larger share of the record is concerned with his dealings with the Sisters of Mercy whose motherhouse he was instrumental in establishing in Portland. For them he became in a special way a trusted confidant, a good provider, a generous benefactor, and an esteemed spiritual father. Mother Warde, the pioneer foundress of the Sisters of Mercy in the United States, lived under Bishop Healy's jurisdiction in the early years of his pontificate. She and some of the other Sisters admitted that they found it difficult to accept him at first. But once they came to know his heart of gold beneath his formal exterior, they became closely attached to him. He in turn gave his best energies to the promotion of their work, the care of their spiritual lives, the fostering of vocations, and the providing for their material welfare. He customarily addressed them as "my dear daughters," and he came each Sunday when he was in Portland to give them a spiritual conference in the endearing Salesian style that he had developed during his years of deeply spiritual training in France.

As one reads through volume after volume of Bishop Healy's letters, his stature among his priests and his relations with them emerge quite clearly. One sees that he was accepted loyally by his many-score priests without regard for his color or mixed racial ancestry. They respected him as one of the outstanding churchmen of New England who had successfully directed the destinies of the larger diocese of Boston for almost a score of years before becoming Bishop of Portland. They knew his high standing with other members of the hierarchy—his close friendship with Archbishop Williams, with Bishop Harkins of Providence, and with Cardinal Gibbons, who often came to Portland as Bishop Healy's guest. They were impressed by his oratorical achievements as the main speaker for the consecration of new bishops, the dedication of new churches, and the funerals of prominent clergy and laity in Boston and elsewhere in New England.

On his part, Bishop Healy governed his diocese and his priests with gentle diplomacy. He fostered a strong and positive policy in the vital areas of Catholic education and church expansion. He deftly handled the delicate relations between the nationality groups under his care (mainly the Irish and French Canadians), and the much more delicate questions of clerical integrity and faithfulness.

For twenty-five years he competently fulfilled the office of bishop. He became a personal friend of both Pope Pius IX and Pope Leo XIII. It was an open secret that he would have been nominated for the archbishopric of Boston if he had outlived Archbishop Williams, and would most probably have been made a cardinal. As it was, the Pope appointed him to an ecclesiastical dignity just a step below that of the cardinalate. He was made an assistant at the papal throne toward the end of his episcopate.

Through it all, Bishop Healy remained an humble, prayerful, and deeply devotional churchman. He loved the pilgrimages to the sacred shrines of Europe and to Jerusalem and its holy places. He wrote glowing accounts of his pilgrimages—none so moving as that of witnessing the mystical experiences of the famous stigmatist, Louise Lateau. Everywhere he went in Europe he was respected as a Catholic prelate and received with undisguised hospitality.

His priests warned him against traveling in the South of the United States, owing to the risk of insult and indignity. Bishop Healy nevertheless traveled often to Baltimore, Washington, and Norfolk, Virginia, in which latter place he spent many months recuperating from illnesses in the Sisters of Charity Hospital. Once he journeyed by boat to New Orleans with his brother Father Patrick Healy. They stayed a fortnight as guests of the Jesuit College. Bishop Healy preached in their downtown Church of the Immaculate Conception. He was even received with honor by the incumbent Archbishop of New Orleans. But it is doubtful whether he ever ventured back to his native Georgia.

At the age of seventy, full of merit before God for his noteworthy achievements in behalf of religion, Bishop Healy died on August 5, 1900, a victim of the heart disease that had troubled him for years.

More than two hundred priests, two archbishops, seven bishops, many judges from the federal and state courts, a large number of state legislators, and more than three thousand of the laity of Portland, Boston, Manchester, and the parishes of Maine and New Hampshire attended his funeral on Thursday, August 9. He was buried, according to his express will, not in the crypt below the Cathedral, but in the Catholic cemetery in the midst of the remains of his faithful flock. There to this day his grave is marked by a tall Celtic cross erected by his people to the memory of the strong man of God who had guided their spiritual life for a quarter-century.

CHAPTER II

In His Brother's Footsteps

ALEXANDER SHERWOOD HEALY, D.D., J.C.D.

1836 – 1875

"His learning, his gentleness of disposition, the depth of his piety made him one of the priests on whom we could always rely. Many hearts will long cherish what was to us his leading characteristic—his guilelessness. With all his learning and experience, his heart was as pure as a child's." In these terms Archbishop John Joseph Williams of Boston summed up his estimate of the personality of Father Sherwood Healy, the second of his family to become a priest.

Like Father James Healy, Sherwood was raised from infancy on the Healy plantation in western Georgia, having been born there January 24, 1836. Instead of being sent to the Quaker schools, however, Sherwood was enrolled from the first at Holy Cross College when his brothers transferred there in August, 1844. With them he was baptized in November the same year.

Sherwood early manifested the same keenness of mind that distinguished his brothers. He led his class consistently at the "Cross." He too was prominent in college exhibitions, reciting poems and delivering original speeches in public while still just a youngster of thirteen and fourteen. In later life Sherwood regretted that he did not finish his college work at Worcester. Upon the departure of his brother Patrick in 1850, Sherwood also went to New York. There, through his brother Hugh, he secured a job as a clerk in a wholesale warehouse on lower Broadway.

For a lad of fifteen, business life was monotonous and distasteful. After two years of the dull clerkship, Sherwood decided to study for the priesthood like his brothers James and Patrick who had already enrolled in seminaries. Sherwood took the road to Montreal's Sulpician Seminary in September, 1852.

The decision to enter the seminary seems to have been a sudden one, though Sherwood had led an angelic and quiet life at the Cross, deeply prayerful and studious. He discovered that Montreal was much more difficult for him than Worcester. He learned French rapidly enough, but took a dislike to the accommodations, the course of studies, and the lack of that uniform kindness that had been shown him at the Cross. For a while, he was in a sea of difficulties about his vocation. James, now studying at Paris, urged him to transfer to the more famous Sulpician Seminary there. This he determined to do, or else give up his vocation.

The major difficulty at Montreal was the weakness of Sherwood's eyes and general health. After a summer spent in Boston under a doctor's care, he was able to depart for Paris, leaving New York on the first day of September, 1853. The leave-taking should have been joyous, but it was marred by tragedy. On the day he sailed, his brother Hugh took a hansom cab with him down to the wharf. He went up the gangplank with Sherwood, helped him with his luggage, returned to the wharf when the ship was about to weigh anchor, and walked over to the place where he was accustomed to rent boats for rowing exercise in the harbor. He hired a small skiff and rowed out into the middle of the river to wave farewell to Sherwood from that vantage point. But while he sat waiting, another ship, going downstream, rammed into his skiff, swamped it, knocked Hugh into the water, and washed his oars away. Hugh, a strong swimmer, managed to recover the skiff and pushed it ahead of himself back to the wharf; but he apparently swallowed some of the contaminated river water, for within a few days he was seized with typhoid, and within a few weeks he was dead.

The grief which Sherwood felt over the loss of his brother was ameliorated, to the extent that environment can ever help in such a situation, by the great attractiveness of his new surroundings. He found St. Sulpice a delightful contrast to the Montreal Seminary. He liked the garden and the fine park at Issy, where he stayed, and he plunged into the study of philosophy with an enthusiastic interest. James was able to report that he was doing wonders in it by the next year, and was again leading his class. He was sharp enough to detect the basic ontologism of the Malebranchian text and to look with suspicion on it. But he followed the great controversies of contemporary French Catholic philosphy with intelligence and mature deliberation.

After two years of theology at the Sulpician Seminary, he decided to transfer to Rome for the completion of his studies. He matriculated at the Apollonio College and there again distinguished himself by a brilliant course. In two more years he was ready for ordination, receiving the sacred anointing in Rome, December 15, 1858. For his brilliance in his theology, he was awarded the degree of Doctor of Divinity. But, envisioning a career of teaching in a seminary, he stayed on for two more years of study under the famous Jesuit theologian Father Peronne. In 1860 he was given the degree of Doctor of Canon Law.

During his time at Rome and in Europe, Sherwood made a hobby of collecting church music. By now a talented and serious musician, he went out of his way to assemble a library of masterpieces of sacred compositions: Palestrina, Capocci, Tertiani, and other Italian composers, as well as Mozart, and the French and German masters of ecclesiastical music. When he returned to the United States, he brought with him one of the outstanding libraries of church music available at the time.

Unknown to himself, his name came up for consideration as one possible choice for the rectorship of the North American College, then in process of being founded at Rome. Bishop Fitzpatrick of Boston wrote to Archbishop Hughes of New York, extolling Sherwood's qualities of soul and mind, stating that at St. Sulpice he was a "model of piety, regularity and good conduct." Yet he added:

> Still it would be useless to recommend him even were he known to the other bishops as well as to myself. His youth would be a fatal objection. There is also another objection which, though in reason less substantial, would in fact be quite as stubborn. He has African blood and it shows distinctly in his exterior. This, in a large number of American youths, might lessen the respect they ought to feel for the first superior in a house. (July 10, 1859.)

Spared disappointment by never having been aware of the opportunity, Sherwood returned to the United States and took up his residence in Boston under Bishop Fitzpatrick's authority, on September 20, 1860. His first assignment was that which his brother had filled upon his return: assistant to Father George Haskins in the House of the Angel Guardian, now in its new location in suburban Roxbury. There, Sherwood endeared himself to the boys in the institution, to the parishioners who attended Mass in the large chapel of the house, and to the various sisterhoods about town to whom he gave conferences and spiritual counsel in the confessional. Bishop Fitzpatrick singled out this assignment for him because he feared for his delicate health. As it was Sherwood did experience a good deal of difficulty readjusting to the severities of the Boston winters.

In 1863, when his brother was obliged to take a six months' leave of absence for reasons of health, Father Sherwood was deputed to fill his place as chancellor of the diocese and assistant at the Cathedral. The arduous work again told on his constitution, and he too was obliged to surrender the office and take a prolonged rest when his brother returned.

During that year and the next, negotiations were under way for the opening of the new provincial seminary at Troy, New York, where the bishops had bought the buildings of the defunct Methodist institution, Troy University. Bishop Fitzpatrick proposed Sherwood as one of the faculty for the new institution, and, upon being approved by the other bishops, Sherwood was so designated on April 24, 1864, while still an assistant at the Cathedral under his brother.

In September of the same year, Father Sherwood departed for the new office in Troy. There as vice-president, professor of moral theology, of church music, and of rites and rubrics, Sherwood ably set the seminary on its course. He was one of the few native Americans on the staff, four of the other priests being imported from Belgium to teach the courses. He was also confessor and spiritual guide of the seminarians, many of whom owed to the mild, pious, and intellectual professor their perseverance in their vocation, and their excellent training for the priesthood.

While at Troy, Father Sherwood composed a seminarians' *Manual of Plain Chant* which was used for years as the textbook in church music. He also composed original pieces, such as the Troy *Magnificat,* a solemn hymn that was sung at church services throughout New England.

The new Bishop of Boston, John J. Williams, took a special liking to Sherwood Healy. He chose him as his theologian for the Second Council of Baltimore in 1866. In 1869, when on the point of departing for the famous Vatican Council, he again selected Sherwood as his companion and theological advisor for the momentous assembly. Sherwood's health had not been good at Troy. His eyes had been giving him so much trouble that, in 1865, he had been obliged to surrender his position as professor of moral theology, and limit himself to his other specialties. He found time, however, to compose the diocesan statutes adopted by the Boston diocesan synod in 1869. It was evident by 1869 that he could not well endure the much more rigorous climate of northern New York. He therefore resigned his position there, and obtained a long leave of absence to recover his health.

Bishop Williams advised Sherwood to combine a European tour with the trip to the Vatican Council as his personal theologian. This they did together, traveling by slow stages through England, France, Germany, Switzerland, and northern Italy before reaching Rome in late November 1869.

The Vatican Council opened on December 8. Father Sherwood Healy took his place in the assembly of more than seven hundred cardinals, patriarchs, archbishops, bishops, abbots, theologians, and generals of religious orders. He followed the progress of the historic deliberations with rapt interest, his well-trained theological mind divining the significance of the dogmatic definitions made by the Council. He daily conferred with Bishop Williams on the theological and political aspects of the decrees under consideration, and counseled him in his thinking and his voting.

Three months of strenuous work and of wretched Roman winter undermined Sherwood's health. He fell ill on Friday, March 18, 1870, with pulmonary complications. By the twenty-sixth he was in such critical condition that he was given the Last Sacraments. In his diary, Bishop Williams records that there was very little hope for his recovery, but Sherwood survived. By the middle of April he was out of danger, and by April 19 was able to leave the hospital for a ride out in the spring air with Bishop Williams, who was greatly relieved at his friend's recovery, as his day-to-day diary shows.

Father Sherwood stayed on at Rome until July 3, continuing in his capacity as theologian for the Boston prelate. He then went to Paris and to some of the French spas in an effort to regain his strength. But his trip was cut short and he returned to the States with Bishop Williams when the outbreak of the Franco-Prussian War put an end to the Vatican Council.

In recognition of his services, Bishop Williams offered Sherwood the post of rector of the Cathedral in Boston soon after his return, on September 27, 1870. Services were still being held in the temporary pro-Cathedral on Washington and Castle Street, a former Unitarian church taken over in 1860. But the new Cathedral was a-building at Washington and Malden streets in the massive proportions that Bishop Fitzpatrick had dreamed of, and Patrick Keeley of New York had designed.

To Sherwood, as rector of the Cathedral, went the task of raising funds to keep pace with the costs of the gigantic enterprise. For this purpose, he conducted two mammoth Cathedral Fairs, one in 1871 and the other in 1874, both of which were hugely successful. For the first one, now that the Cathedral was roofed over, Sherwood planned and executed a series of concerts within the unfinished walls of the new edifice. He trained and conducted the Boston Choral Union for the musicales. The large crowds that attended were treated to a demonstration of his superb musical skill, as represented by the chorus's masterly rendition of sacred music.

During the weeks of the Fair, Father Sherwood published a magazine, *The Cathedral,* that carried articles by himself and his brother James, now pastor of St. James Church in the South End. The magazine ultimately became a monthly, and is still published to this day. The early editions have become collectors' items because of the valuable historical articles written by the Healy brothers.

It was during the five years of his pastorate at the Cathedral that Sherwood reached the zenith of his career in Boston, just as his brother was doing at the next-door parish of St. James. They were pastors of the two outstanding diocesan churches in Boston, vying with one another for the honors as pulpit orators, spiritual directors, promoters of charitable and apostolic enterprises, and leaders in their respective fields of special interest.

The emulation was a holy and fruitful one. It spurred Sherwood to achieve great things in the field of sacred eloquence. Like his brother, he too was in great demand as a speaker. His forceful eloquence graced many of the official occasions of the ecclesiastical year in Boston's many churches. Diary-writing Father Hilary Tucker, another assistant at the Cathedral during the time when both of the brothers were there, awarded the palm for excellence in sacred oratory to Sherwood. In the 1870's he was frequently invited to speak at church dedications and at the laying of cornerstones of churches and other religious institutions around the diocese.

The uniqueness of the Boston situation in the 1870's was not lost on the people. Here were two southern boys, each a pastor in his own right, ruling the two principal parishes of this staid northern city. They were both handsome and brilliant, but the swarthiness of their coloring and the dark bushiness of their hair revealed them as Creoles. They were known and spoken of as colored men. They were loved and respected as competent and holy priests.

Where James clearly had the advantage was in his administrative and business ability. On the bishop's council, of which they were both members, his experienced judgment was followed in financial and in the practical details of routine diocesan life. Sherwood's keen legal mind was deferred to for the latest in canon law and church procedure. He was better acquainted with Roman practice and precedent, and, as secretary of the council and author of the diocesan statutes, he guided the bishop's decisions through the intricate patterns of the Church's legislation.

Sherwood's diary manifests many contrasts to James's diaries for this and other periods of his life. Where James is almost photographically detailed in his descriptions of his experiences and travels, Sherwood's pen turns more to the philosophical, the poetic, even the mystical at times. The inscription at the beginning of his diary reads:

Thought engenders thought. Place one idea on your paper, another will follow it, and still another until you have written a page. You cannot fathom your mind. There is a well of thought which has no bottom. The more you draw from it, the more clear and fruitful it will be.

In his diary he wrote out his sermons, the Italian ones he preached in Rome as a young priest, the later ones in English. They reveal the deeply pensive mood of his mind, the clarity of his spiritual insight, and the facile and graceful style of his writing and speaking. Thus he muses upon life and death in one of his entries:

We live but to die, or rather we die to live. The things of this earth when they pass away really die, their existence is at an end, the end of their creation accomplished. They literally are no more . . . But man to whom all these things of earth converge, man with death dies not. His end cometh not. He is not of the things that were. His mode of existence only is changed. He breaks the relations he held with this world, but he does not pass away and flitter away into nothing. He passes from one sphere to another. He is like a traveller who passes by us, leaving us, is lost to us, but not lost to himself. He continues his route and encounters others . . .

In late 1874 death was not far off for Father Sherwood. He had overworked himself in planning and conducting the second of the great Cathedral Fairs in the fall of that year. He had continued his many routine duties in the parish, preaching every week and sometimes oftener, venturing out into the sub-zero cold on sick calls, and attending the bishop in his official functions both at the Cathedral and elsewhere.

People saw and admired his unflagging zeal, his fidelity to his labors, and selfless spending of his energies for their spiritual welfare. His name was whispered about as a possible candidate for the episcopacy when both the neighboring dioceses of Portland and Hartford were made vacant by the deaths of their bishops. His friends at the Cathedral were somewhat disappointed when his brother was elected as Bishop of Portland in February, 1875, and Bishop Galberry was chosen for Hartford.

They had recompense next month. Sherwood was promoted to the position of pastor of St. James Church. That was recognized as a step to a future bishopric, for the large parish was already becoming known as the "mother of bishops." He moved to his new appointment on April 5. There he took up the last details of the construction work in the still unfinished basilica. He saw that through to completion and dedication.

In May of 1875, Bishop Williams chose Sherwood to read the papal brief in the first important ceremony in the new Cathedral—the conferring of the archiepiscopal insignia of rank on the prelate, and the elevation of the Boston diocese to the rank of an archdiocese. Sherwood achieved his ambition to ascend the pulpit of the new Cathedral on Sunday, May 2. He read in his rich melodious voice the stately Latin of the Pope's decree. Then, descending from the pulpit, he directed the intricate ceremonies for the unique services. His good friend and constant patron, Cardinal McCloskey, sat upon the Cathedral throne and placed on Bishop Williams' shoulders the symbol of his higher dignity and in turn received from him his oath of fidelity to the Holy See and the Church Universal.

Next month Sherwood was in Portland for the solemn consecration of his brother as bishop. He shared the happiness of that day with James, but the recurrence of his lung trouble and his persistent coughing boded ill.

For the grand dedication of the new St. James Church on Harrison Avenue, July 25, 1875, Father Sherwood invited Bishop Healy back to give the main sermon of the day. It was an impressive gesture of brotherly affection, and a tribute to the rightful builder of the imposing new edifice. Sherwood was at the point of exhaustion in the hot weather, his reserve strength having been sapped by his many duties, including the promotion of another gigantic church fair to pay for the building costs.

On August 23 the blow fell. Sherwood had two severe lung hemorrhages. Doctors despaired of him. On September 7 he was taken to Carney Hospital to await the end. All through the month he lingered and on into October. Archbishop Williams came to visit him almost daily. Of those who hoped for his recovery, Sherwood only said, "They think that I can recover, but it is not so; only let them pray for me."

By October 20 the end seemed at hand. His brother hurried down from Portland to be with him at the last. Next morning at nine-thirty, he died peacefully and without a struggle.

His remains were brought to St. James. There he lay in state, fully vested in his pastoral robes, his chalice clasped in his anointed hands. Thousands of the faithful visited the church to pray at his side and to mourn their loss.

At the funeral on the twenty-third, the black-draped basilica was packed to the doors. Archbishop Williams celebrated the requiem Mass for the dead pastor. Four bishops and 150 of his fellow priests of the diocese and seminary were there. The Sisters to whom he had ministered also came to mourn him—Sisters of Charity from Carney Hospital, Little Sisters of the Poor, the Sisters of St. Joseph, the School Sisters of Notre Dame, the Sisters of St. Francis, and those in whose order his own sister Eliza was now living, the Congregation of Notre Dame.

After the absolution, Archbishop Williams, with tears in his eyes, addressed a few words to the congregation. He told them that they did not realize their loss, so short a time had he been with them. He spoke touchingly of Sherwood's gentleness, of the depth of his piety, of the complete trust and confidence he had in him. "He was one of the priests on whom we could always rely," he said. "Many hearts will long cherish what was to us his leading characteristic—his guilelessness. With all his learning and experience, his heart was as pure as a child's." Choking with emotion, the archbishop could utter only a few more words. There were not many dry eyes in the congregation that day.

Sherwood Healy was a saintly priest. He lived a rich spiritual life, and died a martyr to his priestly work. His memory is still perpetuated in the Cathedral he shepherded through to completion. One of the stained-glass windows is dedicated to the humble Georgia boy whose saintliness helped build the living stones of the church while the stonemasons were erecting its massive structure.

CHAPTER III

Georgetown's Second Founder

FATHER PATRICK FRANCIS HEALY, S.J., Ph.D.

1834 - 1910

On entering the main gate to the campus at Georgetown University in Washington, one is immediately confronted with the two monuments to Georgetown's two founders: the large heroic statue of Bishop John Carroll sitting benignly upon his episcopal throne; and, rising up in seven-storied majesty above him, the huge pile of the Healy Building, a monument to the foresight and leadership of Georgetown's second founder, Father Patrick Francis Healy, S.J., president of the institution from 1873 to 1882.

The contrasts between the founders could not be more striking in regard to birth and rearing. Carroll was born of aristocratic Maryland landowners, his father a prominent Maryland merchant, and his mother reputed to be Maryland's richest heiress, Eleanor Darnall. Healy was the son of a pioneer Irish planter and a mulatto slave, and was born February 27, 1834, a full century after John Carroll.

Carroll was reared in the family home at Upper Marlboro, and later at Forest Glen, Maryland, receiving his early education at home. Healy was sent at the age of seven to join his brothers in the Flushing Quaker school on Long Island, New York. He had no family life after that, while John Carroll continued during his youth to move among the prominent Maryland Catholic families with whom his own was connected.

Both boys had early enrolled in Jesuit schools, Carroll at Bohemia College on the Eastern Shore of Maryland in 1747, and Healy at Holy Cross College in 1844. While Carroll's home training gave him the ease, dignity, and polish which characterized him in his subsequent

career, Healy's equally dignified manners were acquired in the course
of his college training and in the novitiate of the Society of Jesus, which
he entered upon completing his studies at Holy Cross in 1850. Carroll's polish and suavity were further enhanced by his enrollment in St.
Omer's College in France for a five-year period of college training, and
his novitiate at Watten, Belgium. And the stamp of Jesuit training,
recognizably imprinted on both men through their perseverance in
the course of Jesuit studies, was apparent in their parallel devotion to
Catholic education, their literary style and speaking ability, their
philosophical bent of mind and temperament, and their unflagging
zeal for duty and for service to the Church.

Patrick Healy emerges as a distinct and lively personality in his
early letters to his Jesuit friends—letters which have been preserved
in the archives at Woodstock and at Holy Cross. Though he is but a
minor character in his brother's diary of 1848-49 at Holy Cross, he
begins to develop as a man with a mind of his own when he decided
to enter the Jesuit order in 1850.

As a young man, Patrick was the most handsome of the Healy
brothers, taller than the bishop-to-be, fair-complexioned, regular of
feature, with a dimpled chin and with smooth, flowing hair, worn in
the style that Civil War generals were to immortalize. He was agile
of mind and body, athletic, interested in sports, yet an eager scholar
when study and classes beckoned him.

His first assignment after his vows in 1852 was that of teacher and
prefect at St. Joseph's College in Philadelphia. From there, he capably
handled the family affairs during the illness and after the death of
his brother Hugh in 1853.

In the fall of the same year, Patrick was transferred to Holy Cross
College to teach in the resuscitated institution which had been sus-
pended for almost two years following the disastrous fire of 1852.
There were only twenty-seven students that year, and Patrick assumed
full charge of disciplinary problems as their prefect. His younger
brother Michael was among the scholars enrolled, and even with him
Patrick had his many troubles. Michael ran away from school a number of times. The reason for his flights was not far to seek. Patrick

wrote of it to Father George Fenwick at Frederick, his spiritual father from the earlier days at Holy Cross (November 23, 1853):

> Father, I will be candid with you. Placed in a college as I am, over boys who were well acquainted either by sight or hearing with me or my brothers, remarks are sometimes made (though not in my hearing) which wound my very heart. You know to what I refer. I have with me a younger brother, Michael. He is obliged to go through the same ordeal. You may judge my situation at periods. "At periods" I say, for thanks to God I have felt this affliction but once since my return hither. I trust that all this will wear away, though I feel, that whilst we live here, with those who have known us but too well, we shall always be subject to some such degrading misfortune. Providence seems to have decided thus . . .

There was not much time left for sensitive brooding in Patrick's very full schedule. He taught rhetoric, French, and mathematics the next year, and in each of the successive years, he moved up with his class, teaching higher grammar in the 1855-56 session, heading the college poetry class in 1856-57, and in his final year at the Cross, teaching again first- and second-year English as well as bookkeeping.

He definitely was of the professorial mold. He liked teaching, and many of his letters portray his interest in his scholars and their progress. His success with them was a tribute to his patience and versatility. At one period, he had a class composed of four Americans, two Canadians, one Irishman, two unsophisticated Cubans, and one *grand Canuque*. He had to call upon his knowledge of French and Spanish as well as his fine qualities of tact, diplomacy, and psychological deftness in order to cope with the situation.

In 1858, after six years, teaching boys in elementary tasks became somewhat monotonous to Patrick. He was assigned to study philosophy and theology at Georgetown. But in the middle of the first semester, he was told to pack up and go to Rome for the rest of his ecclesiastical studies. His diary picks up the tempo of his preparations:

> Great fuss and flurry to get ready in secret. So goes the world. I have told Kelly, Hagen and McDermott . . . New trunk . . . all right . . . off soon . . . all anxiety . . . plenty of bequests . . .

thousands of legacies . . . to his Holiness from children more desirous to see his sights than himself . . .

Patrick sailed from Boston on November 17, 1858, and landed in Rome on December 18, just a few days after his brother Sherwood's ordination. Four months of the Roman winter were as much as Pat could stand. He came down on Holy Thursday with a violent cough and slight hemorrhage, and at the end of the year superiors decided that he should continue his studies at Louvain.

It was in Belgium that he completed his course of philosophy and theology, interrupted by visits from Sherwood and James that always meant excursions about the continent for weeks and months at a time. Bishop Fitzpatrick, who regarded Pat as one of his protégés, also called for his services during the years when the prelate was resting and recuperating at a college in Brussels prior to his return to his diocese in August, 1864.

Next month Patrick was ordained to the priesthood by Bishop Lamont at Liége. He stayed on another year at Louvain, studying for a doctorate in philosophy. This was bestowed upon him after he passed his final examination on July 26, 1865.

The next months were spent in prayer and solitude in Laon, France, for Father Patrick's final phase of training as a Jesuit. In the summer of 1866 he returned to the United States and was assigned to teach philosophy at Georgetown University. Patrick presided over the class in ethics and metaphysics for the Jesuit seminarians then studying at Georgetown. During his first year he was allowed to pronounce his final vows as a Jesuit, February 2, 1867.

The Georgetown catalogue for the following year lists him as professor of rational philosophy, and for the term 1868-69, the additional title of prefect of studies, or dean, is given him. In 1869 he became vice-president of the university, assistant to his old friend and former teacher, Father John Early, whose precarious health obliged him to shift most of the burden of administration onto the shoulders of the younger man.

On May 22, 1873, Father Early had a sudden stroke after dinner, and died two days later. Father Healy was quickly appointed as vice-rector and assumed full charge of the institution. He was officially confirmed by Rome and inaugurated as president of the oldest Catholic university in the country on July 31, 1874.

Even before that time, Father Healy had launched the building of the dream that he wished to make Georgetown. He wanted it to be an American Louvain, housed in splendid Belgian Gothic, and maintaining the high standards of scholastic achievement that he had found in the medieval university.

His first move toward this goal was the laying of plans for the erection of a suitable building to supplement the cramped quarters of Old North, the original brick building which George Washington had visited, and Old South, facing the Potomac on the eminence above the river. Father Healy called in surveyors to make an accurate map of the extensive university campus that spread over the wooded hills for almost a mile. For a while, Father Healy contemplated the transfer of the whole college to a site across the ravine and up on the farther hill where now stands the giant medical center of the university. After consultation with architects and advisors, he determined to build a massive administration, classroom, and residential building to link Old North with Old South, and form a quadrangle with the Dahlgren Chapel on the fourth side.

These plans were submitted to Rome, and, after many delays, were finally approved in 1877. The contracts were then let and the excavations started the same year. By the end of the year the cornerstone was laid with impressive ceremonies. Another year of work saw the seven-story structure at its full height and roofed in. The central tower was completed in July, 1879, rising to a height of 209 feet. Everyone called it from the start "The Healy Building," and though Father Healy's responsibility for it was not officially recognized until after his term of office, his achievement was ultimately recorded for posterity.

The problem of raising funds for the edifice was a grave one. The project had been launched on the pledges of many prominent Catholics in Washington to contribute to the liquidation of the costs. The story goes that when the building was more than half complete, whispers circulating around the city about the dubious "background" of the handsome and hitherto well-liked president of Georgetown suddenly terminated many of the most important contacts that Father Healy had made in the capital. Doors were closed in his face. He was obliged to turn elsewhere in search of funds. His constant financial worries apparently undermined his health. Before his term of office was over, he had to take leaves of absence for long periods, one of which was spent in California, partially in soliciting funds for the new building and partially in rebuilding his shattered health.

Before that came to pass, Father Healy had justly earned his reputation as Georgetown's second founder by his accomplishments in the academic life of the institution as well. To stimulate scholarship and student extracurricular activity, Father Healy induced a number of prominent Washingtonians to establish foundations for annual awards in student competitions. Judge Richard T. Merrick was persuaded to endow the Merrick Medal for oratory and debate. Martin F. Morris donated funds for the Morris Medal in historical studies. Dr. Joseph M. Toner founded the Toner Scientific Medal for progress in natural science. Charles W. Hoffman set up the trust for the Hoffman Mathematical Medal.

These were customarily awarded at the annual commencement exercises, over which Father Healy, in his capacity as president of the university, regularly presided in the years before his health failed. He surrounded himself on the platform with the outstanding Catholic leaders in Washington, and invariably high government dignitaries were also on stage for the impressive ceremonies. For a few of his early years, General William T. Sherman was a guest of honor, despite the fact that he had brought fire and sword to Father Healy's native county in Georgia during his historic march to the sea in the Civil War.

On the platform with these prominent men, Father Healy ably held his own in poise and dignity, in academic gravity and display of oratorical ability, in his distinguished bearing and his fine presence. The Georgetown students of those days were proud of their handsome, well-groomed president, and they received their diplomas from his hands eagerly and with the traditional handshake. At the separate commencement of the Law School (usually held in downtown Washington in Ford's Theatre, the scene of Lincoln's assassination) and that of the

School of Medicine (held in the National Theatre), Father Healy also presided in the full regalia of office and conferred degrees on the new doctors and lawyers.

Among his other academic achievements are listed the modernizing of the curriculum, the Americanization of the university system, the centralizing of the university's libraries, and the organization and development of the Society of the Alumni and the Alumni Association of the various schools of the university.

It was on these alumni associations that Father Patrick depended heavily for the funds necessary to complete and pay for the giant building he had erected. He was successful in raising the needed amounts as construction work progressed, and by 1881 the first rooms in the new building were occupied by classes and the residential section by the student boarders.

The hard and exacting work, and the many worries of his presidential position, gradually undermined Father Healy's health. He had been hospitalized by a recurrent series of illnesses in 1881, and prospects for complete recovery were quite dim. His doctors advised him to resign his position as president of the university. He reluctantly submitted his relinquishment of the honor, and was retired on February 16, 1882. He left Georgetown with the satisfaction of having changed the small college into a great institution worthy of its claim as the foremost Catholic university in the nation.

In subsequent years, Father Patrick spent much time with his brother, Bishop Healy, both in Portland and as a companion on the bishop's annual travels. These the doctors ordered him to take to escape the rigors of Maine's wintry weather, a constant threat to his weakened lungs. Besides, the bishop's unpredictable vertigo required the presence of an attendant priest at his Mass each day. Father Patrick was given this assignment when he was in the bishop's entourage.

Together the brothers traveled quite extensively. They spent vacations in Bermuda, in Norfolk, in New Orleans, in San Francisco, in Canada, and elsewhere in the country. Almost every other year they traveled to Europe, their favorite vacationing spots and their places of pilgrimage alternating in their itineraries and diaries like a Baedeker of the major countries in Europe. They visited Rome and

Naples, Milan and Florence, Geneva and the Swiss lakes, the Rhine cities, and those of southern and eastern France. Both liked Paris and Brussels, and were welcome also at the homes of their many Spanish friends along the Mediterranean coast of the Iberian Peninsula.

In these years Father Patrick was technically assigned to St. Joseph's Church in Providence (1891-94), and to St. Lawrence Church on Park Avenue and Eighty-fourth Street in New York (1895-1906), but he easily secured lengthy leaves of absence because of his health. The *petit mal* that had bothered him intermittently since before 1858 became more grave as he grew older. He was able to tolerate only the lightest of ministries, infrequent Mass, occasional confessions, and a rare sermon.

In 1889, upon the occasion of the centennial celebration at Georgetown, the officials at his old university wished to have Father Healy as one of the main speakers on the final program. He was obliged for reasons of health to forego his share in the celebration of the hundredth anniversary. Even the thought of giving so important a speech had brought on his sickness once more.

His brother's death in 1900 was a severe blow to Father Healy's health. He it was who had the disconsolate task of winding up the bishop's affairs after his sudden demise. To him the bishop had willed all of his personal papers, his sermons, journals, diaries, and letters. Patrick sorted these out from the official diocesan records and then took them to Holy Cross College to deposit them in the archives of the Alma Mater from which both he and his brother had graduated in successive years half a century before.

There was little else to his career after the turn of the century. Father Patrick was assigned as spiritual father at St. Joseph's College in Philadelphia in 1906. Two years later, he was transferred to the infirmary building at Georgetown for his last days. He finally passed away peacefully at Georgetown on January 10, 1910, and was buried almost within the shadow of the Healy Building in the campus graveyard.

In due course, the structure erected by Father Patrick became known as the Healy Building. Along its spacious corridors are hung the oil paintings of all of the past presidents of Georgetown University. Up to the present day, the well-executed picture of Father Patrick Healy, S.J., hangs in its place of honor along with the other men of renown who governed the proud institution. Georgetown is richer in tradition and in human wealth because of the strenuous achievements of this humbly born son of the Church who gave his full strength and sacrificed his health to raise the university to full stature in the academic world.

CHAPTER IV

Good Father Gus

FATHER AUGUSTINE TOLTON

1854–1897

In the same year in which Bishop Healy was ordained a priest in faraway Paris, a second son was born to two Catholic slaves in a humble slave cabin on a plantation near Brush Creek, Ralls County, in northeastern Missouri not far from Mark Twain's city of Hannibal on the Mississippi.

The father, Peter Paul Tolton, had been baptized by Father (later Bishop) Peter Paul Lefevre on one of his missionary tours. The colored man was then and continued later to be a slave of the Hager family, Catholics of Ralls County. Falling in love with a Catholic slave girl of the nearby Elliot plantation, he married Martha Jane Chisley in St. Peter's Church in Brush Creek. Martha Jane had been baptized a Catholic in infancy in her native Meade County in the Catholic section of Kentucky. Raised as slave of the Manning family, Martha was given as part of the dowry when one of the Manning girls married a Missouri man named Stephen Elliot. Thus she came to live with them in Ralls County, a loyal and devout Catholic notwithstanding her humble status as a domestic slave.

As her own children came along in the years after her marriage, they were duly baptized in the Catholic Church. Her second son was born on April 1, 1854. He was given the baptismal name of Augustine, though the church's baptismal register simply lists him as the colored child born on April 1 and the property of Stephen Elliot. Mrs. Stephen Elliot stood as sponsor. Father John O'Sullivan performed the ceremony and entered the date as May 29, 1854.

Two more children were born before the outbreak of the Civil War in 1861. All during these years the young couple prayed for freedom. The Dred Scott Decision whereby the famed Missouri slave was returned to bondage by the Supreme Court of the United States in 1857 had seemed a final blow to their hopes.

But with the fall of Fort Sumter and the start of hostilities, it seemed time for Peter and Martha to make a break for freedom. Peter decamped to join the Union Army. His life in freedom was a short one. He died in a hospital in St. Louis during the war.

Martha Jane also determined to reach the promised land of freedom across the Mississippi in Illinois. One night she took her four children, one a babe in arms, and fled hurriedly through Ralls and Marion counties until she reached the river. There she was challenged by some Missourians who tried to apprehend her as a runaway slave. Federal soldiers who happened along at the time rescued her, and with their aid she crossed the river that same night, some miles south of Quincy, Illinois.

Young seven-year-old Augustine never forgot that thrilling escape. Years later he recalled how, together with his older brother and his younger sister, he ran himself out of breath to keep up with his frightened but determined mother. She had her heart set on Quincy and freedom. She attained both. The family settled down in the comparative peace of Quincy, free at last.[1]

Martha Jane Tolton, though illiterate, was a remarkably devout woman. She ruled as a religious matriarch in her small domain. She taught her children the Ten Commandments, raising them to keep God's law. She courageously went to work to support the family. In time the two older boys joined her at the large Harris Tobacco Factory at Fifth and Ohio streets to help earn enough for the family.

[1] A fictionalized treatment of the dramatic escape has been widely circulated, depicting young Tolton as a lad of sixteen when the family made the dash for liberty. The above account is based on two separate but concordant reports, one in a speech by Father Tolton given at the First Colored Catholic Congress in Washington, January 1-3, 1889, and reported in the *American Catholic Tribune,* a Negro Catholic weekly, for the next week, page 18; the other, an interview with Father Tolton and his mother by the renowned editor of *St. Joseph's Advocate,* the Josephite Father, Dr. Green, who wrote it up in October, 1886, pp. 186-87.

For twelve years young Augustine worked as a tobacco stemmer and factory hand. Eight of these years he was directly under the supervision of the owner's brother. For three other years he labored under the foremanship of a "pleasant Irishman," named McKinney.

Owing to the seasonal nature of the work, the factory was idle for more than three months a year. It was during this time that Augustine attended "winter" classes at the public Lincoln School. Attending Mass at St. Peter's Church along with the white Catholics of the parish, young Augustine and his brothers came to the attention of the pastor, Father P. B. McGirr. He decided to admit the Toltons to his parish school. In doing so, he stirred the wrath of his Irish congregation. The parents threatened to take the white children out of the school if the Toltons were allowed to attend. But the pastor and the Sisters of Notre Dame both insisted that the black children stay. Stay they did, and the white children likewise.

"I learned the alphabet, spelling, reading, and other things in St. Peter's School, and partly by hearing others read at home," Father Tolton later said. He cherished the memory of his teachers, Sister Sebastian, Sister Mary Eustatius, and Sister Herlinde, the last of whom would later teach in Father Tolton's own school.

Augustine worked part-time around the school and the church during the slack season at the factory. He tended the furnace for six years at St. Peter's. His spirit of devotion impelled him to spend long hours in prayer in the quiet church.

On the day of his first Communion, while he was still at the Sisters' convent, Augustine met Father McGirr. The pastor, noting the glow in his eyes, encouraged him to study for the priesthood. In pursuance of this, Augustine applied for admission into the ranks of the Franciscan Fathers who staffed St. Boniface's Church and St. Francis Solano (later Quincy) College.

Nothing came of the application. But Father Schaeffermeyer and other Franciscans began to take a special interest in the boy. Father Schaeffermeyer admitted him to St. Boniface's German Catholic school, but soon afterward Augustine had to withdraw, because he did not know his grammar and because of the opposition of some of the parents of German children in the school. By way of recompense, Father

Astrop, later pastor of St. Boniface's, and Father Theodore Wegmann began to give Augustine private tutoring. Father Wegmann taught him Latin for two and a half years, from May, 1873, to October, 1875. He also gave Augustine private lessons in Greek, German, English, history, and geography, as a sort of introduction to his high-school work.

In 1875 Martha Jane secured a position as a housekeeper for a priest in one of the northeastern Missouri parishes. She took her small family with her, Augustine going along in hopes of keeping up his studies under the new priest who promised to tutor him. For eleven months they stayed in Missouri. The atmosphere was very unsuitable to Martha Jane—Negroes were still being kidnaped and sold as slaves in Missouri, notwithstanding the emancipation.

Back in Quincy, Augustine went to work again, first in a horse-collar factory, and later with the soda firm of J. J. Flynn and Company. The Franciscans of the local Catholic high school tutored him before work in the morning, and at later sessions in the evening. He continued to be deeply religious and to yearn for the priesthood. He joined the Temperance Society at St. Peter's Church, became the standard-bearer in its processions, and faithfully kept the teetotaler pledge: he never tried liquors of any kind, nor did he even know how they tasted.

In later years, Father Tolton gave credit to the German Franciscans for opening the way to his career. Father Michael Richardt, whom he met in 1877, asked Augustine to help him do something for the un-catechized colored Catholic children of the town. Augustine went about gathering them together for Sunday school in St. Francis' school-house. He helped them with their prayers and was so successful a re-cruiter that his forty children became the nucleus of a one-room school taught by Sister Herlinde.

Father Michael was impressed with Augustine's intelligence, liveli-ness of mind, piety, and modesty. He spoke to Bishop Peter J. Baltes about Augustine's desire to be a priest, and as the bishop was then on his way to Rome for his ad limina he promised to secure admission for the colored boy to the College of the Propaganda there. He was un-successful. Father Michael then wrote to the Father General of the Franciscans, asking that he intervene to pave the way for the unique aspirant. This time the answer was in the affirmative.

There was jubilation in the Tolton home over the good news. The students at St. Francis College took up a collection to help finance the trip. The bishop donated fifty dollars, and the Franciscans added their mite. On February 15, 1880, Augustine left Quincy for Rome. He sailed from Jersey City on the *Westlicher* the following Saturday, February 21, accompanied by three Franciscans who were also on the way to Rome. Augustine first saw the Eternal City on March 10, and was admitted to the College of the Propaganda two days later. In another week, he received the clerical garb, and plunged into his studies in earnest.

Augustine found the Italian teachers "lovely and fatherly," especially Professors Checci, Conrado, and Levi. He made friends with the prefect of the Propaganda, Cardinal Giovanni Simeoni, and with Monsignor Satolli, later Papal Delegate to the United States. "All were my friends," he said, "they loved me, though I cannot say why."

The young student distinguished himself by a brilliant course at Rome. He took the propaganda oath on May 6, 1883, and was tonsured a week later by Cardinal Lenti. In 1884 he received the minor orders from Cardinal Parocchi. He progressed in the normal stages to the priesthood, taking the first of the major orders in 1885, and looking forward to 1886 as the year of his ordination.

There was some question as to whether he would be ordained for the foreign missions or for the United States. He told of the incident thus:

> When on the eve of going to St. John Lateran to be ordained, the word came expressing doubt whether I would be sent here. It was said that I would be the only priest of my race in America, and would not be likely to succeed. All at once Cardinal Simeoni said: "America has been called the most enlightened nation; we will see if it deserves that honor. If America has never seen a black priest, it has to see one now. Come and take an oath to spend your whole days in your own country."

Augustine took the oath, and on Holy Saturday, April 24, 1886, he was solemnly ordained to the sacred priesthood in the Basilica of

St. John Lateran, Cardinal Parocchi again performing the ordination ceremony.

On Easter Sunday the newly ordained priest offered Holy Mass on the High Altar of St. Peter's, usually reserved for the Holy Father himself. Over the tomb of St. Peter, he brought to a close his preparation at Rome and began his life as a fully qualified priest and apostle.

Cardinal Simeoni decided that Quincy was the proper place for Father Tolton's missionary work. He bade his neophyte goodbye on June 13, 1886, and missioned him to America. In company with an Irish gentleman, the young priest toured the continent and England until the end of the month, sailing from Liverpool on June 26 and arriving in New York July 6. His first Mass in the country was said at St. Mary's Hospital in Hoboken, where he had been sheltered before sailing Romeward. He had promised the Sisters then that if he were ordained, he would say his first Mass in their chapel.

Next Sunday, St. Benedict the Moor Church, at Bleecker and Downing streets in New York City, was the scene of his first solemn High Mass. He sang at ease with his powerful voice, standing erect the full six feet of his height, and making an impressive figure flanked by the two white priests who assisted him as deacon and subdeacon.

Homecoming to Quincy was a gala day for Martha Jane and her son. On July 18 Father Tolton offered a solemn High Mass in St. Boniface Church.

Toward the end of the month, on July 25, Father Tolton was named pastor of St. Joseph's Catholic Church for Negroes. The parish had grown out of the catechism class that Father Tolton had gathered for Father Michael Richardt in 1877. Each year there had been a few more converts and child baptisms, and Sister Herlinde's school had been kept up, save for a brief period after 1880 when the provincial had ordered its closing. The congregation occupied a former Protestant church which belonged to St. Boniface's parish. This was turned over to the colored parishioners for their use as a church upstairs and a school in the basement.

The small (seventy feet by thirty-six) building was taken over by Father Tolton as his first parish. It had been neatly equipped with oil paintings for stations of the cross, and with an altar shrine of the

Blessed Virgin to the left and one for St. Joseph to the right of the main altar. There were eighty members in the congregation when Augustine assumed charge. They were poor, desperately so, and the total annual collections did not amount to more than a hundred dollars.

Father Tolton addressed himself to the task of running the demoralized parish. He and his mother lived nearby in what was known as the "old seminary." Together they braved the future; but it looked dim for the young priest. In the course of his first year nine colored men came to see him. They wanted to become Catholics, but each with the proviso that he could keep his current wife. To most of the prospective women converts, he might have said what Christ said to the woman at Jacob's well, "He whom thou now hast is not thy husband."

Normal family life was rare. The children hardly had shoes and clothes enough to attend school regularly. The prospect of spending the day in the warm schoolroom was by itself enough to induce them to continue through the winter months. Sister Herlinde and Father Tolton nevertheless continued to battle for them. They kept the school open, and persevered in their work for the parishioners.

There were external compensations to offset the frustrating work of the depressed parish. Father Tolton was often invited away from Quincy to lecture and preach. He spoke at the First Catholic Colored Congress in Washington in 1889. He addressed assemblies of Catholics in Boston and New York. Cardinal Gibbons invited him to Baltimore to preach and minister to the colored people.

Unafraid, Father Tolton ventured deep into the South. In 1890, at the invitation of Bishop Gallagher of Galveston, Texas, Father Gus preached in the Cathedral to a predominantly white congregation. He made a striking figure in the pulpit, his red cincture contrasting with his black cassock just as did the red pompon of his biretta. The wearing of the special red colors made the altar boys believe he was a bishop. But that privilege was merely the sign that he had been trained in the College of the Propaganda in Rome.

Both in the Cathedral and in the Jesuit church at the east end of the island next to St. Mary's University, Father Tolton heard confessions of both white and colored, as he did in Quincy.

Elsewhere in the country also Father Tolton was received with

honor as a Catholic priest. Newspapers all over the country played
up his unique role as the only full-blooded black priest in the American
Catholic Church. He was a prophet not without honor in the South
and in the East.

But back in Quincy, it was the same story. Whites came to the
St. Joseph's Church out of curiosity for the novel experience. They
contributed generously to the upkeep of the church. But Father Tolton
made no progress among the colored. The non-Catholics were very
strong in the community. Their revivals were the big social affairs
of the Negro people. To them the non-Catholic boys took the girls
who had been trained in the small school, and they were soon lost
to the Church. The young boys were enticed away by the demoralizing
influences in the slums. Secret societies among the non-Catholics kept
alive the prejudices against the Church.

In 1889 an opportunity finally opened up for Father Tolton in
Chicago. A wealthy philanthropist, Mrs. Anne O'Neill, donated ten
thousand dollars toward the establishment of St. Monica's Church for
colored Catholics. The archbishop offered the post to Father Tolton.
He secured authorization from his bishop for a transfer to the new
venture. In 1889 he took up his residence at St. Augustine's Church
on Prairie Avenue in Chicago, and in the next year opened St. Monica's
Chapel in the twenty-second hundred block of South Indiana, in the
heart of the Negro slum neighborhood.

There again the minor and major frustrations of the slum apostolate
added to the difficulties of the work on the other side of the color
line. It was no reflection on Father Tolton that his work did not
prosper with spectacular achievements. He was personally a solid man,
true as steel, well versed in his clerical matters, fully capable of delivering sermons that were sound in theology, useful in applications,
and forcefully presented to the people. He was proud of his color,
aglow with devotion to his race and his people, affectionate toward
his mother, and faithful to his parish duties and his priestly vows. His
one relaxation was a pinch of snuff now and then, prescribed as a
potent protective against the winter's cold in the Windy City.

Father Tolton also conducted services in St. Mary's Church basement, where a small colored congregation had been assembled a few

years previously through the efforts of the St. Augustine's Society.
He later built a small chapel at Thirty-sixth and Dearborn streets
where he celebrated Mass for the first time in 1893. The chapel was
named St. Monica's and it remained the center of colored Catholic
life for more than thirty years.

Father Tolton fitted easily into the clerical life of Chicago. He made
friends with the more than a hundred priests who served the expanding metropolis. It was with them that he journeyed to Kankakee during the first week of July, 1897, to make the diocesan retreat. It was an
excessively hot summer, and on the way home, Friday, July 9, he was
stricken by the heat. Rushed to Mercy Hospital, he lingered throughout the day, but died that night. He was only forty-three.

His remains lay in state at St. Monica's all day Sunday. Thousands
of Catholics from all over the city filed through the small church to
pay their last respects to the dead pastor. At the funeral on Monday,
over one hundred priests crowded the sanctuary and the first pews
to say the office of the dead and attend the requiem. The eulogy was
pronounced over the humble priest by Father Mooney, the chancellor
of the diocese.

As he had requested, his body was taken back to Quincy for burial.
His mother accompanied the sad cortege, together with her daughter
Anna, now Mrs. Pettes, and her other son. Representatives of Catholic
Negro organizations from Chicago also journeyed down for the last
rites. Twelve priests of Quincy met the body at the station, and a large
crowd filled St. Peter's Church to overflowing for the funeral. St.
Joseph's little church was no more. It had died of inanition when
Father Tolton had gone to Chicago, and his small flock had been scat-
tered by adversity and migration.

One of the largest crowds ever to form a procession to the cemetery
trailed after the hearse and the carriages bearing the clergy and the
family. Father Tolton's body was laid to rest in St. Peter's Cemetery,
Father Kerr conducting the last service. Old Father McGirr was one of
the pallbearers, thus carrying out his final act in the vocation of
Augustine Tolton. A modest marker was erected over the grave. But
the real monument to Father Tolton is the procession of other colored
priests who have followed in his footsteps, having understood the true

significance of his vocation as a pioneer in the erasing of unwritten laws, and in the elimination of unspoken prejudices. More than any-one else, Father Tolton dispelled the doubts and suspicions that re-mained as vestiges of the thought-ways of whites from the pre-Civil War days. He proved that, given the intelligence, holiness, courage, and the perseverance he manifested in his holy life, the full stature of a good priest could be achieved by men of his background and origin.

CHAPTER V

First Josephite Father

CHARLES RANDOLPH UNCLES, S.S.J.

1 8 5 9 – 1 9 3 3

The coming of "Daddy" Uncles to the altar was an almost inevitable event. It stands to reason that after two and a half centuries of colored Catholic life in Maryland there would sooner or later arise a lad inspired by the Holy Spirit with the special vocation to be a priest forever.

It was to be expected also that out of Baltimore, as the center of Catholic life in Maryland, there would spring the first fruits of the fullness of Catholicism among the Negroes of the state. Half a century before, three colored Catholic ladies had banded together to form the first sisterhood for Negro Catholic nuns in the country, with its original motherhouse in Baltimore. Known as the Oblate Sisters of Providence, the congregation had grown from its inception in 1829 until at the time of the Civil War it numbered many dozens of Sisters. The colored nuns conducted a Catholic Academy in Baltimore for children of the well-to-do Negro Catholics. They also taught Sunday school catechism classes for children of public schools. It was out of these latter classes that Charles Uncles emerged as one of the first colored boys whose footsteps were set on the road to the altar through the influence of the good Oblates of Providence.

The years of faithful labor on behalf of the colored Catholics of Maryland and Baltimore by the Sulpician Fathers and the Jesuits were also to bear first fruits in Charles Uncles' vocation.

For years the Sulpician Fathers had been caring for the spiritual welfare of the Baltimore colored Catholics. They had been providing a special Mass each Sunday in St. Mary's Seminary Chapel on Paca Street. However, in 1859 the Jesuit superiors in Baltimore assigned

Father Peter L. Miller, S.J., to the full-time apostolate among these and other old Catholic families, many of whom had strayed away from the Church owing to economic conditions and lack of interest on the part of the pastors. Father Miller secured the remodeling and reconversion of the basement of St. Ignatius Church as a chapel for the colored congregation, naming it after Blessed Peter Claver, the Jesuit apostle of the Negro slaves in South America.

Father Miller then began the laborious task of bringing back into the active stream of Catholic life the many nominally Catholic families of the neighborhood. It was slow, tedious work. The Uncles family was among those ultimately brought to membership in the new church. Thus, though Charles Uncles was born on November 6, 1859, he was not baptized until April 2, 1875, when he was sixteen years old.

His father was a machinist working for the Baltimore and Ohio Railroad. His mother, the former Anna Marie Buchanan, though she had attended the Oblate Sisters' school for a few years, was not able to have her children baptized until after the new St. Francis Xavier Church for the colored had been opened on Calvert Street in the 1860's.

Meanwhile, young Charles had been educated in a private school conducted by a Mr. W. A. Willyam, a cultured gentleman of color who tutored the children of the moderately well-to-do families in the colored section of Baltimore.

Charles later attended the public schools of the neighborhood, and before he had reached the age of sixteen had also enrolled at one of the secondary schools, working part-time as a journalist and a printer from 1874 to 1879 to help finance his way through school.

In 1878 he attended the Baltimore Normal School for colored teachers-to-be, and qualified for a position as a teacher. From 1880 to 1883, he was occupied with the tasks of training the young in the Baltimore county public schools.

At the time, Catholic circles in Baltimore were witnessing the inauguration of a new era in the Church's apostolate among American Negroes. In 1863, shortly after Emancipation, Archbishop Spalding had purchased a large building at the corner of Calvert and Pleasant streets in downtown Baltimore and had dedicated it under the patronage of St. Francis Xavier as the first Catholic church in the United States for the use of an all-colored congregation. The many hundred Catholic Negroes who had been attending Mass in a body in the basement church of St. Ignatius down the street now took possession of their new spiritual home and formed the nucleus of a steadily expanding parish.

It was in this new church (which had formerly been a Protestant church and a convention hall) that young Charles attended Mass as a young man, made his first Communion and received the Sacrament of Confirmation in 1878.

Here too he became acquainted with the priests who encouraged his vocation—the Mill Hill Josephites who came to Baltimore in 1871 and took charge of St. Francis Xavier Church as their first pastoral work for their special apostolate in America.

The story of their foundation in England by Cardinal Vaughan is too well known to bear repetition here. But it did seem to young Charles that this was finally an answer to the many prayers that his family and fellow Catholics had been pouring forth to God for decades and even centuries. Some years before, Father Herbert Vaughan had toured the country to survey the plight of the emancipated colored Americans. He was impressed everywhere he went by the necessity for a clergy wholly dedicated to the work of Christianization among the Negroes. On his return to England, he founded at Mill Hill the Society of St. Joseph, and by 1871 had a small group of four priests assembled as the first Josephites. In the autumn of that year he and his four priests went to Rome and asked Pope Pius IX to assign them to a mission field among the Negroes. The Holy Father, having recently approved the decrees of the Second Plenary Council of Baltimore that appealed for missionary priests to devote themselves to the apostolate of the emancipated blacks, commanded the Mill Hill Josephites to place themselves under the direction of Archbishop Spalding of Baltimore.

In December of the same year, the band of five missionaries arrived in Baltimore. They were given a glad welcome by the archbishop, and he arranged to turn over to them the Church of St. Francis Xavier in Baltimore as their first American pastorate. It was there in the years following 1871 that Charles Uncles came to know Father Vaughan and his first four companions, Fathers Cornelius Dowling, James Noonan, Joseph Gore, and Charles Vigeront. He felt the warm enthusiasm of their fervor in carrying out their vow to dedicate themselves forever to the service of the colored Catholics. He felt drawn to follow their footsteps; but across his path lay the barriers set up in the high schools and the seminaries that prepared boys for the priesthood.

Years went by before a way opened for him. It was 1883 before he learned that he could secure admission to the Canadian seminaries just as Bishop Healy and his brother Father Sherwood Healy had done. He sent in his application to the St. Hyacinthe's College in Quebec, and was accepted there for the class of September, 1883. Five years later he was graduated with top honors in his class.

It was only then that he was able to enroll in the Josephite Seminary in Baltimore. In 1887 the Josephites had opened their own seminary under Cardinal Gibbons' jurisdiction on Pennsylvania Avenue and St. Mary's Street in what was formerly the old Western Maryland Hotel. The cardinal arranged that the seminarians should attend class with the other Baltimore seminarians in St. Mary's Seminary, under the Sulpician Fathers.

Father John Slattery, who had been instrumental in sending Charles to Canada for his clerical studies, and who was currently the superior of the American Josephites, asked the Sulpicians in the course of the next year whether they would be willing to admit Charles to their classes along with the other seminarians.

The Sulpicians vacillated in their decision. They finally submitted the matter to a vote of the student body in the seminary. According to Father Slattery's report, made public at the First Colored Catholic Congress in 1889, every one of the white seminarians voted in favor of the opening of St. Mary's doors to the colored seminarian. Father Slattery lost no time in informing Cardinal Gibbons of their favorable vote. The cardinal said that if any of them had voted against it, he would have bowed his head in sorrow.

Charles therefore returned from his voluntary exile in Canada during the summer of 1888. He had already completed one year of theology and was thus prepared to take his place with the second-year theologians. He looked forward to the additional year, more as another, closer step toward ordination, than as a new experiment in the field of relationships between Americans of different color. His experience in Canada had given him full assurance that he could handle himself with distinction in a mixed group, and could adjust himself to the white mentality without a major disruption of his equanimity.

At the Paca Street School, Charles mingled with the two hundred men from all over the South who were preparing for holy orders. As a more mature student, he had little difficulty adjusting to the situation, and his added years (he was nearly thirty at the time), together with his polished manners and pleasant personality, made him a genial companion even for the prejudiced southerners. One of the students, who later became Bishop of Galveston in Texas, recalled that Charles always took first place in the large class of seminarians at St. Mary's, even outdistancing the future bishops and archbishops.

It was a memorable day in the history of the Baltimore archdiocese when Charles Uncles went up to the altar with twenty-five other deacons to be ordained a priest on December 19, 1891. Cardinal Gibbons, who just a few years before had received the red hat for his liberal leadership of American Catholics in the formative years of the burgeoning daughter of Mother Church, was the ordaining prelate. He delivered a long and instructive address. He was conscious of the fact that he was ordaining the first colored priest to be given the Sacrament of Holy Orders on American soil. All of the others had hitherto been ordained in Europe. Charles Uncles was the pioneer American colored priest: born, reared, and ordained in the United States.

Christmas that year was doubly gay for the congregation of old St. Francis Xavier Church. The Mass at dawn was the first solemn High Mass of the first of its boys to be raised to the dignity of the priesthood. An immense congregation flooded every corner of the edifice, more than had packed it for Henry Clay's nomination to the presidency or for the secession declaration of the Maryland legislature which had met within those very walls in 1861.

Father Slattery, the superior of the Josephites, preached a glowing sermon to the elated and attentive flock.

Father Uncles' experience and talent as a teacher marked him for a classroom career. He was assigned shortly after ordination to teach in the minor seminary at Walbrook, a suburb of Baltimore. There at Epiphany Apostolic College he began a long career of more than forty years of teaching young seminarians.

Year after year he inducted the young men into the mysteries of Latin and Greek and trained them further in his own elegant mastery of English. He became known early among the seminarians as "Daddy" Uncles, and his kind, genial, self-assured attitude in the professor's chair made him a favorite among the boys.

Besides teaching, he took on a large share of the spiritual direction, instruction, and molding of the seminarians. He was one of the regular confessors whose grill-side manner was sympathetic and evocative of the best in the struggling saints-to-be. He never held himself aloof from the students, being careful always to remain approachable and easy to meet, so that he inspired confidence and invited trust. The nickname of "Daddy," pinned upon his person by the quick-witted neophytes, aptly expressed their appreciation of his fatherly relations with them.

Notwithstanding his height (he was more than six feet, two inches tall), Father Uncles could unbend with the smallest of his students, and could joke and laugh with the jolliest. He could tell an earthy joke like the one about the man who had a piece of dog bone grafted on his injured leg, and still not scandalize the innocent. And he felt sufficiently at ease on the delicate issue of race to find chuckles where others found gloom. His standard joke, when he passed the drugstore in which the seminarians were buying an afternoon soda, was to step in the doorway and ask them, "Are niggers allowed in here?" Then he would order a huge bowl of ice cream and eat it with the zest of a minor seminarian.

In class, he was a fresh-air enthusiast. He insisted on having the windows opened even on the coldest winter day. And he kept his scholars awake by his complete mastery of the subject and the student mind as well. He taught the old textbook of Greenough, until he knew it by heart. Ultimately he prepared his own edition of a text in the field, after many years of urging on the part of the staff and the students who wanted a short cut to the attainment of a minimum Latinity.

Aside from one year spent on the mission band, Father Uncles' whole career was dedicated to classroom work. He traveled South on the mission circuit one fall and winter, but he did not like the Jim Crow system. He even prevailed upon the priests to drive him by car from one mission to the next so that he could be spared the indignity of the segregation system on the buses and trains. He was not a success at the revivalism of the mission work, and so he returned to the classroom the following year, glad to be back among the congenial pupils of the seminary.

It is a pity that he did not use his very great literary talents in behalf of the Catholic press and especially of the colored mission apostolate. The editor of the *Colored Harvest* was constantly asking him for articles for the mission magazine. Finally, in 1909, Father Uncles contributed a substantial and capable piece entitled "The Catholic Church and the Negro" for the October issue. It is a well-reasoned and dispassionate analysis of what the Roman Catholic Church teaches and practices, does and says in favor of "my people." He reaffirms the Church's universality, stating that it knows "no North or South, no East or West, no distinctions founded on race or color." It is for all countries and all mankind, he insisted. He urged his readers not to hold the Church or religion responsible for the perversity of pseudo-disciples who neglect to follow the teaching of the Church because of avarice, greed, or cold barbarism.

The article manifests the breadth of his reading and the depth of his scholarship. He cites the story of Toussaint L'Ouverture as a Catholic who liberated his nation. He quotes from Archbishop Ireland to the effect that prejudice must be banished from the sacred circle of the Catholic Church whose solemn dogma is the equality of all men before God. He quotes Pope after Pope in condemnation of slavery, and even adduces the testimony of non-Catholic historians such as Guizot, Macaulay, and Lecky to shore up his contention.

The broad range of his historical knowledge is also apparent in the ease with which he culls instances even from African history. And he summed up the major features of the American Catholic Church's efforts on behalf of the colored in this country.

The man reveals himself in his good, flowing style, his lofty and classical allusions, his command of language and felicity of expression. He could have been a renowned litterateur, but he preferred to be just a seminary professor, dedicated to the hidden tasks of preparing young fledglings for the winging toward the altar.

In Christmas week of 1916, Father Uncles celebrated in Baltimore his silver jubilee as a priest. He chanted a solemn High Mass in St. Francis Xavier Church on January 7, with Auxiliary Bishop Owen D. Corrigan presiding in place of the aging Cardinal Gibbons. Church dignitaries, priests, religious, laity, and dozens of his former pupils filled the church for his jubilee. There were gala observances in the parish school and in the parish hall during that week, and Father Uncles, surrounded by his near relatives and friends, accepted the tribute with a charm and grace that befitted the dear old "Daddy."

In the mid-twenties, the Josephite Fathers decided to move their minor seminary and novitiate from Baltimore to Newburgh, New York, just outside of Poughkeepsie on the Hudson. They built a new and well-equipped college, and transferred their students from Walbrook to the more spacious setting on the lower Hudson.

Father Charles was among the professors chosen for the staff of the new institution, and he succeeded in transplanting some of the atmosphere and tradition of the old school to the new by keeping up the same pattern of intimate relationships between teachers and students that had prevailed in Baltimore. He again became an institution in the new seminary. He continued year after year the patient task of imparting a solid foundation in the Church's language to the incoming scores of aspirants to the priesthood.

By 1924 the infirmities of age were beginning to creep up on him. He still continued his routine classwork, but he had slowed down considerably in the pace that he was wont to set for himself and his students. He did not ask to be taken out of the grind of steady teaching and placed as an assistant in a sinecure. There were rumors to the effect that he had some mild ambition for the pastorate of his home parish, St. Francis Xavier in Baltimore, and that when this was not granted him, he had refused to accept any other parochial assignment. It hardly fits in with his retiring, spotlight-shunning personality, but the rumor persisted. He lived it down by faithfully adhering to the religious life and the routine of his dedicated tasks.

In the last years of his life, he was frequently incapacitated by many illnesses, not the least of which was a weakened condition of the heart that left him often gasping for breath after a strenuous day of class.

It was in the heat of the insufferable July of 1933 that Father Uncles reached the end of his life. He knew that death was approaching, and on July 20 had asked for the last Sacraments. Shortly after the doctor and the priest had administered some relief for his suffering body and soul, he passed peacefully to God, still in the harness of his position at Epiphany Apostolic College in Newburgh.

There in the chapel his body lay in state over the weekend while his many relatives and friends from Baltimore came to pray at the bierside. For the funeral on Monday twenty-five priests assembled. A large number of nuns and laity also joined the family mourners. Father Pastorelli, the superior of the Josephites, offered the solemn requiem Mass, and Father Daniel Rice, S.S.J., delivered the final eulogy over "Daddy" Uncles.

Father Uncles' body was buried temporarily in Calvary Cemetery in Newburgh, but later it was more fittingly entombed in its last resting place in the new graveyard on the seminary grounds. There a monument was erected to the memory of the first colored priest to be ordained on American soil.

In evaluating the career of Father Uncles, one must place it in the setting of the wide variety of ministries open to the Catholic priest. Some critics have surmised that Father Uncles was averse to the colored apostolate because he shunned notoriety and did not go on any barnstorming tours of the mission fields. While one can appreciate the reluctance of a cultured man to engage in zoological exhibitionism, one must recognize that there are many forms to the colored apostolate, just as there are many roles for average priests to play in the rich and variegated life of the Church.

The role of the seminary professor is a vital one. As a teacher of future priests who were to dedicate their lives to missions among colored, Father Uncles was in a position to form the mentality of the young seminarians while they were still amenable to education, especially in the area of attitudes toward the colored as a people. "Daddy" Uncles' quiet influence spread through generation after generation of young Josephites, dispelling preconceived notions about the intellectual inferiority of the Negro, quietly confirming their minds in regard to the possibility of full Christianization of the colored man, and generally endearing the seminarians to the people among whom they would spend their lives. Many a future difficulty in the ministry was thus strangled in its cradle. Much heartbreak on the part of the priests-to-be and their future congregations was fended off by the gentle influence of the clear-eyed, gray-haired teacher.

His passing was mourned by the seminarians. But his influence lived on in their lives and in the spirit of the Josephite apostolate, the largest and most successful one among the American Negroes thus far.

CHAPTER VI

Missionary and Pastor

JOHN HENRY DORSEY, S.S.J.

1873 - 1926

It was a farsighted Josephite superior, Father John R. Slattery, who personally sponsored the first colored boys aspiring to be priests in his order. He had stated his convictions about the urgent need for a colored priesthood in his articles in the *Catholic World* in 1883 and 1884. And he had backed up his words with convincing action. Already, before the establishment of Epiphany Apostolic College in Baltimore, he had sent at least one colored seminarian to England to study in the Mill Hill Josephites' Seminary near Liverpool. Upon the opening of Epiphany, he had summoned James Brown back to Maryland, but unfortunately, within the next year, the young man took sick and died.

Father Slattery nonetheless continued sponsoring vocations for colored lads who manifested the necessary intelligence, piety, and good conduct.

In the 1880's a young lad named John Henry Dorsey came to Father Slattery's attention. John Henry had been born in Baltimore on January 29, 1873, of a family that had long been Catholic on his father's side, though his mother, Emmaline Snowden Dorsey, was a convert. Notwithstanding the necessity of sending the four boys and their one sister to public school because of the color line in Baltimore parochial schools, the Dorseys had raised their children as pious Catholics. All had been baptized in St. Francis Xavier Church, and thither the family continued to come for Mass, traveling the not inconsiderable distance from northwest Baltimore to the downtown location where young John Henry and his brothers could serve on the altar.

It was the boy's obvious goodness and piety as a Mass-server that drew Father Slattery's attention to him as a possible candidate for sacred orders. His perseverance in his duties as an altar boy all through the higher grades convinced Father Slattery that John Henry had a true vocation.

In 1888 Father Slattery arranged for John Henry to matriculate at the minor seminary of St. Thomas in St. Paul, Minnesota, where Archbishop Ireland, proclaiming a non-segregation policy and denouncing racism in fiery terms, had opened the way for the admission of colored students.

Next year, however, Father Slattery was able to open his own preparatory seminary in Baltimore, in the suburban neighborhood called Walbrook. John Henry was among the first to enroll at the new Epiphany Apostolic College. He scored high grades in his class during his minor seminary days, and after finishing at Epiphany, he transferred to St. Joseph's Seminary in Baltimore and followed in the footsteps of Charles Uncles by attending classes at St. Mary's Seminary along with the white seminarians. Though he did not lead the class as Charles Uncles had done before him, he ranked high among the leaders, keeping steadily at his books and, in fact, overworking himself to that end.

The strain affected his health. He became ill in 1893, missed class for a considerable length of time, and was advised to interrupt his philosophical studies for a year. He therefore took Father Slattery's offer of a teaching position at the new Josephite School in Richmond, Virginia, and taught also for a time in Baltimore.

By 1897 his health had been regained. He resumed his study of philosophy with the September class, and paced himself successfully through the rest of the course. Along with his class, he was ordained by Cardinal Gibbons in the Baltimore Cathedral June 21, 1902.

It was a great personal triumph for Father Slattery and a great joy for Father Dorsey when the newly ordained priest sang his first solemn High Mass in St. Francis Xavier Church in Baltimore on June 22. Father Slattery preached the sermon to a crowded church, filled with well-wishers and with the numerous relatives of the Dorseys. His three brothers, his sister, and his happy parents headed the family delegation. Father Slattery congratulated the congregation on this second priestly vocation to come from their deeply religious families. He reaffirmed his belief in the urgent need for more vocations saying:

> Today after twenty-five years of labor among and for the colored people, I am absolutely convinced that the Catholic Church will make little progress in the converting of the Negroes of our Southland unless she succeeds in getting a large body of colored priests.[1]

He denounced as utterly foreign to the Church's main lines of tradition the hostility of certain people to the development of a native colored clergy. He put his finger on the source of much of this hostility when he declared: "The spirit of the political party inimical to the Negro, to which for good or ill the bulk of Catholics belong, dominates many Catholics. It is this un-Catholic sentiment which looks askance on the Negro priests."[2]

Father Slattery was fully confident that the Catholic Negroes generally wanted to have their own priests ministering to them. He had addressed the first Colored Catholic Congress in Washington in 1889, at which Father Gus Tolton was honored enthusiastically by the leading colored Catholics in the country. At that time Father Slattery had declared that the way they received Father Tolton proved that the colored Catholics of America definitely wanted their own priests.

He had added that "as soon as we have a great many colored priests, things would change south of the Potomac."

To show his sincerity in this matter, Father Slattery immediately assigned Father Dorsey (who gave much greater promise of being a pulpit orator than Father Uncles had) to tour the colored missions of the country.

He visited all of the large cities of the North, starting with Washington, whose two colored parishes had sent large delegations to attend his ordination and first Mass in Baltimore. Later in the fall, he began his crucial swing through the South. The same eager acceptance on the part of colored Catholics greeted him as he stopped at each of the missions in Virginia, Alabama, Mississippi, Louisiana, and Texas. His

[1] *American Catholic Historical Researches,* 20(1903), p. 18.
[2] *American Catholic Historical Researches,* 20(1903), p. 93.

sermons attracted large turnouts wherever he went. In Alabama, Booker
T. Washington heard him speak and complimented him on his oratory.
In the rural areas of Louisiana, particularly in Palmetto where Father
Peter LeBeau (the first native Louisiana Josephite) was pastor, the
congregation wept with joy at seeing one of their own at the altar of
God. One of the accounts of his first missionary tour sums up the im-
pression thus:

> Father Dorsey has visited most of the Josephite Churches and
> received a most cordial welcome. . . . He has the zeal of an
> apostle, talents of the highest order, and a mind equipped with
> a thorough knowledge of Catholic theology.[3]

At the end of his full year of spiritual barnstorming, Father Dorsey
was assigned to the mission band permanently. He was based at the
newly opened St. Joseph's College for Negro Catechists, founded at
Montgomery, Alabama, to be a "Catholic Tuskegee" and modeled
after the now famous institution that Booker T. Washington had
established not far from the Alabama capital.

Besides teaching and helping in the spiritual formation of the
dozens of colored Catholic students who enrolled in the small "college," Father Dorsey continued his work of ambassadorship for good
will among Catholics of both races. Bishop Allen of Mobile, who had
approved the Montgomery venture, invited Father Dorsey to say Mass
and to preach in his own Cathedral in Mobile where he pontificated
for the occasion.

It was in this capacity of clerical statesmanship that young Father
Dorsey made his most lasting impression in the South. He had a
kindly and genial presence, his twinkling eyes accentuating an ever-
smiling countenance. His broad forehead and prominent chin gave
strength and intelligence to his features, and his stocky stature and
barrel chest commanded attention and respect as well. When he
preached, it was with the impassioned love of truth that was redolent
of the Hebrew prophets of old, and was most often in the strong
Biblical language that had become his mother tongue. His yearning
for the salvation of souls was evident in the unflagging dedication of his

[3] *The Colored Harvest,* (1903), p. 422.

vast strength to the task at hand—preaching, visiting the sick, reclaiming the fallen-away Catholic, and crying his battle cry, *"Da mihi conversos!"* (Give me converts!)

There was one other ambition which Father Dorsey secretly nurtured, and which Father Slattery seconded. The young priest strongly desired to be the first colored pastor in the Deep South. He constantly prayed for his own church, his own congregation, and his own parish. He and his fellow Josephites fully accepted Pope Leo XIII's encyclical on the need for native clergy everywhere, as in the Philippines;[4] but still, Leo XIII had gone to his reward in 1903, before a single colored priest had been appointed to a pastorate in the South.

In 1905 the opportunity finally arrived. A vacancy suddenly occurred in a mission church founded at Pine Bluff, Arkansas, by an ex-Confederate soldier, Monsignor John Loisy, and rebuilt by Father John Ferdinand, S.S.J., after he took over in 1898. Father John Henry Dorsey was proposed to the Bishop of Little Rock, Most Reverend John B. Morris, as a possible successor to the former pastor. The bishop approved the appointment, and in October, 1905, a southern parish finally welcomed its first colored pastor.

For four years he remained as pastor of the little community. He proved himself an able administrator of parochial affairs, a successful sponsor of the 200-pupil parochial school, and a good spiritual director for the Holy Family Sisters from New Orleans who staffed the school.

In October, 1909, he was again assigned to the mission band to give his unique influence a wider play and to counteract the untoward rumors that had been spread among the Catholic Negroes of New Orleans and the Gulf Coast as a result of Father Plantevigne's unhappy experience there, as we shall see in a subsequent chapter.

For the past year or more, Catholic colored leaders had been planning the foundation of a fraternal order called the Knights of Peter Claver. In the preliminary meetings in October, 1909, Father Dorsey had played an important part, though the initiative in the foundation came from Father Conrad Rebescher on the part of the clergy (then

---

[4] The Josephites published their endorsement of the Pope's strong plea for a native clergy in *The Colored Harvest* for 1903, page 434.

pastor of Heart of Mary Church in Mobile), and from Gilbert Faustina, a successful cigar manufacturer in Mobile.

On Sunday, November 7, 1909, the solemn foundation of the Knights of Peter Claver was celebrated in Mobile in an all-day observance. At the pontifical High Mass in Mobile's Cathedral in the morning, Father Dorsey preached the sermon while Bishop Allen presided from his pontifical throne. It was a powerful plea for fraternal co-operation and the leading of exemplary Catholic lives on the part of the Knights. It set the spiritual tone for their organization, and when the initiation of the forty original members was climaxed that evening by solemn benediction of the Blessed Sacrament, everyone was convinced that the new fraternal order would be a great spiritual asset to colored Catholic America.

Father Dorsey served as national chaplain for fourteen years, from 1909 to 1923. He unfailingly attended the annual conventions and was usually featured as one of the main speakers on the program. The lay members had full confidence in his judgment and often appealed to him for guidance during the not infrequent storms that beset them in the early years. Some of the oversolicitous clergy, who demanded almost too much of a voice in the affairs of the order, precipitated many disputes with the duly elected lay officials of the order. In the midst of the wrangling, in which some bitter remarks were exchanged on both sides (even in the pages of a newspaper published in Baltimore by Father Dorsey's brother), the Knights appealed to their national chaplain to solve the difficulties.

Father Dorsey quite understandably tended to side with the lay leaders who had both law and right in their favor. He therefore requested the clergymen who had attacked and criticized the lay leadership to pledge themselves to conciliation and future abstention from the disturbing attacks. However, his fellow Josephites reserved their own right to speak out when they wished. Father Dorsey was thus obliged to let time heal the breach that he could not remedy.

Meanwhile, Father Dorsey's major and most successful enterprises were his inspiring revivalistic missions, conducted year after year up and down the reaches of the South. He teamed up with Father John Albert, S.S.J., and other missionaries to give two- and three-week missions in practically all of the Josephite parishes as they spread rapidly throughout the South. A full record of his missionary labors would read like a spiritual temperature chart of the congregations tended by Josephite pastors from Baltimore to Texas.

Father Dorsey's appeal was even broader than this. He also gave "revivals" to non-Catholics as the first step toward the establishment of a Catholic church in many a hitherto non-Catholic neighborhood. Thus in the fall of 1909, while based on St. Joseph's College in Montgomery, Father Dorsey gave a two weeks' mission to non-Catholics in Birmingham, Alabama. The result was a nucleus of twenty-five converts who were later formed into a Catholic parish.

Notwithstanding his busy itinerary, Father Dorsey kept a diary of his mission work, and excerpts from this were published from time to time in the *Colored Harvest*. These give us a glimpse of the killing pace he and his fellow missionaries set for themselves in their apostolate to the much-neglected communities of Negroes in the South. In 1913 he records his labors during a mission in Lexington, Kentucky, from November 25 to December 3. Next day he departed for a pre-Christmas revival in Meridian, Mississippi. In January, 1914, he conducted a mission for non-Catholics in Memphis, first driving all over the city to address colored audiences in meeting halls, Protestant churches (the Amen Corner at the Metropolitan Baptist Church sang out its approval of his pulpit oratory), and even at the University of West Tennessee. His energetic work before and during the mission resulted in the conversion of more than three dozen persons to the Church. And his permanent impression of Catholic good will toward his fellow Negroes was reciprocated in a spontaneously organized luncheon in his honor, attended by all of the leading professional men in the colored community.

The stepped-up pace of mission-giving continued through the year. Father Dorsey went from Memphis to San Antonio where he gave two missions, then to Galveston, Houston, and Ames in Texas, and back to Meridian, Mississippi. His duplicated success at this latter place inspired the pastor, Father James Wendel, of the Society of the Divine Word (S.V.D.), with the renewed conviction that the colored clergy was the hope for the conversion of the Negro. In a comment on Father Dorsey's missions in Meridian, he later wrote:

> If we had a hundred colored priests to labor among their own race, they would be hailed as a hundred kings by a people who hunger for their ministry. Let any reader tell me why we should not be able to have these hundred colored priests![5]

Into the summer, Father Dorsey persevered in his untiring and zealous work. He preached in south Louisiana at Plattenville and at Klotzville, and in St. Dominic's Church in New Orleans' Carrollton section. In this latter place there were 152 converts, 250 fallen-away Catholics brought back to the faith, and a total of 4,500 communions during the mission.

Along the Gulf Coast, Father Dorsey preached in Pascagoula, Mississippi, in Mobile, and Prichard, Alabama. Up the east coast he traveled, giving missions in Norfolk and in Portsmouth, Virginia. Such was his fame that even the white Knights of Columbus in Norfolk invited him to address their meeting. Non-Catholic Negro organizations like the Y.M.C.A. and an order of colored women also insisted on hearing him. He spoke in theaters and in Baptist churches, always on the theme of the Catholic Church and its work among the colored folks of the South.

In 1915 it was the same onrushing story. In January he was in Dallas for a mission of three weeks, extended because of the special demands of the crowds that flocked to St. Peter Claver Church for his talks. The same month, he had participated in the launching of a new parish in the uptown section of New Orleans where the Sisters of the Blessed Sacrament had just bought the buildings of old Southern University to set up the beginnings of Xavier University on Magazine Street. In the auditorium of the new Catholic foundation, Father Dorsey assembled the neighborhood Catholics and laid the groundwork for the now flourishing parish of the Blessed Sacrament.

His annual visits around the circuit of the Catholic missions in the South became fixtures in the civic life of the Negro communities. Such was his success that even the non-Catholic ministers began to

[5] James Wendel, *Our Negro Missions* p. 42.

take special precautions against the extension of his influence. In Mobile in 1916 the Baptists and Methodists pitched revivalist tents within earshot of the Pure Heart of Mary Church so as to disrupt by their singing and music the sermons that Father Dorsey preached. His followers nevertheless continued to multiply. He counted more than seven hundred fallen-away Catholics in one parish, brought back by his personal contact and his mission work. He made more than fifty-four converts from Protestantism in one of his missions there. He wrote:

> The locality is in a religious frenzy. Every night when our bell peals forth, all the bells of the Protestant Churches ring out in a melody of discord.[6]

Through the war years he kept up his routine of missioning and lecturing in the South. In 1917 his itinerary included Galveston, Memphis, Vicksburg, San Antonio, Walter (Mississippi), and Baltimore. It became apparent to everyone that he could not maintain the exhausting pace much longer. The same ill health that had forced him to interrupt his seminary studies now plagued him. He had to give up active work and retire to St. Joseph's Seminary in Baltimore, where he tried in the next few years to recoup his health.

By 1923 Father Dorsey had recovered sufficiently to assume charge of St. Monica's Church in Baltimore, a slum church in the waterfront section of the city, where a small group of a few dozen colored families attended Mass along with some Italian immigrants, Chinese converts, and even Indians.

With this mixed congregation, Father Dorsey labored during his last years, old age settling upon him prematurely, and all of the infirmities of body and of disposition making life quite disagreeable for him. Gone was the glamour of his exciting career as a missionary. Gone too even his chaplaincy of the Knights of Peter Claver, which he had resigned in 1923. He had remained loyal and faithful to his pledge as a Knight of Peter Claver, and had even risked the wrath of some of his fellow Josephites in defending them.

On one occasion in Mobile, while giving the first week of a mission

[6] *The Colored Harvest* (October, 1916), p. 4.

to the men, he had invited all of the Knights to come to Communion. One of them, prominent in the order, had been refused the Sacraments by the pastor because he was sending his daughter to the public high school, owing to the fact that the colored children were not admitted to the white high schools for girls, and no colored Catholic secondary school had yet been established. Father Dorsey sided with the Grand Knight, and gave him absolution in confession, and Holy Communion when he approached the altar rail. The pastor in retaliation called off the second week of Father Dorsey's mission and asked him to leave his parish.

It was incidents such as this that had contributed to Father Dorsey's breakdown. But he still continued to function as a priest at St. Monica's for three years after his recovery.

It was in 1926 that the last tragic act in his career was completed. In a dispute over some disciplinary action taken by Father Dorsey in regard to one of the school children, the father of the child, an ex-convict, became enraged at the pastor. Encountering him in the school yard, the homicidal maniac seized a heavy block of wood and struck Father Dorsey over the head with it, knocking him down and fracturing his skull.

Father Dorsey lingered on in the hospital, dying finally on June 30, 1926. His good friend, Father Charles Uncles, celebrated the solemn requiem Mass for the funeral. Two other colored priests, Father Joseph John of the Lyons African Missionaries, and Father Norman DuKette, recently ordained for the Detroit archdiocese, were deacon and sub-deacon for the farewell service.

Father Dorsey's tragic end, the story of which was grossly distorted by rumors and gossip among the whites, came to be regarded as evidence of a full-scale rejection of the colored priesthood by the colored Catholics of America. As it traveled the racial rumor routes down through the South, the story became twisted into the alleged "lynching" of their own priest by the colored congregation to which he was assigned.

Nothing could have been farther from the truth. Father Dorsey was mourned and missed by thousands. He was looked upon as the vanguard of a whole legion of colored priests to be raised up by God for the special spiritual help of his own people. His untimely breakdown from overwork and his tragic accident in Baltimore were severe blows to the hopes of Catholic Aframerica.

The damaging effect of the rumors could not be erased for years. They still persist in certain white circles of the South, even in clerical circles otherwise thought to be well informed. These distorted rumors still impede the wholehearted development of a colored clergy in the very region where God needs men of color most urgently.

Perhaps more than anyone else, Father John Dorsey implanted firmly in the collective consciousness of both colored and white Catholics the idea of the feasibility of the colored priesthood. His life and especially his missionary work were a clear demonstration that, notwithstanding the noble work and the grand gains of the white missionaries among the Negroes of the nation, the key figure in the future apostolate could not help but be the well-trained, capable, devout, and energetic colored missionary, pastor, and apostle.

It was with a consciousness of the historic import of his mission that Father Dorsey drove himself relentlessly during his brief years as a missionary. There were criticisms from the sidelines that he was more of a showpiece than an actual apostle, that the colored folks flocked to the churches to hear him as a man rather than receive his ministrations as a priest. However, the impressive number of his converts and the lasting influence of his life in Aframerica both testify that his mission as a priest was of equal importance with his symbolism as a "race man"—a Negro pioneer in a hitherto unexploited field of action.

His fire did burn him out prematurely, but not in vain. It ignited the flame of the love of God in many a young colored boy's heart, and the desire for a priest-son in many a Negro mother's breast. To these little flames would later come the fuller fire of the Holy Spirit inspiring the burning love of souls and the ardent ambition to dedicate more lives to God in the priesthood of His Church.

CHAPTER VII

Yeye Mobali: *Real "He-Man"*

ADRIAN ESNARD, C.I.C.M.

1879 – 1947

If you take a large map of Africa and trace the Congo River a thousand miles up its arching course through the Belgian Congo, you will come to the name of Lisala, a river town that now boasts of its own airport.

In 1910 the crude jungle town was the end of the journey for a pair of young missionaries, assigned by the Belgian Scheut Fathers to the task of establishing a mission in the hitherto unevangelized area.

Across half the world to this destination Father Adrian Esnard had sped to realize a wish he had conceived as a lad of four. A native of New Orleans, he had been born on January 7, 1879, the fourth of eight children, five boys and three girls. He was baptized in the historic old church of St. Mary's next to the Ursuline Convent in the French Quarter. As the scion of an old French Creole family, he had, like many others of mixed parentage, enrolled for his elementary and secondary schooling at the Jesuit College of the Immaculate Conception on Baronne and Common streets. Later, with his two older brothers, he also attended for a time the Jesuits' St. Charles College in Grand Coteau.

The family home in the French Quarter (where his father ran a furniture store) was often visited by priests of the nearby Church of St. Augustine. Father Joseph Subileau, a silken-bearded patriarch stationed at the church for forty-nine years, deeply impressed four-year-old Adrian. "I want to be a priest like Papa Bileau, and wear a long beard," the child declared one day. His father used this to shape his ways in virtue. "If you want to be a priest like Papa Bileau, you have to be good!" This was his constant admonition when the youngster got into childish mischief.

However, it was a visiting Belgian priest, Father Alphonse C. Kettles, who was the deciding influence in Adrian's choice of his field of labor. Recruiting seminarians for the foreign missions, Father Kettles dropped in at the Esnard home. He asked the pious mother whether she would give up her son to be a missionary-priest. She called her son in. "Would you like to try the *petite seminaire* in Belgium?" The sixteen-year-old lad was enthusiastic. "Oh, yes, *ma mère*," he answered. "Would you study hard?" "Oh yes, yes, *ma mère*," he repeated.

Thus it was that in 1895 Adrian Esnard enrolled at the College of St. Nicholas in Waes, Belgium. There he made a reputation for himself as a lively and intelligent scholar. The reports going home to his parents gratified his mother, but made his father believe that he could become a doctor or a lawyer. His father did not want him to be a missionary.

In 1899, upon completing his work at St. Nicholas College, he cabled his parents for permission to go to Lourdes on a pilgrimage. There beneath the statue of Massabielle, he made his final decision. Though he had toyed with the idea of becoming a member of the Pères Blancs (White Fathers), his confessor had advised him to consider the Immaculate Heart (Scheut) Fathers. He sent another cablegram to his parents. "I've made a decision. I'm joining the Immaculate Heart Fathers."

Letters were exchanged. His father tried to persuade him to return to the States and become at least a diocesan priest so that he could be near home. Adrian felt God calling him to surrender fully to a life of mission toil. Besides, he felt that he could not become a diocesan priest, particularly in New Orleans.

His parents finally gave their consent. He entered the novitiate of the Society of the Immaculate Heart near Brussels on September 7, 1899. A year later on the feast of the Nativity of the Blessed Virgin, he pronounced his religious vows. A year after this, his parents visited him in Scheut. His father tried to persuade him to become a doctor, a lawyer, or at least a diocesan priest. "No, *mon père,* I'd not be a priest if I could not be a missionary," Adrian said. "Well, I see you have a real vocation," the father finally admitted.

For five years Adrian studied philosophy, theology, and mission languages, first at Scheut, and then at Louvain. There he was ordained to the missionary priesthood on June 17, 1905. Only after this did he return home for his first solemn High Mass which he said in old St. Augustine's Church in the French section of New Orleans near Esplanade Avenue.

A distant cousin of his mother, Father Theophile Wircher, who was a Father of Mercy stationed in New York City, came to New Orleans to preach the sermon at the memorable ceremony. Old Father Joseph Subileau was still pastor, still stroking his long white beard, and still exciting holy envy in young Father Adrian to grow a beard like that. It was not long before he was allowed to try his chin at rivaling Father Subileau. One of his first missionary assignments was to the Philippines. He headed a mission band sent out by the Scheut Fathers, having been chosen as superior because of his dual mastery of French and English, and because he would thus be a very able intermediary between the Belgian missionaries and the American Government then in power in Manila.

The petty government officials in the Philippines took a different view of the matter. They found Father Adrian's Creole background to be objectionable. They refused to deal with him as head of the mission. Finally, in 1908, they insisted that he be recalled to Belgium. It was a severe blow for the young priest, unaccustomed to this sort of narrow bigotry which he had encountered neither in the free-and-easy atmosphere of Catholic New Orleans, nor in the equally tolerant Belgian schools. All that he had to show for his time in the Orient was a bushy black beard that was fast rivaling Father Subileau's in length.

Father Adrian's ambition to be a missionary was not smothered by this first rebuff. He volunteered for the Congo mission, and soon after his return to Europe, he was again on a ship bound for the adventures of the mission.

Arriving in the Congo in 1909, he was first assigned to the Kangu (Mayombe) station to learn the language. In 1910 he was transferred to Nsona-Mbata, but was there only a few months when he was called to penetrate a thousand miles deep into the Congo hinterland. With a

Father Baeten, he set out for Lisala to found the new mission of Boyange-St. Paul.

It was here that Father Adrian proved himself to the natives and to his fellow missionaries to be "yeye mobali"—a real he-man. To him they all looked in awe and admiration as he carved his mission compound out of the bush and built up the most thriving Christian settlement in the whole vicariate of Lisala.

For two years Father Baeten tried to keep up with the pace that Father Adrian set in his struggle against the ever-encroaching bush and the prostrating heat. When Father Baeten had to give up, Father Adrian was appointed superior in 1912, thus assuming the responsibility for the whole mission station.

Teaching the natives to make bricks and to build solidly the structures of the mission was a trying task. He wanted a lordly and imposing church of which he and his newly won Christians could be proud. But when it was almost finished, it suddenly collapsed. Father Adrian corrected the structural defects in his next plans, and went ahead to rebuild the church. Soon after it was dedicated, it burned down. He rebuilt it once again, and it still stands, with its high bell tower and its nicely proportioned lines as a monument to his indomitable determination.

That same iron will pushed through the construction of the other sections of the mission compound: the school, the large rectory, the convent for the Sisters, the hospital, and all of the farm buildings.

In Boyange on the extensive lands, Father Adrian laid out a date-palm plantation that became the best in the whole region. It prospered so much that he was able to support the missions of half of the vicariate on the proceeds.

But the fruits that he sought most eagerly were those of the spiritual realm. He planted well, sowing the seeds of God's grace in the backward children of the Congo lowlands. He mastered their language and taught them their faith both through sermons, catechism lessons, and hymn-singing with his deep booming voice. He won his children's hearts by teaching them Negro spirituals, leading them in the rhythmic melodies by beating time with his hands on his knee as he sat, or clapping as he stood. He sang them the Creole French hymns of New

Orleans as well as the devotional Breton hymns of France. The native people came to love the bearded patriarch whose fearsome beard was offset by the shining, soft eyes of his deeply spiritual and fatherly countenance.

Under the African sun, Father Adrian became nut-browned and weather-beaten. The great bushy eyebrows grew like a protecting hedge over his eyes, weakened by the fierceness of the sun. His beard billowed out into a majestic and patriarchal sign of his pre-eminence among the beardless natives. But in spite of the towering power of his presence, he retained his happy disposition and tempered his iron discipline over the new Christians with a love that bound them together in a community which became the model of the whole vicariate.

For ten straight years he stayed with his neophytes in the depths of the Congo. Finally, in 1923, his superiors decided that he should have a sabbatical leave for a few months. They sent him back to America to visit his family, to give lectures on the missions, and to collect donations for the support of new missionary enterprises.

Before the vacation time was over, he was speeding back to his second home in the middle Congo.

"Yeye mobali" received a royal welcome when he returned to his native tribesmen. They were glad to have their smiling, courageous, iron-willed spiritual chieftain back again, even though it meant more work for the innately lazy, sterner sermons for the lax, and tightened discipline in school and in the village.

His corps of assistants and fellow missionaries, who worked out of the large center of Boyange in caring for the mission stations in the surrounding villages, were also happy to have Father Adrian with them once more. They prevailed on him to sing the songs that gave them their only entertainment in the upper country. Father Adrian boomed out with his favorite "Sonny Boy," the song he always sang for the reunions of the Fathers.

As he surveyed his mission and his flock, he could not help but be proud of it and of them, especially when he compared them with others he had visited on his way to and from his vacation. His 2,500 communicants were one of the largest Christian communities in the Congo. Notwithstanding the thatched roof that still covered the lower roofs over the side aisles, his church was by far the most imposing in all of the upcountry. His mission gardens and walks were beautifully laid out and set off by hedges and rows of palm trees. Even the roads on the plantation were kept in better repair than those elsewhere washed out by the heavy rains of the tropical summers.

Father Adrian resumed the routine missionary life once more. His one diversion was an occasional foray into the bush in quest of big game. He had become an expert hunter and a good shot, despite the eyeglasses he had to wear. In his best years, he could shoot a heron through the neck at a distance of a hundred yards. Even the younger tribesmen were envious of his skill and energy on the hunt. He was "yeye mobali"—a real he-man.

After he passed his fiftieth birthday in 1929, however, he began to show signs of failing. His health began to give way under the relentless tropical sun. In 1931 his superiors recalled him to Belgium for a rest cure. Upon his arrival there in late June, he received a cable telling him of his father's death on June 2.

In the fall of that year, after he had recovered his health, the Scheut superior again allowed him to come home for a visit to his aging mother. He spent several months with her before the restlessness of the missionary spirit impelled him to ask for a reassignment to the Congo. At the age of fifty-two he began all over again as he had in 1910.

Superiors assigned him to a virgin field at Mbaya, which, like Boyange, lies just a few degrees from the equator in the heat-infested bush. There Father Adrian shaped another mission out of the wild land. Everything had to be built: house, church, school, hospital, plantation. In a few years he had raised it all. He had won new hundreds of the people to the faith. He had established himself as the spiritual patriarch of the region.

His long years of experience with the natives had given him a vast fund of knowledge and a shrewd and sharpened judgment. Even government officials came to consult him about their projects and programs for the betterment of the Congo. His influence was felt up and down the river from Leopoldville to Stanleyville.

All the while he remained a simple, devout priest. He was scrupulous in saying his breviary daily. He often spent more than three-quarters of an hour for his daily Mass. And his soul was so attuned to the will of God that he often ran out of the confessional because hearing all of the offenses against God was too hard for him to bear.

His mother died in January, 1939, and Father Adrian suddenly felt old and tired as he approached his sixtieth birthday. Sickness and the infirmities of age crept up on him. He tried to ignore them, for he did not want to rest or retire. He wanted to stay on the job as a missionary to the end. In 1945, at the age of sixty-six, he was still outdistancing the younger men in his missionary achievements. He was still the joy of the community, teaching the younger priests how to sing so that the natives would be captured for God by their love for music.

From his post deep in the back country, he followed the progress of the war and the establishment of peace in 1945. He wrote in a letter of February 16, 1946:

> By this time I guess all the boys are back and we must thank God fervently for having protected them and brought them back safe and sound. Let us hope that 1946 will bring peace to the world just as 1945 brought us victory. But what is Victory without peace? I may be blind, but I cannot see a single country where they now enjoy real peace, and there is a very dark cloud which covers the world and seems to spread out more and more. I speak of communism. I cannot understand how England and America can allow Russia to act as she does. The Russians like the others promised that all countries could freely choose their own government and she imposes everywhere a communist government without consulting the people. Why don't they allow Russia itself to have free elections? And still, Russia protests against England because England insists upon free elections in Greece. May God in His divine bounty grant us all real peace.

The last of his wars came to an end within two years. He succumbed to the tropical fevers early in 1947 and was sent down the river to the clinic at Leopoldville. There he lingered for a few months, hoping to regain his health, but telling Father Polle who was with him, "If God should call me, I will have served Him for forty-three years. I put myself under the Mantle of Jesus, and pray for His Mercy that He will grant me a place near Him in heaven."

On Saturday, June 18, 1947, "Yeye Mobali" went home to God, full of holy days before God and men. His Christians mourned him. Out of their hard-earned money, they raised funds for more than a thousand Masses for his soul.

Father Adrian was buried in the mission graveyard at Leopoldville, far from the land he owned as his native country. He retained his American citizenship all his life. He held no bitterness toward America for the pettiness of its officials who expelled him from American possessions in 1908. But I know at least one American who hangs his head in shame that his great country did not treat this great man of God with the reverence and respect he deserved.

While Father Adrian's birth certificate clearly indicated his race as "colored" and thus places his case outside the realm of conjecture, an investigator runs into numerous other cases similar to his that elude verification.

Historically, there is the nebulous story about "Father Paddington," often referred to as the first colored priest. He is supposed to have been a West Indian whose ship, driven off course by a storm, took refuge in Charleston harbor during the days of Bishop England. The doughty prelate is said to have given him hospitality in his home when the local authorities were about to give him the accommodations of their jail. Another version tells of Bishop England's ordaining of a colored priest during the first half of the nineteenth century. But it is now conceded that if this happened, it must have been while Bishop England was in San Domingo as Papal Legate, and not while functioning as bishop in North and South Carolina.

Another rumor that eluded checking told of how two brothers, born of colored parentage in the South, went North and were ordained as priests, serving for years in some unnamed northern diocese under the name of "Father Green." This seems to be but a fourth-hand version of the Healy story.

Still another case is that of Father Amadee Guyol, S.J., who belonged to the southern province of the Society of Jesus. He was believed to have been a colored priest because, while he was stationed in New

Orleans, some colored folks from the French Quarter would come to the Jesuit College and ask to see "Uncle Amadee."

It turns out upon investigation that Father Guyol's father married a mulatto Creole after the death of his mother, and raised a second family with whom Father Guyol was on good terms. His other brothers ultimately ostracized the second wife after the death of her husband, and drove her and her children out of the paternal home. They went to St. Louis to live. The story reaches full circle within a few years when Frater Philip Allen, S.V.D., now studying at St. Augustine's Seminary in Bay St. Louis, will follow his great-uncle's path to the altar of ordination.

Another whose course briefly ran parallel to that of other priests included in this volume is Father Sebastian Arjonilla, a native of Stann Creek, British Honduras, where he was taught by the Sisters of the Holy Family. He was known as Spanish and "white" down there, but when his classmates Philip Marin and Alban Velasquez entered St. Augustine's Seminary, he accompanied them. After a few years he transferred to Notre Dame Seminary in New Orleans. He was ordained for the New Orleans archdiocese and is still a pastor in good standing there.

A final case that is still in the "hear-and-tell" stage is that of a colored boy born in Pass Christian, Mississippi, who was sent, according to the story, to the seminary in Louvain, Belgium, by Monsignor John Prendergast, former pastor of Our Lady of the Gulf in Bay St. Louis, before the first World War. He is said to have been ordained in Louvain for one of the dioceses in the British West Indies where he rose to become vicar-general. It is added that he visited Monsignor Prendergast in Vicksburg in 1938. Thus far, investigation has not revealed whether this is simply a black-coffee rendering of Father Esnard's story or is that of a separate person whose life should be included in this volume.

CHAPTER VIII

Capitol Hill's First Colored Priest

FATHER JOSEPH C. BURGESS, C.S.Sp.

1 8 8 0 – 1 9 2 3

There have been colored Catholics living on Capitol Hill in Washington since before the laying out of the city and the building of the national Capitol itself. In the decades before Congress chose the Potomac site for the capital, the lands on Capitol Hill were the property of Daniel Carroll of Duddington, cousin of one of the Catholic signers of the Declaration of Independence, Charles Carroll of Carrollton.

Daniel Carroll was a rich landowner and slaveholder who lived in Duddington Manor and there raised all of his family and his bondsmen as Catholics, holding religious services and even Mass for them in the manor chapel when an itinerant Jesuit missionary passed through on his travels.

In 1790 Daniel Carroll acceded to George Washington's request that he surrender his plantation with its majestic sweeping view of the Potomac, to be the location for the proposed center of government of the newly born United States. Carroll took recompense in the form of some lots in the future city, and on one of these he built his own home at Third and "C" streets, S.E., just a few squares from the Capitol. He continued to have religious services in his new mansion for the Irish workers who built the Capitol and for the family and domestics of the Catholic household.

In due course, when a church was built at Second and "C" streets, S.E., on a plot of ground donated by Carroll for the purpose in 1821, a gallery was provided to accommodate the free men of color and the Catholic domestics of the neighborhood who attended Mass along with the white Catholics. In old St. Peter's the colored parishioners were baptized and married, confirmed and buried, as was expected of all Catholics. Even after Emancipation, the colored continued to frequent St. Peter's despite the erection of the special Church of St. Augustine's across town in the Northwest district.

It was in one of these Catholic colored homes on "B" Street between First and Second streets, Southeast, just across the street from the Library of Congress and a stone's throw from the Capitol grounds, that a baby was born to a devout young couple on January 22, 1880. He was baptized in St. Peter's Church as Joseph Burgess. Notwithstanding the constant prayers of his parents for increase, he remained an only child, and was carefully nurtured in their modest home on "B" Street.

His father earned a living by working at odd jobs, among them that of a billboard poster. His mother supplemented the family's meager income by running a dressmaking establishment with her sister, Laura Simpson. Together, the parents were thus able to raise young Joseph properly and send him to the nearby public school. The St. Peter's Catholic School did not admit colored boys, and St. Augustine's School was too far away for the young boy in the 1880's.

Two years before his birth, however, a group of the Capitol Hill and Southeast colored Catholics had petitioned Archbishop Gibbons in the name of the eight hundred Catholic parishioners of Capitol Hill's two parishes, asking for adequate care for their spiritual needs. The petition set in motion events that led, during Joseph Burgess' young boyhood, to the establishment of another colored Catholic parish in the Capitol Hill area. It was opened in 1894, as St. Cyprian's Church.

Under the new pastor, Father James Matthews, who had been summoned from Anne Arundel County two years before to organize the parish, Joseph became the first altar boy in the new church. It was located at Thirteenth and "C" streets not far from Lincoln Square.

Halfway between his home and church, the Oblate Sisters of Providence, a colored Catholic sisterhood with headquarters in Baltimore, founded St. Ann's Academy in 1892. Joseph enrolled in the new school and quickly became the outstanding student in the small group of thirty-six who comprised the student body. Joe was a diligent and brilliant pupil in comparison with the others. He led his class without effort, and became a favorite with the Sisters, especially Sister Clementine who also tutored him privately to keep him busy and active.

Joe was a resourceful boy. To support himself through his school years, now that his mother was ailing and unable to continue her dressmaking, he secured a printing press. After learning to operate it skillfully, he set himself up as an amateur printer, and in this way earned enough for his expenses during his school years.

His teachers remembered him as a pious boy who was serious and religious, never rough and rowdy. He was well groomed and handsome. Though well liked by the girls, he never went out with them, not even on parish picnics across the river in Anacostia during the summer. Sister Clementine encouraged him in his secret desire to become a priest, and Father Matthews, whose faithful altar boy Joe remained through his late teens, also urged the young lad to aspire to the sacred dignity.

In 1898 it was decided that St. Ann's Academy had given Joe all of the education it could supply. Because he was the only boy ready to graduate, the commencement exercises at the end of that year were held for him alone, as the first graduate of the school. Sister Clementine was there to share the happy program and to listen to the valedictory speech that young Joe delivered. After the ceremony he whispered to her, "I'm going to make you happy again, I'm going to become a priest."

His mother had died during his last year at school, and though Joe grieved over it long and deeply, he bore up bravely under the loss. It freed him from one of the ties that might have held him back from his vocation. The next summer, shortly after his graduation, he submitted his application to Epiphany Apostolic College near Baltimore. He asked the Josephite Fathers to accept him as a candidate for the priesthood in their seminary.

In the fall of 1898 he packed up and left Washington for the first stage of his journey toward the priesthood. At the new seminary in Walbrook, a suburb of Baltimore, Joe quickly became accustomed to the routine of the ten-year-old institution. Though there were other colored students in the mixed school during those years, Joe somehow did not like the life that the Josephite seminarians were training to lead.

In 1902, when twenty-two years old, he transferred to the Holy Ghost Fathers' School at Cornwells Heights, Pennsylvania, and the following year was admitted to their novitiate. On August 15, 1904, he pronounced his religious vows as a Holy Ghost seminarian, and three weeks later he set sail for Europe to study at the Holy Ghost School of Theology in Chevilly, France.

It was in France that he was ordained on July 14, 1907, as a priest forever. The same day he made his apostolic consecration, dedicating his life to the missionary apostolate of the Holy Ghost Fathers.

His return home to Washington for his first High Mass was a triumphal occasion for St. Cyprian's parish. He was the first colored priest from Washington, and the first boy from the parish to achieve the heights of his priestly ambitions. The alumni of St. Ann's quickly organized for a grand reception. A special program in his honor was held at the school after the solemn Mass. Sister Clementine was there to welcome her former pupil, to receive his priestly blessing, and to speak to him in French now that he had mastered the language she taught him years before.

Father Matthews gave him a hearty welcome as his special pride and protégé. He arranged for Father Burgess' first sermon in the city, a short exhortation on the necessity for Christian education. People drank in his simple words. They knelt later at the altar rail to receive his blessing as one of their own.

His brilliant career in the seminary, however, stood in the way of his missionary work. Because of his facility with letters and books, Father Burgess was assigned to teach in the seminary at Cornwells Heights in Pennsylvania. He accepted the hidden life of the seminary professor, and buried himself in his books and classes. He became a favorite of the Sisters of the Blessed Sacrament in Cornwells Heights, and was often invited to say Mass in their chapel and to give them exhortations and conferences. He was not an emotional or revivalistic speaker. He talked plainly and well, and though he was a trifle nervous, he manifested his energetic temperament mainly by walking rapidly and being somewhat Gallic in his gesticulations.

Occasionally, during his twelve years as a seminary professor, he traveled into the South to do missionary work or to substitute for a chaplain during the summer months. He was assigned to Rock Castle, Virginia, as a chaplain for one of the schools there, and had other assignments that were part-time and limited to vacations.

His first missionary call was to the primitive mission of Haiti. In 1919 he was based at the College Saint Martial in Port-au-Prince during the American occupation of Haiti following the first World War. Superiors believed that his American citizenship (the Haiti missionaries were mostly French) and his mastery of French would make him a good intermediary between the French and Americans, and his colored background would ingratiate him with the natives. Unfortunately, there was little chance for him to display his native talents. His health broke down in the tropical climate and he was obliged to return to the States.

One of the stories he used to tell of the perils of mission life in Haiti manifested his sense of humor in a grim sort of way. He said that one of the natives from the bush came to the primitive village in which he was at one time located, and told him that a sick man wanted to have the priest. Father Burgess followed him on foot for miles out into the steaming jungle. Finally, the sharp-toothed, wild-eyed native turned on the young priest and snorted, "Father, you'd better turn back and go home, I feel like eating you!" One look at the man in that state of emotion convinced Father Burgess that he had been tricked by a headhunter and was in danger of losing his head. He sped back to the village before the man's appetite ran away with him.

Back in Cornwells Heights, Father Burgess recuperated enough to resume his routine work as a priest. His father meanwhile had become old and feeble. Father Burgess was obliged to go down to Washington and arrange for his accommodation at the Little Sisters of the Poor. There the faithful old man was sheltered and cared for until his death some years later.

Sister Clementine was also invalided during these latter years. Father Joe visited her to comfort his old teacher to whose prayers and encouragement he felt he owed his vocation. She died in 1921 and his Masses for her shortened her brief stay in Purgatory.

It was during 1920 that Father Burgess became the center of a controversy that raged in the pages of the *Crisis*. It was touched off by an article entitled "The Catholic Church and the Negro Priest," by a colored man named George Joseph McWilliams. The writer declared that he had applied to be admitted to St. Joseph's Seminary in Baltimore and was turned down by the Josephites because he was colored. The article appeared in the January issue, and the next month Father Hanley wrote to explain that the man had been rejected not because he was colored but because he had misrepresented himself and had been caught in untruths and inaccuracies that manifested character defects undesirable in a candidate for the priesthood. "At the time of Mr. McWilliams' application, there was a colored student in the college, and at the same time two other colored candidates had been accepted," Father Hanley asserted.

Still the controversy continued. McWilliams applied for admission into the Fathers of the Holy Ghost and was likewise rejected. He wrote a wholly imaginary account of the interview with the priest who examined him, in the course of which McWilliams, now an irate apostate, declared that the priest had said that Father Burgess had never been what a priest should be, and that no colored man had ever been a successful priest anywhere in the world, not even in Africa. He further accused Father Park of saying:

> We have no colored students and are not going to take any. Almighty God does not want a colored man for a priest. He is absolutely unfit morally, physically, and effectively. Prejudice, sentiment and authority are against it, and one with a sound mind ought to know that God does not want him. Colored people don't want them, and the white people can't use them. This is the decision of the U.S. Catholic Councils, and if you do not accept it you are in vain.

It was obvious to anyone that a diseased mind had produced this tirade against Father Burgess and his fellow priests. In defense of Father Joe, his provincial wrote, "Father Burgess is a talented and

exemplary member of the Congregation of the Holy Ghost." And
Father Park issued a categorical denial of the McWilliams statement:

> This is absolutely untrue. On the contrary, I sympathized
> with the gentleman, told him to persevere in prayer, etc.,
> and added that if he really had a vocation, our Divine Lord
> would certainly give him the opportunity to follow it.

To demonstrate how high a standing Father Burgess maintained in
the Holy Ghost congregation, his superiors that year appointed him
assistant pastor in St. Joachim's Church in Detroit. In this French-
Canadian parish, Father Burgess continued his ministry to the end
of his life. He was well accepted by the French-speaking parishioners
and by the rest of the English-speaking clergy as well. He became a
fast friend of Bishop Gallagher and also of Mayor Thompson, the
latter often inviting him to his country home for dinner.

For both of these dignitaries and for other pastors around the city,
Father Burgess made use of the mechanical hobbies he had cultivated
for the past fifteen years. He had been experimenting with a device
known as "radio telephony" at a time when very few homes possessed
"radios." Father Burgess had mastered the secrets of the new invention
and had constructed a number of experimental receiving sets. He personally built the first sets that the bishop and the mayor installed in
their homes. In fact, it was rumored around Detroit that he had invented a secret mechanism (a radio direction finder, possibly) that the
Army bought and used during the first World War.

There was also a rumor current in Detroit and in colored circles
along the eastern seaboard that Father Burgess was the inventor of
the famed Burgess Battery. One still hears this repeated in clerical
circles to the present day. It is of course a pure fantasy, with no foundation in fact. The actual inventor of the battery was Charles Frederick
Burgess, a white man, native of Oshkosh, Wisconsin, a noted professor
at the University of Wisconsin, where he founded the department of
chemical engineering and devised and patented a number of improve-
ments on the dry-cell batteries of the period.

Father Burgess had no connection with Professor Burgess, nor with the Burgess Battery Company. All of the patents are held in the name of the famous inventor, none in the name of the humble and retiring priest.[1]

It was not in the field of mechanical inventions, but in the obscure and routine work as a parish assistant that Father Burgess passed the last years of his life. Some of the parishioners knew that he was a colored priest, but not all of these would even tell their children this fact. Other parishioners did not realize that he was a Negro, and even to this day are surprised by inquiries such as I made about the parish reaction to the presence of a colored assistant.

Father Burgess shouldered his share of parish duties. Both of the other priests at the church, Fathers Sheridan and Schultz, could also preach and hear confessions in French, the former as a result of his seminary years in France, the latter because he was a native Alsatian. Notwithstanding the stories about his being overworked, Father Burgess did not undertake more than the usual amount of labor for a parish priest. He had in fact much leisure time for the pursuit of his hobbies, and was certainly not "worked to death," as one account intimated.

Rather, because of the still-lingering effects of the tropical diseases he had contracted and never fully thrown off, Father Burgess seems to have been well cared for in his Detroit years.

The tropical ailments caught up with him in 1923. He was admitted to St. Mary's Hospital with kidney and other organic disorders. He did not respond to the doctors' treatment or to the weeks of excellent care that the Sisters gave him. On November 4, 1923, he piously passed away at the age of forty-two.

His good friend Bishop Michael Gallagher celebrated the requiem Mass for the funeral at St. Joachim's on Wednesday, November 7. The remains of Father Burgess were buried in the Mount Elliot Cemetery.

The Detroit papers gave him only a passing few paragraphs of notice when he died. He created no greater ripple on the surface of history than many a thousand of humble, obscure, and faithful priests,

[1] All of the details of the Burgess battery inventions are fully elaborated in Alexander McQueen's *A Romance in Research: The Life of Charles F. Burgess* (Pittsburgh: The Instruments Publishing Company, 1951).

but he is still remembered by the people to whom he ministered. One pious old soul did not want to lend me his portrait that still stood on the central mantelpiece in her parlor. "At night," she said, "I often talk to him. He was a holy priest."

CHAPTER IX

The Broken Heart

FATHER JOHN PLANTEVIGNE, S.S.J.

1871 – 1913

Acadian Catholic Louisiana did not long lag behind Creole New Orleans and Catholic Maryland in raising in its spiritual seed bed a number of pious religious lads who aspired to the priesthood.

The first of these to be ordained was Father John Plantevigne, who came from an old colored Catholic family in Pointe Coupee parish (County), more than a hundred miles up the Mississippi from New Orleans.

The river town of Pointe Coupee in the center of the parish had been for more than 150 years a scene of French Catholic activity. Capuchin and Jesuit missionaries had stopped off there to administer the Sacraments even before the first church was built in 1738. The Catholic community shared in the changing fortunes of the colony as it passed from French, to Spanish, to American hands in the course of the next hundred years. In the early nineteenth century, Father Antoine Blanc (later Bishop and Archbishop of New Orleans, 1836-60) was pastor of the Church of Pointe Coupee. On his missionary journeys, he baptized the children of the plantations in the area, both white and colored.

There was a background of great bitterness between the two races because of the disorders of the War Between the States. The Federal troops had arrested the Catholic pastor of Pointe Coupee because he was one of the leading spirits in the resistance to the Unionists. In the course of their progress up the river, Farragut's men had burned the Church of St. Francis at Pointe Coupee in retaliation for the sniping at them that went on day and night. Feeling ran high against the

Yankees and all they stood for—emancipation, equality, and republicanism.

It was in this milieu of war-engendered animosity that John Joseph Plantevigne was born, October 22, 1871, on a small farm near Chenel, just a few miles from Pointe Coupee and Fausse Riviere, later called New Roads. His mother died when he and his brother Albert were still quite young. They were raised by his strictly Catholic grandmother. She kept them loyal to the Church notwithstanding their attendance at the small country public school in which they received their elementary education.

From the time they were in their teens, John and Albert picked cotton to earn enough money for their keep and their schooling. Both were bright and intelligent lads, and for a while John in turn taught in the simple one-room schoolhouse down the road.

In 1897, at twenty-six years of age, John and his brother went down the river to New Orleans and enrolled in Straight College on Canal Street, a Protestant institution operated by the Congregationalist Church's American Missionary Association. It was here that the brothers parted ways. John's deep religious feelings were inextricably bound up with the Catholic Church. He felt called to be a priest. He learned of the progressive and optimistic attitude of Archbishop Janssens, who had insisted that the colored priest was to be the instrument in the hands of God to evangelize his colored brethren. Before his first year at Straight was finished, John sent in his application to the Josephite Seminary in Baltimore. He was admitted for the term beginning in September, 1898.

His brother Albert remained at Straight College. He left the Catholic Church and joined the Congregationalists. Within a few years, he became a minister in the Puritan Church, serving for a time at one of their New Orleans churches. He married a New Orleans girl, and in 1901 the American Missionary Association financed his return to his native parish to start a Protestant church and school for the neglected children at Pointe Coupee. He worked successfully at the pioneer task for four years until 1905.

Meanwhile, John Plantevigne had traveled to Baltimore and entered

Epiphany College in Walbrook, just outside Baltimore. He threw himself into the training for the priesthood with a maturity and seriousness that soon made him a model of religious observance. Men noticed his deeply religious piety, his frequent and lengthy visits to the Blessed Sacrament even outside the appointed times, and the unspoiled innocence of soul that shone through his untroubled eyes.

The superiors of the seminary at length appointed him as custodian of the sacristy. In that office he took special care of the sacred vestments and of the altars in the community chapel. (He was neat and clean about his own person.) He kept the altar linens immaculate and spent long hours cleaning the sanctuary and sacristy to make them spotless for their holy functions.

Graduating from the minor seminary in 1901 with a good mastery of Latin, John transferred to St. Joseph's Seminary on Pennsylvania Avenue in Baltimore. There he pursued the study of philosophy and theology. He advanced with his class through all of the minor orders, and was halfway through his course when shattering news came to him in 1905.

His brother had been well received in his home parish for the first two years of his school work. But furious white opposition arose against him when he projected and started a high school for the colored in 1904. He and his wife and three children were threatened with violence if he pursued his plans. Undaunted, he went ahead with his educational work. One day, while returning from the Oscar post office a few miles down the road from his school, Albert was ambushed by two white gunmen who shot him in cold blood, blowing the back of his head off, and leaving him and his dead horse on the open road to terrorize the Negroes in the vicinity. His widow and his grandmother fled with the three children to Baton Rouge. Sometime later one of the men suspected of the killing was in turn himself slain as though in retribution.

The tragedy was a severe blow for John Plantevigne, now a young ordinand looking forward to the reception of Holy Orders. Nonetheless, John redoubled his determination to vindicate his church and to dedicate himself to work for his neglected people. His ordination date was advanced almost a year. He and his classmate, Father John

Albert, S.S.J., were ordained on September 21, 1907, in the St. Joseph Seminary Chapel in Baltimore, Bishop Alfred A. Curtis officiating.

The new priest was given leave to return to his native parish for the offering of his first solemn High Mass. He stopped in New Orleans on the first Sunday of October and offered Mass in St. Katherine's Church on Tulane Avenue, the first colored Catholic church in the Crescent City.

Then, notwithstanding the warnings of his relatives who urged him to stay away lest he meet with the same fate that befell his brother, Father Plantevigne entrained for Pointe Coupee.

He was welcomed at the train by Father Louis Savoure when he arrived at Chenel, Louisiana.[1] His old pastor, who had regularly sent him funds for his seminary expenses, willingly allowed him to say Mass in his church on a weekday for his relatives and friends. It was all done quietly and without publicity, in order not to excite the frenzy of those who had conspired to do away with his brother.

Later in the month, he spent some time in Baton Rouge with his grandmother and his sister-in-law, offering Mass in the convent at the parochial school where the Sisters received him in a kindly fashion. He returned to New Orleans to continue his new priestly pilgrimage, and his performance of his sacred duties so impressed the colored Catholics of St. Katherine's Church that they asked him to stay with them as their pastor. The Holy Family Sisters welcomed him to their

---

[1] One of the legends still current in south Louisiana about the Plantevignes seems to be a strange mixture of the stories of Albert LeForest Plantevigne and Father John, his brother. According to the story (which was not verified by Albert's widow, nor confirmed by on-the-spot checking), a self-appointed delegation of whites is supposed to have met the train at the New Roads station when Father Plantevigne was scheduled to arrive. They supposedly formed a cordon around the Jim Crow car and would not allow him to get off the train. Thus they allegedly blocked his attempt to say Mass in New Roads. The widow of his brother affirmed to me that Father Plantevigne did say Mass in his home parish of Chenel, but did not even want to go to New Roads for Mass there, though the Negro friends of the Plantevigne family gave a benefit program for him, to raise some money as a gift to the newly ordained priest. Father Plantevigne did not appear at the program, mainly because the enemies of his brother were still in New Roads. He did, however, pay his last respects to his brother by blessing the simple grave on the grounds of the now-abandoned school.

chapel in their convent on Orleans Street just behind the Cathedral in the French Quarter. There too he chanted High Mass during his stay.

This cordial welcome was balm to the wounds he had received in his first tragic contact with racial prejudice against his family. He returned to Baltimore to continue his preparation for the dual battle before him.

His Josephite superiors decided that he should have special training as a missionary to equip him for a career in the footsteps of Father Dorsey, who was creating a profound impression in the South by his stirring missions.

Father Plantevigne therefore enrolled with Father Albert at the Catholic University of America in Washington. There in the Paulist Fathers' special school for missionaries in Protestant America, the two young priests studied under Father Walter Elliott and Father Alexander P. Doyle, C.S.P. At their Brookland Mission House, Father Plantevigne learned many of the secrets of dealing with the anti-Catholic mind. He wrote and practiced and rewrote his sermons in preparation for a long career of mission work.

The career started in February, 1908, with a three weeks' mission at the new Church of St. Barnabas on Biddle and Argyle Avenue in Baltimore. The Paulist Father Doyle opened the mission and then turned it over to the neophytes, Fathers Plantevigne and Albert. Together the two young priests spent themselves in preaching, catechizing, hearing confessions, reclaiming lost sheep. They combined pulpit work with neighborhood visiting, going into the slums in quest of fallen-away Catholics and prospective converts. They baptized many children of Catholic families, instructed adults in their religion, and ended up with a total of seventy converts from Protestantism as their first conquests for the faith.

During the subsequent months, while continuing their training at Catholic University, the pair of missionaries-to-be took turns in Baltimore at gathering in the harvest at St. Barnabas by follow-up work. They thus continued their catechetical classes and convert work for months after the mission closed.

It was this thorough and systematic method of reviving Catholic life that the missionaries planned to follow as a team during the next few years. In the fall of the year they began with a spectacular mission at St. Joseph's Church in Wilmington, Delaware, October 11-25. One of the special attractions for the mission was the hundred-boy choir from St. Joseph's Colored Boys' Home in Clayton, Delaware. But the center of attraction, according to the Wilmington *Standard and Times,* was the "presence of Father Plantevigne, the colored missionary, who won the admiration of his auditors by his prepossessing appearance and his forceful eloquence." Several non-Catholic ministers attended the services out of curiosity. They heard, but did not heed, Father Plantevigne's "Plain Facts for Fair Minds," and his talk on "Why I Am a Catholic."

Father Plantevigne's engaging manner and handsome looks made him the idol of the youngsters in the parish. One day while giving them a talk he asked, "How many of you want to be priests?" All of the boys and most of the girls too raised their hands in response.

From Wilmington, the missionary team traveled down to Norfolk, Virginia, for their first attempt below the Potomac. One week was devoted to rejuvenating the faith of the Catholics. The second was centered on the non-Catholics—with the netting of twenty-five converts.

The missionaries perfected their methods and proceeded on their tour of the South. December found them at St. Peter's Church in Pascagoula, Mississippi, where they gathered in a like number of neophytes. January was spent in Alabama, with missions at St. Luke's in Axis, St. Peter's in Chastang, and at a Baptist church in Fairford. February and March were likewise devoted to the Alabama missions, one in the small town of Bellefontaine, and the other running through three weeks of March, at the Pure Heart of Mary Church in Mobile. At this latter place there were more than 230 persons brought back to the Sacraments, and thirty converted to the faith.

Father Plantevigne had his heart set on a scheduled mission at St. Dominic's Church in New Orleans, the first Josephite pastorate there, under the care of Father Peter O. LeBeau, who, like Father Plantevigne, was from Pointe Coupee parish. Archbishop Blenk had just turned over to the use of colored Catholics in the Carrollton section of New Orleans the old frame church that formerly housed the congregation of Mater Dolorosa parish. That very month of March, 1909, Father

LeBeau had transferred the scene of his activity from the Petite Prairie region near Washington, Louisiana, to the new parish in Carrollton. The mission was designed to be a new start in colored Catholic life in New Orleans' uptown section.

Father LeBeau's request for missionaries had gone to Father Samuel Kelly who had the previous year erected a house for mission headquarters at Pascagoula, Mississippi. The southerner expected that Fathers Kelly and Albert would come to give the mission. When he was informed that Father Plantevigne had been chosen for the task, he objected strenuously. It was known that he was not in favor of using colored priests in the South. He presented his objections to Archbishop Blenk, who wrote to Father Plantevigne asking him to refrain for the present from coming to New Orleans to give missions.

Father Plantevigne, who had built up high expectations for a triumphal re-entry into Louisiana, took the disappointment as an end to all of his hopes. He was prostrate under the shattering of his fondest dreams. He wrote to his superior in Baltimore, Rev. Justin McCarthy, S.S.J.:

March 27, 1909

Dear Father McCarthy:
  Bishop Blenk has refused to have me give the mission in his city. This comes to me as a thunderbolt I never expected. Father Albert says that you expected it all along and yet you never said a word to me to guard me against this awful blow. Now my life is a perfect wreck.
  Take me away from here immediately for I shall never again be satisfied here. Place me somewhere where I shall be alone. You expect to open a place in Florida. Put me there, if the bishop has no objection to me, or put me at Chastang, if the bishop will have me. As to the mission band, do not think of it in connection with me any more.
Yours,
J. J. Plantevigne

Under the same emotional backlash, Father Plantevigne wrote also to Archbishop Blenk, complaining of the discrimination and prejudice that he detected in the banning of his appearance in New Orleans. The prelate hastened to write back to him to correct the misapprehension under which the young priest labored:

Archbishop's House
1205 Esplanade Avenue
New Orleans, La.
March 31, 1909

Rev. J. J. Plantevigne
Scranton, Mississippi

Dear Father:

From your letter of the 23rd. inst. it is clear that you put an entirely wrong construction of my motives in advising that you refrain for the present from taking part in a mission to be given to the dear colored people of the parish of St. Dominic, New Orleans.

It is no ill will to you nor to your race that induced me to give this advice—quite the contrary is the case, for I am certainly determined to take all the best and most prudent means to advance the interests and welfare of my spiritual children of the colored race. Just at present, when I am contemplating and seriously examining the ways and means of successfully promoting their religious interests, I deem it right and proper to expose myself and the work in hand to no risk that might be run by over-zeal or any action that might stir up prejudices and suspicions calculated to endanger the real progress that I have just as much at heart as you have. I do not doubt that when the right time comes, you will be able to do excellent work in this diocese for your own people, and I believe that that time is not far off. Until then, the exercise of Christian resignation and the spirit of humble obedience cannot but prepare you all the better for effective and successful work in this large field of our dear Lord's vineyard.

With blessing,

Yours devotedly in Christ
James H. Blenk
Archbishop of New Orleans

In colored circles in New Orleans, the failure of Father Plantevigne's plans for his mission at St. Dominic's caused no little stir. Sympathizers wrote to him to express indignation at the canceling of his mission.

Others threatened to expose the bishop's action in the public press. Father Plantevigne wrote to the Apostolic Delegate, Monsignor Falconio, to complain of the unjust treatment and to criticize the attitude of the bishop. He continued to take it as a personal affront. For a while, it looked as though he were going to fight for full recognition and redress. "I mean to see this thing through," he wrote Father McCarthy. "There are certain things about which one must keep quiet but there are other things that quietness don't help." However, his cries were to no avail. Fathers Albert and Kelly gave the mission at St. Dominic's. Father Plantevigne was left behind at Pascagoula.

There the suspicious colored non-Catholics (and some Catholics as well) continued in their belief that though he was a priest, he did not "have all of the powers of a white priest."

All through the month of April, Father Plantevigne remained at his post. He wrote to the Archbishop of Chicago to request a position in his diocese, perhaps the post made vacant some years before by the death of Father Tolton. The Chicago prelate wrote back that he would continue the mission in Chicago under the direction of his own priests for the present.

The combination of shock and despondency gradually undermined Father Plantevigne's spirit. Though he might have continued to give missions in Mississippi and Alabama, he felt that his whole career was in a shambles. He was therefore recalled to Baltimore for his health's sake. His missionary career was actually at an end. Before June he was assigned to the post of assistant pastor at St. Francis Xavier Church on Calvert and Pleasant streets in Baltimore.

In Washington in June, 1909, where he went for a conference of missionaries, Father Plantevigne took occasion to express his views on the Jim Crow system that had barred his way in the South. The Baltimore *Afro-American Ledger* for June 26 reported that he started a flood of debate by remarking:

> The blood of the Negro boils in resentment of a "Jim-Crow" system in the Catholic Church. The doors of the Church must be opened full width, not a side entrance, if the Negro is to be saved by the Catholic Church. Negroes have followed their masters into the Catholic Church, but have fallen away in great

numbers because they have not been given an active part in the organic life of the Church. Social circumstances compel us to compromise. This is unfortunate, because it loses the Negro and fails to develop true religion among the whites, for true religion is charity.

The Negro wants Catholic priests, non-Catholic people are accustomed to colored ministers and refuse to enter the Catholic Church under white priests.

As though to bear out his contention that colored Catholics wanted their own priests as pastors, a large group of colored Washingtonians next year sent a petition to Cardinal Gibbons for the erection of another colored Catholic parish in southwest Washington for the hundreds of families living there, but excluded from the school and from all but minimum attendance at St. Dominic's Church. They asked to have a colored priest who would work for the uplift of the race and especially for the education of the neglected children. They named Father Plantevigne specifically as the priest they desired to have for their pastor and spiritual leader.

The young Josephite priest was nevertheless kept on as assistant pastor in Baltimore. It is not even known whether the Washington petition was ever revealed to him. He continued in his routine duties at St. Francis Xavier Church for the next few years. Only occasionally did he emerge from obscurity to lecture, and when he did his theme was always the same. In an article later reprinted in *Our Colored Missions* he returned to the question of what must be done to win the colored man over to the Catholic Church, and, after winning him, how best to keep him within the fold:

Many are inclined to make of these questions a problem hard to solve. I say there is no problem at all if we go on and do God's work without hesitating on account of social or racial conditions. But as soon as we begin to compromise with principle, we at once give birth to a problem insoluble in its every aspect, a problem which will become more and more entangled by every new method we advance for its solution, and one which will stand impregnable to every effort of the most zealous men we have in the field.

Why? Because we are to deal with a people who have been

made to feel that they are looked upon as inferiors and who resent this most stubbornly. The respectable colored man sits ill at ease in a Jim-Crow car, or a theatre, but his very blood boils, his sense of religion rebels against a Jim-Crow system in the Catholic Church because he associates the Church with Christ, with God, Who is "no respecter of persons."

This discrimination against him by some has caused him to mistrust the efforts of the most earnest among those who have and are endeavoring to bring him to Christ, and this is a deplorable fact, since among the white priests we have men who are so earnest in their endeavors, so untiring in their zeal for the welfare of the colored race.[2]

One can see the reflection of a sensitive spirit and a deeply wounded soul in these lines. Father Plantevigne brooded over the discrimination he had experienced in the Deep South. The story was bruited about the colored neighborhoods of Baltimore that he was a man with a broken heart.

Within two years he was a broken man. He contracted tuberculosis and wasted away. The disease even affected his mind, and for a while he was confined to Mount Hope Sanitarium. He recovered his mental health, but his lungs were far gone.

In 1912 he was hospitalized at St. Agnes Hospital in Baltimore, there to await the end. His sister-in-law came up to visit him from Baton Rouge, and his Baltimore friends also filed in to console him. But the ravages of the disease were ineluctable. He sank gradually, and on January 27, 1913, at the age of forty-two, he died. His sister-in-law, as his closest relative, urged the church authorities to bury him in Baltimore. She did not know what would happen if the body were brought to Baton Rouge or to Chenel for burial from the Catholic churches in those troubled places.

Cardinal Gibbons personally conducted the funeral of this third colored priest ordained in his diocese. He gave the blessing over the remains and then preached a simple and eloquent sermon, comparing Father Plantevigne's work of liberation from sin with the great work of Lincoln in emancipating the Negro from slavery. Of the dead priest, he said:

[2] *Our Colored Missions,* 25 (October 1933), p. 146.

In him you have lost a true priest—a man of God. He was a
priest possessed of uncommon intellectual attainments, and he
was no less remarkable for his high moral qualities and for his
burning zeal for the salvation of souls. He possessed to an
eminent degree the three marks, to my opinion, which charac-
terize the Negro race: a deep religious sentiment, a great
warmth of affection, and an unfailing gratitude to their bene-
factors. . . .

The faithful and devoted Catholic folks of St. Francis Xavier parish
took up a collection and erected a large bronze plaque to the memory
of Father Plantevigne. It still hangs today in the vestibule of their
church in Baltimore as a perennial reminder of the great-souled priest
who worked among them for the last years of his life.

The loss of Father Plantevigne was a great blow to the apostolate
among the American Negroes. The tragedy of his life was also a set-
back in the development of the colored priesthood. Cardinal Gibbons'
advisors voted against the ordaining of any more colored priests in
Baltimore. Elsewhere in the country other people also tended to neglect
the careful examination of the full details of his sad and tragic case,
and instead made the hasty generalization that his untimely breakdown
and death were owing mainly to racial qualities that unfitted the colored Catholic man for aspiration to the priesthood.

Fortunately, some of his fellow Josephites had already taken up the
matter directly with Rome. Father Joseph Anciaux, pastor of the first
church in which Father Plantevigne had given a mission, had written
a famous "Red Book" complaining of the neglect of the colored apostolate on the part of some of the American hierarchy. As a result the
Holy Father ordered the establishment of the Catholic Board of Colored Missions and the promotion of the work in all of its aspects.

Not long after the death of Father Plantevigne, his fellow missionary, Father John Albert, wrote an essay on "How to Convert the Colored Race," which Father John E. Burke, director of the Catholic
Board for Colored Missions, transmitted to the Apostolic Delegate
along with his report on progress in the field.

On September 1, 1913, Father Albert took up his pen further to in-
form the delegate, and through him the Holy Father, of the reasons for

expanding the colored priesthood. He gave five cogent reasons to support his urgent case for colored priests in the United States:

1. Outside of Catholic centers, the white priest is a "Persona non grata" in the religious life of the colored. This feeling is held by both white and colored of the South.

2. "Like wants like." The rank and file of the colored race want their own priests. This axiom is philosophically correct, and if colored Catholics were more numerous, experience would teach it.

3. If we cannot preach a vocation sermon to colored youth, we cannot convert the race. I wonder whether any race can be converted without the aid of a native clergy.

4. The most positive opponents of a colored clergy assert that it is fifty years too soon. But we know that it will take even more than fifty years to obtain even a small number of colored priests. Therefore all should agree that it is high time to lay the foundation. . . .

5. During the past six months out of twenty-four applications for admission to Epiphany Apostolic College (the preparatory school for the training of priests to convert the colored) fourteen or fifteen were from colored youths. I believe every one of these was refused admittance. Can this be the Will of God? How long, O Lord, will thy Church close the priesthood gate in the face of this race of people?

Some of the southern bishops were beginning to see the wisdom of Archbishop Janssens' insistence on the development of a colored clergy for the apostolate among the southern Negroes. Two of them, Father Albert wrote to the Apostolic Delegate, had recently suggested a possible solution—the establishment of a new society or order of colored priests governed for the present by a white abbot. These priests, being "religious," would not come much into contact with the secular clergy or the hierarchy. This, Father Albert noted, was an important point on account of the prejudice existing in the South. Father Albert also added that the bishop under whom he was then working, Most Reverend John B. Morris, of Little Rock, Arkansas, had recently offered ten thousand dollars as a foundation for the motherhouse of the order, should it be placed within his diocese.

As we shall see in the sequel, this plan was taken up and developed as an interim stage in the process of integrating the colored Catholic priest into the American Catholic clergy.

CHAPTER X

The Fighting Archbishop's Protégé

FATHER STEPHEN L. THEOBALD

1874 – 1932

No one ever accused Archbishop John Ireland of taciturnity. He ruled his archdiocese of St. Paul at the top of his powerful lungs. He made himself the most vocal of the liberal wing of the American hierarchy, and his voice was heard up and down the country during the last decades of the nineteenth century and the early part of the twentieth.

On the race question Archbishop Ireland voiced the stand of Catholic liberals in many historic and impressive statements. In an address on January 1, 1891, on the occasion of a commemorative service for the anniversary of Lincoln's Emancipation Proclamation, he restated the Catholic position on slavery and racism in terms that are still vibrant today. He cited Leo XIII's declaration that slavery was opposed to religion and to the dignity of man, was a relapse into barbarism, and was lamentably unchristian and inhuman, a denial of Christian principles and Christian virtues. He urged his hearers:

> Let us on this emancipation day thank God for the blessings of Christianity. The spirit of Christian freedom is today poured out upon the nations of the earth. The mighty social wave which is now lifting upward upon its crest the masses of the people in all lands is but another manifestation of the same heavenly spirit.
>
> Let us do our full duty. There is work for us. I have said that slavery has been abolished in America; the trail of the serpent, however, yet marks the ground. We do not accord to our black brothers all the rights and privileges of freedom and of a common humanity. They are the victims of an unreason-

ing and unjustifiable ostracism. They may live, provided they live away from us, as a separate and inferior race, with whom close contact is pollution. It looks as if we had grudgingly granted to them emancipation, as if we fain still would be the masters, and hold them in servitude.

Strong words those, and evidence of a strong man's convictions. Archbishop Ireland would have no compromises on the race question. He was irreconcilably opposed to racism, to prejudice, to the dual standard of law and justice, and to the artificial barriers of the caste system. He plainly demanded of his audience:

Let the Negro be our equal in the enjoyment of all political rights of the citizen. The Constitution grants him those rights; let us be loyal to the Constitution. If the education of the Negro does not fit him to be a voter and an office holder, let us for his sake and our own, hurry to enlighten him. I would open to the Negro all industrial and professional avenues—the test for his advance being his ability, and never his color. I would in all public gatherings and in all public resorts, in halls and hotels, treat the black man as I treat the white. I might shun the vulgar man, whatever his color, but the gentleman, whatever his color, I would not dare push away from me.

This forthright exposition of his Catholic convictions in the matter of relations between the racial groups set Archbishop Ireland in the forefront of the Catholic liberals in this area of social thought. Colored Catholics came to look upon him as one of their most intelligent champions, and they were constantly reassured by statements such as he once made to a colored congregation:

I know no color line. I will acknowledge none. I am not unaware that this solemn declaration of mine shall be deemed by many upon whose opinion I set high value, as rash and untimely. Yet I fear not to make it. I am ahead of my day. But the time is not distant when Americans and Christians will wonder that there ever was race prejudice.

Inevitably, these strong statements on the race question evoked a query that was put to the archbishop some time later:

"Would you admit a colored student into your seminary?"

The archbishop thundered out his reply, "Yes!"

"Suppose a large number of students should object or embarrass this student for the priesthood because of his color, what then—?"

The archbishop exploded, "I would expel all such students, for their act would prove conclusively to me that they were unworthy of the high office to which they aspire. There is no room in the Catholic Church for racial prejudice."

The question passed out of the theoretical realm into the practical in 1905 when Archbishop Ireland finally discovered a young colored man with the signs of a vocation to the priesthood and with the necessary talents to guarantee the success of his pioneer experiment. The applicant was Stephen Louis Theobald, a native of Georgetown in British Guiana, where he had been born on July 5, 1874. He had been educated during the eighties at St. Stanislaus College, a Jesuit college in Georgetown. There he received a solid foundation in the rudiments of the faith and of letters.

Transferring to the governmental institution of Queen's College after finishing his philosophical studies at the Jesuit School, Stephen had prepared himself for law school by passing the examinations with a brilliant record. He then secured admission to Cambridge University in England and pursued his law studies until he obtained his degree in 1905.

It was in that year that he realized his vocation to practice the higher law of the love of God. He read the stirring speeches that Archbishop Ireland had been making in the United States, and so he wrote to apply for admission to the St. Paul's archdiocesan seminary.

This was a challenge and an opportunity for the archbishop. He accepted Stephen Theobald after the preliminary examinations, and directed him to report to the seminary in Minnesota in the following fall. There Archbishop Ireland took the thirty-year-old seminarian under his wing as a special protégé.

Stephen's brilliant achievements in his studies justified Archbishop Ireland's confidence. Within five years he was ready for ordination. On June 8, 1910, Archbishop Ireland anointed him with the sacred oils and made him a priest forever. His first assignment retained him on the Cathedral staff as the archbishop's expert in canon law cases.

Father Theobald's ambition to be a pastor in his own church was realized soon after. He was appointed to the Church of St. Peter Claver in St. Paul, Minnesota, and there given charge of the mixed congregation of white and colored who frequented the twenty-year-old church.

It was in this plain, devotional, and well-arranged church that Father Theobald served out his entire life as a priest, shepherding his flock for twenty-two years. The new pastor lavished upon the church all of his well-trained taste in art. He managed to raise enough money to equip the sanctuary with three altars of white marble, the main altar being set off with a high reredos, and above this a large mural depicting St. Peter Claver in his great apostolate for the colored in South America. Father Theobald had a deep devotion to his patron saint, tracing its origin back to his days in British Guiana, not far from the site of the saint's forty years of labor for the Negroes at Cartagena in Columbia, South America.

Under St. Peter Claver's auspices and protection, Father Theobald year after year fulfilled his pastoral duties toward the poor and the sick, toward the rich and the erring, with an unfailing courtesy and noble generosity. His tact and diplomacy came to be known all about St. Paul. He was revered as a saintly priest. His diminutive stature and quiet, bespectacled countenance secured for him a ready welcome in the hearts of his parishioners and fellow citizens.

His quiet influence soon began to spread beyond his parish. In 1914 while in Baltimore, he met Dr. Thomas W. Turner, who spoke of organizing a Catholic colored federation along the lines of the National Association for the Advancement of Colored People. Father Theobald was enthusiastic about the plan, and he co-operated with Dr. Turner and the other colored Catholic leaders who eventually banded together as the Federated Colored Catholics. Dr. Turner thought so highly of Father Theobald's talents as a diplomat that he asked the young priest to represent the colored Catholics in the NAACP's annual convention. Still both he and Father Theobald realized the need for a Catholic organization also to work for improvement of race relations within the Church.

In 1917 the first steps were taken toward this in the organization of the Committee Against the Extension of Race Prejudice in the Church.

They made use of the Catholic press and of personal correspondence to combat racism in the ranks of Catholics. They called for official action on the part of the Papal Delegate, the American cardinals, archbishops, and bishops against the practice of excluding Catholic Negroes from Catholic schools, and especially from seminaries. Father Theobald remained in the background as their spiritual director, and kept in close contact with their work.

In 1919 the group mellowed its name to "The Committee for the Advancement of Colored Catholics," and adopted a more personal approach through the appointment of committees to call upon leading churchmen and directly state the cause of colored communicants in the Church. They continued their work through the public press and through letter writing for the redress of wrongs committed against Catholic Negroes by their fellow religionists.

Finally, in 1925, the group expanded into a national organization called the Federated Colored Catholics of the United States. It was in and with this organization that Father Theobald did his best work for the betterment of interracial feeling within the Church.

Meanwhile, he had been continuing his own scholarly apostolate by writing articles for publication. One of these, which appeared in the *Records of the American Catholic Historical Society* (December, 1924), shows the breadth of his scholarship, the tough-mindedness of his approach to the whole race question inside the Church, and the balance of his analytical powers. He was apparently stirred into writing the article "Catholic Missionary Work among the Colored People of the United States, 1776-1866" by a similar article that had appeared just the year before under almost the same title by Miriam T. Murphy. Miss Murphy's article was a "sweetness-and-light" analysis of the work of Catholics among the colored population in the country.

Father Theobald was miffed by the glaring omissions in Miss Murphy's former article. He covered much of the same ground, but corrected historical misapprehensions created by Miss Murphy's treatment. Where she had been content, for instance, to refer to Abbé Jean Moranville's work for the "poor Negroes" in Baltimore, Father Theobald cited the more important work of Father Joubert in establishing there the colored sisterhood of the Oblates of Providence. Where she had been eulogistic about slave-owning Bishop Flaget to the extent of holding that his canonization was possible, Father Theobald scouted the very idea of praising a man who had thus held his fellow human beings in bondage.

Father Stephen was equally vigorous in his realistic appraisal of the work of Bishop England and of other straddlers on the slavery issue. Where Miss Murphy had very gently indicated that his theory of slavery was "doubtless" open to question, Father Theobald was forthright in his denunciation, showing how shrewd politicians like Van Buren played for Catholic support on the issue by quoting the southern and border-state bishops. Father Theobald stated:

> Thus it is clear that the American bishops indorsed the institutions of domestic slavery, basing their attitude on their interpretation of the Holy Father's letter in which, as they held, a clear distinction was made between the African Slave Trade and domestic slavery, and this in spite of their knowledge that, apart from the alleged good treatment accorded to Catholic slaves by their owners, the horrors of the African slave trade and still more were to be found in the institution in the South.

His long training under Archbishop Ireland is evident in Father Theobald's strong indictment of the politically-minded bishops. He affirmed that they had indirectly contributed to the hardships of the Negro by participating in the political upheaval over the slavery issue, though he admitted that it was a painful thing for him to tell. He showed the fighting spirit of the liberal archbishop of St. Paul when he wrote:

> In view of the foregoing, what, I may ask, becomes of Archbishop Spalding's claim that the church stood aloof from the political issues leading up to the Civil War? Simply this, it amounts merely to a distinction between the church's official and unofficial interference.

It was this strong, no-nonsense approach to the stark issues involved in racism that made Father Stephen Theobald assume giant stature among colored Catholics throughout the country. They knew him as their champion, as the uncompromising defender of their human rights, and as the inspired and well-informed leader in their fight for Catholic principles and practice within the Church.

The climax of his prestige among colored Catholics was reached at the annual convention of the Federated Colored Catholics held in St. Louis in 1931. He was chosen as the celebrant of the Mass with which the convention opened at the St. Francis Xavier College Church next to St. Louis University, on Sunday, September 6, 1931. There was a huge procession through the streets of St. Louis before the Mass, led by the boys' band of St. Elizabeth's Church, and comprising representatives of all of the St. Louis colored societies, the Catholic Knights of America, the Knights of Peter Claver, as well as the White Friends of Colored Catholics, the Knights of Columbus Zouaves, and the St. Louis University Jesuit seminarians. Two bishops viewed the parade, Archbishop John Glennon and Bishop Johannes, his auxiliary. Archbishop Glennon spoke at the Mass on the unity of all races in the Church, and referred to the kiss of peace between Father Stephen Theobald and Father Edward Kramer, the deacon of the Mass, as a symbol of peace between the white and the colored Catholic groups.

That evening, at the mass meeting held in the St. Louis University auditorium, Father Theobald was the featured speaker on the program. His talk was entitled "Our Hopes and Aspirations." It was a glowing tribute to the Church as the hope of his people and the only ultimate solution of all problems of national, racial, and social cleavages. He urged productive harmony and peace to overcome the minor frictions both within the Federation and within the Church. He insisted on constructive and conservative co-operation, maintaining that the Church does not propagandize in protest, seeking questionable notoriety in glaring headlines, but works quietly and persistently for justice, right, and peace. He maintained that the Roman Catholic Church would not stand for any discrimination against the Negro because of accidental conditions such as color. "If there is any," he stated, "it is due to lack of listening to the voice preaching the law of brotherly love." The Church, by insisting on essential things of life and on the immortality of the human soul, was the only institution, he declared, that could get at the roots of racial discrimination.

The fearlessness of Archbishop Ireland again manifested itself in his outspoken protégé. He launched into a vigorous attack on the color line in St. Louis, and even in St. Louis University, on whose platform he was speaking. He deplored the segregation policies of Catholic institutions and schools in the area, though he found excuse for them in the state laws that forbade a mingling of the races in certain types of public facilities. But he denounced as unfair the practices of Catholic hospitals, controlled by religious sisterhoods, of receiving non-Catholics as long as they were white, and refusing to receive as patients Catholic Negroes.

Notwithstanding the gloomy picture, he prophesied that it would not be many years before they would be able to witness the presentation of diplomas from St. Louis University to colored boys and girls. This prophecy was greeted with great applause, and it was repeated when he averred that he would go back to St. Paul and organize an attack on the segregation policies of St. Louis Catholic institutions unless they changed their racial program.

This combination of fearless defense of principle and untiring work for the betterment of his people endeared Father Theobald to colored Catholics all around the country.

Back in St. Paul, his church became a center for special services. Thousands attended the novenas he conducted for the saint-of-the-hour, the Little Flower, St. Theresa of Lisieux, to whom Father Stephen had a great and childlike devotion. Many non-parishioners crowded into the Church on Aurora and Farmington to hear his simple sermons and touching prayers.

He became a well-liked friend of all the clergy in the diocese and was welcomed for dinner at their hospitable residences without any reference to racial taboos.

Even the Sisters in the religious communities accepted him as one of their priestly visitors and confessors, and Father Stephen liked to tell, in his broad-minded way, a story that illustrated a good point in human relations.

> I went one day to call on some Sisters. I knew them very well, and they knew me very well, so well that they forgot who I was. One of the Sisters heard I was calling, and rushed into the parlor saying, "Father, I would not keep you waiting. I

have been working very hard today," And then she forgot herself and said, "I have been working like a nigger." Now the good lady did not intend to insult me at all. But you can see what is going on in their minds.

He had just celebrated his twenty-second anniversary as pastor of St. Peter Claver in the summer of 1932 when he was suddenly stricken with appendicitis. He was rushed to the hospital on Friday, July 8, and immediately operated on to remove the appendix. It was too late. A rupture had occurred during Mass, and by the time the appendectomy was performed, peritonitis had set in. He lingered for four days, during which Archbishop Murray was constantly at his bedside. On Tuesday night, July 12, he quietly went home to God, the prelate saying the prayers for the dying as he slipped into unconsciousness.

Father Stephen Theobald's funeral was attended by more than a hundred priests and five bishops. Over a thousand mourners were turned away from the thronged church, as persons from all stations in life in St. Paul endeavored to catch a last glimpse of the plain and humble pastor who had ministered so devotedly to them all through the years.

One witness reported that he had seldom seen an outpouring of people so genuinely and sincerely sad, so open in their confession of affection for their lost shepherd. "He is remembered by many whose hearts learned a new song through him, whose souls leaped to new spiritual vision under his unfailing tutorship."

The national Catholic weekly, *America,* eulogized him by saying that his life and character are a refutation of the fears alleged by those who would deny the honors of the altar indiscriminately to members of the Negro race.

CHAPTER XI

In Monastery Gardens

FATHER JOSEPH ALEXANDER JOHN, L.A.M.
FATHER ARCHIBALD (AUGUSTINE) DERRICKS, O.SS.T.

The role of the religious orders in the development of the colored priesthood in the United States is recognized as the central and all-important one. The education of the Healy brothers by the Jesuit order opened the way for their achievements in the clergy of the last century. One of them was even incorporated into the order, becoming an outstanding Jesuit, head of the oldest Jesuit institution in the country, and representative of the Jesuits of the eastern seaboard in the General Congregation of the order.

The German Franciscans of Quincy played a significant role in the burgeoning of Father Tolton's vocation and his successful attainment of orders in Rome. Though the Josephites of the early days were not a full-fledged religious order, they functioned partly as a religious order and partly as a group of clerics available for service under the various bishops of the country. Whether or not they were then a fully constituted order, they are at present; and for the last few decades have played a notable part in the sponsoring and encouragement of vocations.

We have seen too that the Immaculate Heart Fathers and the Holy Ghost Fathers also pioneered in the induction of colored religious into their ranks and in raising them to the dignity of priesthood. Subsequently we shall have occasion to elaborate on the effective moves made by the Society of the Divine Word in the development of the colored clergy in the country.

In this chapter, we turn our attention to two early religious-order priests who are included in the roll of American colored clergymen. Though neither was born in the United States, both came to the country early in life and were ordained for labor in the colored apostolate here. We shall see that the career of one of them was very significant in the promotion of the colored priesthood, mainly because his failures modified the direction that it might have taken.

FATHER JOSEPH ALEXANDER JOHN, L.A.M.

1 8 8 0 – 1 9 4 4

The more significant of these two was Father Joseph Alexander John, L.A.M., a member of the Society for the African Missions who were popularly called and designated the "Lyons African Missionaries" because of their origin in the French city of Lyons.

Joseph John was born on the little island of Carriacou, one of the beautiful gems of the British West Indies near the coast of South America, which belonged ecclesiastically to the archdiocese of Port of Spain, Trinidad. He remained on Carriacou from his birth on August 22, 1880, until as a young boy finishing grammar school, he evinced some signs of a priestly vocation. There were no minor seminaries or colleges (high schools) in the missionary archdiocese of Port of Spain. He therefore went to work in the islands, filling odd jobs until he was twenty-five years old. In 1905 he went to live and work in New York, still hoping for a chance to become a priest.

The missionaries of his native land were instrumental in securing his admission to St. Joseph's College for Negro Catechists in Montgomery, Alabama, in 1907. After a year, he entered the Josephite's Epiphany Apostolic College in Baltimore for minor seminary work, with the understanding that he was to matriculate elsewhere for higher studies. The Josephites did not have any missions in the British West Indies, where Joseph John wanted to work, and they could not promise him admission to their group or ordination at the hands of Cardinal Gibbons.

In June, 1913, a year before the outbreak of the first World War, the thirty-three-year-old seminarian obtained entry to the ranks of the White Fathers, a French-African Mission society founded by Cardinal Laviguerie and maintaining a house in Canada for the recruitment of French-speaking missionaries to work in French Africa. Joseph enrolled with the White Fathers in Canada, and was sent by them first to Laval University in Quebec, later to Holland, and then to their house of studies in Carthage, North Africa. There he remained for about one year when his health failed in November, 1917. He was told that this showed that he had no vocation. Disconsolately, he left the religious order, and set about recovering his health.

It was soon discovered that the indisposition was only minor and temporary. Nevertheless, back in New York, Joseph went to work as a butler in the turbulent postwar metropolis, still harboring the desire to become a priest.

A new opportunity opened for him in 1921. Father Ignatius Lissner of the Lyons Society of the African Missions had come to the United States from France and had established a mission among the colored Catholics in Augusta, Georgia. After ten years of almost fruitless work among them, Father Lissner wrote, in 1916, that the "future of the mission to the Negro lies in the colored sisters, brothers, and priests."[1]

Father Lissner therefore undertook to found a seminary that would train both white and colored students for the priesthood. It was in 1919 that he succeeded in opening St. Anthony's Mission House at Highwood (near Tenafly), New Jersey. He was backed in this project by Cardinal Van Rossum, speaking for His Holiness Pope Benedict XV, who encouraged the establishment of the seminary for the training of colored priests. The Lyons African Missioners supplied professors of theology and philosophy from France. Joseph John was one of the first colored students to be accepted. In his class was also another Negro lad, William Floyd, and, together with the white students, these seminarians progressed rapidly in their theological studies. By 1923 both were ready for ordination. The ceremony was scheduled for June 13, at the hands of Bishop John J. Collins, S.J., formerly Missionary Bishop

[1] *Annual Report of the Commission for Catholic Missions to the Colored People and the Indians*, 1916, p. 22.

of Jamaica, B. W. I., who was then stationed in retirement at Fordham University.

Unfortunately, young Floyd's health was not strong. He fell ill before the ceremony and was obliged to withdraw. Undaunted, Joseph John went on alone to receive Holy Orders.

It was in St. Benedict the Moor Church on West Fifty-third Street, in the old colored neighborhood which had been New York's "Little Africa" before the swarming of Harlem, that the first colored priest was ordained in New York, on Wednesday, June 13, 1923.

The following Sunday, June 17, he celebrated his first solemn High Mass in the same church, surrounded by a representative group of the clergy who were thoroughly in favor of developing the colored priesthood in the country: Father Lissner and his fellow Lyons African Missioners, Fathers Laude, Schlecht, Barthelen; Monsignor John Chadwick, pastor of St. Agnes Church in New York; Father Thomas O'Keefe, pastor of St. Benedict's, and Monsignor John E. Burke, director general of the Catholic Board for Mission Work among the Colored People, who delivered the sermon.

It was a triumphant day for Monsignor Burke. He had seconded the foundation at Highwood by supplying the needed funds from the Mission Board's revenues. He set the keynote of gratitude to God for the ordination of New York's first colored priest. He extolled Father Lissner's Mission House as a great opportunity for colored Catholic boys who would be educated for the priesthood free of charge, and, if found worthy, would be ordained as priests like Father Joseph John. He affirmed that he had for years been a staunch advocate of the necessity of colored priests in the United States. He added:

> We who are working among the eleven million colored people in the United States are planting the seeds. Thank God, we can already see consoling results. I believe the harvest is to come for the colored priests of the United States. We need colored priests. We need colored Sisters, and, thanks be to God, they are coming. Obstacles must be overcome, and prejudices must die. . . . The white race has not the monopoly on the benefits of the Redemption—the grace of God can work in the soul of a black man as efficiently as it can in the soul of a white man. . . . Agitate in prayer for colored vocations. Agitate

among yourselves that the idea may spread. Agitate by coop
erating with those who have taken up the work of educating
young colored men and girls for the priesthood and the sisterhood.

Father Burke ended his highly oratorical sermon by generously wel-
coming Father Joseph John into the ranks of the clergy, and bidding
him go forth to his divine mission with a stout heart full of trust in
God's grace.

It was publicly announced that Father John's mission work would be
among the Negroes in the South. Yet none of the bishops in whose
dioceses the Lyons African Missioners were laboring would take the
step of assigning Father John to a pastoral position in the Deep South.
True, most of the mission posts manned by the LAM's were in Georgia, where the prospects for the peaceful welcome of a colored Catholic
priest were not too hopeful. In fact, at that time, owing to the ravings
of Tom Watson and the ridings of the Ku Klux Klan, even the existence of white priests in Georgia was precarious.

Father John was consequently assigned to teach at St. Anthony's
Mission House as "professor of English, Literature, Latin and Homiletics." There were only nine pupils in the nascent seminary at the
time, six novices and three postulants. Father John shared teaching
duties with Fathers Lissner, Wierle, Schlecht, and Imback.

It became apparent that the seminary would not thrive. Modeled too
rigidly on the European pattern, it was not adapted to the American
boy. No provision was made for recreation, save the dubious entertainment of raking leaves and doing other chores around the house.
Even when it was moved to Tenafly later, it failed to attract vocations.
There were rumors among the Negro Catholics that Father Lissner
aspired to be the head of a nation-wide diocese made up of all colored
Catholic churches, thus deepening the cleavages of the segregation
system. Another factor in the lack of interest in the seminary was the
Africa-orientation of the staff, especially Father Lissner, who had been
a missionary in Dahomey, Guinea, and the Gold Coast, and who
reportedly preferred the simple African native to the American Negro.

At all events, Father John was granted frequent leave from his light scholastic duties in order to give missions and accept invitations for services elsewhere. He was a guest of St. Augustine's Church in Washington not long after his ordination. There the congregation was treated to the first solemn High Mass ever celebrated in the country by three Negro priests together. Father John was celebrant. Father Dorsey and Father Uncles of the Josephite order were subdeacon and deacon respectively.

In the summer of 1924 Father John became the first Negro priest to offer Mass in Cleveland. He went there at the invitation of Father Thomas E. McKenney, pastor of the Church of Our Lady of the Blessed Sacrament. In that imposing church, the young colored priest offered the Holy Sacrifice before a mixed congregation. Next year, he gave a mission at St. Augustine's Church in East St. Louis, Illinois, and traveled about elsewhere in the country as well.

However, Father John had difficulty adjusting himself to American ways. For a good part of 1924 he was tentatively assigned as assistant pastor at St. Augustine's Church in Louisville, but there he remained withdrawn, uncommunicative, and dissatisfied. He confided to one of his fellow colored priests, "These Americans, you can't tell when they're sincere."

In 1925 he returned to the motherhouse of the province at Tenafly. He was living there when the energetic Father Edward C. Kramer was made director general of the Catholic Board for Mission Work among the Colored People. Father Kramer discovered that Father Lissner had given up his endeavor to secure a permanent pastorate for Father John. Instead, the old patriarch had offered Father John this odd consolation, "You will live in the room next to me; and we will be good friends."

This did not suit Father Kramer. He secured an agreement from both Father Lissner and Father John that if he could obtain a pastorate for the young colored priest, his superior would assign him to it. Quite a bit of persuasion was needed to convince the two. To Father John, the director general spoke plainly, "Father, you are first a priest of Jesus Christ, and then a member of the Society of African Missions."

Some time before that Bishop Nussbaum, the Passionist bishop of Corpus Christi, Texas, was transferred to the diocese of Marquette in

Michigan. Many of the Passionist priests who had been loaned to the diocese under Bishop Nussbaum were withdrawn. Bishop Ledvina, the newly consecrated ordinary of Corpus Christi, issued a desperate call for priests to staff the churches of his diocese. When Father Mark Moeslein, C. P., pastor of the Holy Cross Colored Catholic Church in Corpus Christi, left the diocese, Bishop Ledvina wrote to Father Kramer asking him urgently to secure a priest for that church. Father Kramer saw this as an opportunity for Father John. The bishop readily accepted the colored priest, stipulating only that Father Kramer also secure some colored Sisters to teach in the grammar school in the parish. This the resourceful director general managed to do.

Father John assumed the pastoral role at Holy Cross Church in the latter part of 1927. He gave thorough satisfaction to the bishop, and was well accepted generally by the colored people in the South. He was soon elected as the national chaplain of the Knights of Peter Claver at their annual convention in Opelousas, Louisiana.

There were difficulties in Corpus Christi. Some of the parishioners, still attached to their former pastor who had founded the mission, and to the Holy Ghost Sisters who had been teaching in the school, did not take kindly to the foreign ways of Father John, nor did they readily accept the Holy Family Sisters. There were personality differences between Father John and the Sister Superior, the kind that could and often do happen even in the best of parishes.

After two years of unsuccessful efforts at resolving these conflicts, Father John had sense and courage enough to tell the bishop that, with his permission, he would withdraw from Holy Cross Church.

By this time, Archbishop Pius Dowling, O.P., of Trinidad, had made a bid for Father John's services in his native diocese. Thither he went in 1929. He received an appointment as pastor of the parish in Cedros on the West Indian island.

For fifteen years Father John faithfully fulfilled his office of resident pastor at Cedros. He was revered as a good, hard-working, venerable priest. Among his own people, bound to him by native ties of common ancestry and culture, Father John at last found his true vocation in life. He led his flock well through calm and—literally—storm. A cyclone destroyed his church building within the first two years of his pastorate.

Under his leadership, his parishioners erected a small but beautiful edifice to replace the demolished one.

Ten years of successful ministry among the Trinidadians led Archbishop Dowling to move officially toward incardinating him into the archdiocese of Port of Spain in Trinidad. With the consent of the Congregation of the Propaganda in Rome, Father Lissner gave the colored priest his exeat. Father John officially joined the archdiocese which he could never have entered if opportunities for his pursuit of his priestly studies had not been opened to him in the United States. America had given him what the islands could not provide. Though he had found it difficult to adjust to American ways, he always owed his attainment of the goal of the priesthood to his friends among the clergy in the United States.

In the early 1940's, the stomach ailment that had plagued him during his studies again threatened him. This time Father John did not recover. In 1944 he died piously in the Lord.

With him were buried the hopes of Father Lissner for the development of a colored clergy in his congregation.

FATHER AUGUSTINE DERRICKS, O.SS.T.

1 8 8 7 – 1 9 2 9

Like Father John, Archibald Augustine Derricks was a native of the West Indies. His birthplace was Samana, a village in the republic of San Domingo, where he was born of non-Catholic parents, John Derricks and Henrietta James, on February 19, 1887. Until the age of seventeen, he pursued his education in the public schools in his homeland, growing up as a strict and partisan Protestant. In 1904 he came to the United States to study for the Protestant ministry, and, as he later admitted, to fight the Catholic Church.

In pursuit of his education, he enrolled in the high-school department of Howard University in Washington, and during his first year there he continued to study the standard anti-Catholic literature available at the institution.

Visiting at the home of a good Catholic family, however, he was abruptly halted in his antagonism toward the Church. One of the girls in the home put on her hat and remarked that she was going to confession.

"Surely you don't believe in such nonsense," Archibald taunted her. The child answered that she had sense enough to believe in it, and she explained the words of Christ from the Bible to justify her belief in the forgiveness of sin in confession.

Archibald was arrested by the child's simplicity and faith. He began to examine the other side of the Catholic question, and before the year was over, he began to take instructions and was baptized in 1905.

He continued his college work at Howard University, participating in the Catholic life of St. Augustine's parish in Washington, and eventually feeling himself called to the priesthood. He applied to the seminaries around Washington. He received courteous but disappointing rejections. He continued to pray and hope for an opening of the path to the altar.

In 1920 news spread throughout the country that the Divine Word Fathers had opened a new seminary at Greenville, Mississippi, for colored aspirants to the priesthood. Derricks sent in his application and was accepted as one of the first candidates.

Already in his thirties, Archibald was disappointed upon his arrival in Greenville to find that Father Christman had provision only for the first grades of a minor seminary, and was not at all prepared to offer any philosophy or theology courses to the enrollees. Archibald, therefore, after a short time with the institution, acknowledged to the rector that he had made a mistake in coming down, and left to return to the North.

He went to Asbury Park, New Jersey, and opened a little store there within the confines of a parish operated by the Trinitarians. Becoming friendly with one of the Italian priests, Father Anthony Giovannini, O.SS.T., Archie told him of his aspirations to become a priest. Father Anthony took an interest in the intelligent and mature man. He sent a petition to Rome, asking that Archibald be admitted to the order. Word soon came back that Derricks should go to Italy and enter the novitiate at Livorno in Tuscany. There on May 5, 1921, he received the colorful habit of the Trinitarians, and was welcomed into membership in the order that had been founded in the twelfth century by St. John de Matha and St. Felix of Valois for the redemption of Christian captives taken by Ethiopian regiments and other Moslem raiders who harassed the coasts of Italy and Spain by incessant invasions.

Renamed Frater Augustine of the Ascension, he remained in the monastery of St. Ferdinand in Livorno until May 6, 1922, when he pronounced his simple vows and was sent to Rome to study philosophy and theology at the Gregorian University while living in the Trinitarian monastery of St. Chrysogonus. On May 20, 1925, Augustine pronounced his solemn vows and became forever Augustine of the Ascension, O.SS.T.

In August of the following year he was raised to the subdiaconate, and in November to the diaconate. Finally, after six years of study and prayer, he was ordained to the sacred priesthood on June 11, 1927, in the basilica of St. Chrysogonus.

After another year of study in Rome, Father Augustine was missioned to the United States. He served for a short while in Father Giovannini's parish in Asbury Park, and then was appointed as assistant in the Italian parish of St. Ann's, in Bristol, Pennsylvania. There his mastery of Italian (he could speak four other languages besides) enabled him to function as a useful and respected priest. The duties were light at St. Ann's, and so the pastor urged Father Augustine to take speaking engagements around the country to promote the apostolate. He went on an extended tour of the States, speaking in many churches and before gatherings of colored Catholics in many places.

He was in Cincinnati in early September for the convention of the Federated Colored Catholics of the United States. His picture appeared in the souvenir program along with those of Fathers Tolton, Dorsey, Uncles, Theobald, DuKette, and John. He made an impressive sight with his striking Trinitarian habit, the flowing white collar draped over his shoulders, the large colorful crosses on his blue cape and his white cassock catching the eyes of the assembled delegates. His face was a kindly, smiling one, and his dark skin and broad nose set off the serenity of his eyes and the wistful holiness that suffused his countenance. People sensed his deep religious piety, and were quick to notice his priestly reserve, and his forthright attitude toward the faith and the Church.

Outside of his speaking engagements, Father Augustine kept to the obscure routine of the assistant pastor in Bristol. He became well known in Catholic circles, especially among those interested in the colored apostolate. The Sisters of the Blessed Sacrament invited him to Torresdale, Pennsylvania, in the summer of 1929 to conduct their annual pilgrimage at St. Michael's Church. He was there again welcomed by the faithful colored Catholics who had been bereaved but two years before by the death of Father Burgess.

For some time, Father Augustine had been troubled with stomach pains. In October, 1929, they were diagnosed to be chronic appendicitis. The doctors decided that he should go to New York for the routine operation.

In St. Francis Hospital on October 17, Father Augustine underwent surgery. Complications set in. He lingered for five days, and died on the evening of October 22, meeting God with the same meek, uncomplaining, and trustful spirit that he had shown in patiently waiting for his vocation during all of those long years.

People flocked to pray for him at his coffin-side in St. Ann's Church in Bristol, where his body lay in state until time for the obsequies. A solemn requiem mass was sung before the congregation of both whites and colored, weeping for their lost pastor. He was buried on October 26, in St. Mark's Cemetery outside of Bristol.

His obituary declared that God had given "just a glimpse of another noble colored priest to his people that they might long all the more ardently for many more such as himself, and do all in their means and power that worthy members of the race should ascend the altar of God. . . ."

In his footsteps would follow many another candidate for the holy ordination, in other branches of the Trinitarians, and in many other religious orders as well.

CHAPTER XII

Benign Dean and Jubilarian

FATHER NORMAN DuKETTE

1 8 9 0 –

In the midst of the Civil War, a small group of Negro Catholic men in Washington knocked on the door of the White House and asked to be permitted to see President Abraham Lincoln. They had a petition that must have struck the President's whimsical sense of humor. With generals, cabinet members, and congressmen flooding the corridors and rooms of the executive mansion, these men made Lincoln forget the war for a brief moment. They stated that they wished to have the permission of the chief executive to hold a lawn party on the White House grounds for the purpose of raising funds to build the first Catholic church for the Washington Negroes.

It was a request much easier to grant than the many coming in from the battlefields. Lincoln readily assented. He instructed the delegation to clear the matter through the proper channels. General D. B. French, superintendent of buildings in the often siege-conscious capital, refused to grant the permission unless the President's signature was obtained. The chairman of the committee, Gabriel Coakley, returned to the White House and camped on a chair outside the executive offices. President Lincoln, rushing from a cabinet meeting to a military conference, stopped in the hall and asked Coakley if the permission had been cleared. Upon explanation, Lincoln went back into the cabinet room and then and there signed the official authorization. He later attended the lawn party in person, bringing a large part of his cabinet with him to help contribute to the building of St. Augustine's Catholic

Church, erected on Fifteenth Street between L and M streets, just a few squares from the White House itself.[1]

In 1874, with a congregation of more than two thousand colored Catholics, the parish was able to build a large and imposing structure that for more than half a century remained the center of Negro Catholic life in Washington and, patronized as it was by a large body of white parishioners as well, a fine demonstration of co-racial relationships in an otherwise divided community.

As more of the colored Catholic families of the counties of southern Maryland moved into Washington, the parish expanded greatly during the latter decades of the nineteenth century. One large family from St. Mary's County was the DuKette (or Duckett) clan. One of the DuKette boys, John, had married Laetitia Greenleaf soon after the Civil War and had established his home at 2225 Ninth Street, N.W., in the vicinity of Howard University, newly founded by the famed head of the Freedmen's Bureau, General Howard. It was in this modest home that Laetitia bore twenty-six children, eighteen boys and eight girls. There were four sets of twins, the last of which were born on November 2, 1890. One of these twin boys died soon after birth, but the other survived and was given the name of Andrew at his baptism in St. Augustine's Church on November 30 of that year.

As Andrew grew up, the family named him "Norman." The young lad liked it so much that he took it for his confirmation name when Cardinal Gibbons conferred the Sacrament on him in March, 1903. By that time Norman had almost finished his years at the old Mott School, a public school on a hill overlooking Seventh Street not far from the campus of Howard University. He later spent a year, 1905-6, at the Armstrong Technical High School on P Street.

In 1907 the first steps were taken toward the realization of the ambition he had conceived during his years of serving Mass at St. Augustine's Church. Father Plantevigne visited St. Augustine's Church not long after his ordination, and returned often during his year of study at Catholic University, 1907-8. Norman came to know him very well.

[1] The correspondence between Lincoln and the parishioners and the full account of their dealing with him is given in *America*, 38 (February 11, 1928), pp. 432-33.

To him he revealed his desire to become a priest. Father Plantevigne's advice to Norman was that he should go to Detroit where the clergy, and especially Father Gabriels of that city, were much in favor of promoting vocations among colored boys.

Not long after, at the age of seventeen, Norman joined the migrants to Detroit. He was still undersized, slight, and not too robust. He had little chance of employment in the booming automobile industries, but he did secure a job as a stock and file clerk in the county building in Detroit. Then he began his ten-year-long quest for admission to a seminary.

To one after another of the diocesan seminaries and religious orders Norman patiently wrote letters of application. Father Joseph Wuest, C.S.Sp., founder of the first Catholic colored mission church in Detroit, wanted Norman to join the Holy Ghost Fathers. He wrote to their superior, Father Phelan, but was refused admission.

Months went by between his requests and the answers, even to those which asked only for admission to Catholic colleges. Finally, in 1916, Norman received an acceptance by Columbia College of Dubuque, Iowa. The same day, in a later mail, came a letter from St. Thomas College in St. Paul, Minnesota, the seminary where Archbishop Ireland had educated Father Theobald for the ministry. Norman accepted the Dubuque college offer and prepared to enter that fall.

Bishop Gallagher of Detroit agreed to sponsor the aspirant. He arranged to pay for the major expenses of his education, but he was soon relieved of this burden. A generous white widow, who had taken an interest in Norman upon meeting him in church, assured the bishop that she would pay for Norman's tuition and other incidentals. From then on, his financial worries were few. The widow, who had god-mothered almost a hundred priests in this way, regularly sent him spending money, often adding enough for his clothes and shoes and even his vacation trips.

Norman justified the confidence of the bishop and the widow in his scholastic abilities. He made fine grades at Dubuque. In June, 1917, his report card showed perfect marks of 100 in conduct and application, in Christian Doctrine, and in medieval and modern history. He made

95's in Latin and in ancient history, 93 in mathematics, and 90-92 in English literature, composition, rhetoric, and elocution.

He grew sturdier under the school's regime. As a war measure, the high-school boys were organized into a Reserve Officers' Training Corps. Norman was soon at the head of his battalion and before the end of the year was commissioned as a reserve lieutenant. He was graduated from high school in 1918 and continued on in his college work, securing his academic degree in 1922. He transferred to the major seminary in St. Paul, Minnesota, in 1922.

During the following year, however, misfortune overtook the young seminarian. He contracted pleurisy and pneumonia along with a touch of typhoid. Falling ill in November, he fought the sickness intermittently throughout the whole of the wretched winter, missing much of his school work and baffling the doctor by his failure to respond to treatment. Finally, in March the doctor advised him to give up his seminary work for a year and go away for a change of climate and diet. Norman dug into his cash savings to buy a round-trip ticket to Denver. It proved to be a ticket to health and to the priesthood as well.

Arriving in Denver one blustery March afternoon, Norman sought out the nearest Catholic church to perform his devotions. Father McDonough, pastor of the Jesuit church, befriended him, obtained a room for him with a Catholic family nearby, and thus set Norman on the road to recovery. Having been almost sleepless for seven weeks, the exhausted traveler went to bed and did not awaken for thirty hours. When he arose, Norman knew he was on the mend. The bracing air of Denver restored him completely to health. He recovered his strength enough to go to work both there and in San Jose, California, during the summer months, returning to the seminary in the fall to resume his studies for the priesthood.

After winning his bout with illness, things ran according to schedule for Norman. He was advanced with his new class to the minor orders, and finally, on February 7, 1926, together with twenty-five other seminarians of the Detroit archdiocese, he was ordained in the Cathedral in Detroit by Bishop Joseph Plangens, auxiliary to Bishop Gallagher.

St. Augustine's in Washington prepared a huge celebration for the first of its sons to become a diocesan priest. Several monsignori attended the first solemn High Mass, one of whom personally represented the Apostolic Delegate. The crowd was so great that fifteen policemen were required to handle traffic at the corner of Fifteenth and L streets. Two hundred white alumni of his alma mater, now called Loras College, assembled for the honoring of their fellow student. His mother, now almost eighty years of age, received the blessing from his anointed hands and uttered her Nunc Dimittis. She joined him in Detroit shortly thereafter and enjoyed a year of her son's success before she died in 1928.

In Detroit, Bishop Gallagher assigned Father DuKette to the Cathedral but allowed him to accept the invitations that poured in from all over the country begging him to offer Mass in various cities of the North and the South. For the greater part of a year, he toured the States, saying Mass and preaching all through the East, and as far South as New Orleans, where he was for a month the guest of his former pastor and friend, Father Joseph St. Laurent, S.S.J., pastor of St. Peter Claver Church.

In 1927 Bishop Gallagher appointed Father DuKette to his first pastoral work, the founding of the Church of St. Benedict the Moor in Detroit. For a whole year he worked to start the new church and assemble the congregation. An old Protestant church building had been purchased for the purpose. It served well until one fatal day when an overheated furnace exploded in flames during Mass and sent the building up in smoke. Father DuKette had to rescue the Blessed Sacrament from the building and flee for his life without finishing the Mass.

Other troubles also beset him in Detroit. In early May of 1929 he received some unwanted notoriety because of a misunderstanding with a policeman that almost resulted in tragedy. After attending a play at the University of Detroit one night, he returned home with a severe headache. Before going to bed, he decided to buy medicine for it at a neighborhood drugstore. His efforts to find one open at that midnight hour were futile. Pausing to look into a display window, Father DuKette was accosted by a policeman who mistook him for a prowler. The officer did not know the priest, and, seeing a scarf around his neck (Father was not wearing his Roman collar), he became suspicious. He ordered Father DuKette to come with him to the nearby filling station.

The policeman put in a call to the police station, telling the priest that he was going to take him in the police wagon for questioning. Fearing the complications that might arise, and also feeling conscious of his own innocence, Father DuKette stepped out of the filling station and vanished into the night. The policeman gave chase, shouting for him to halt, and finally shooting at the fleeing figure. The bullet struck Father DuKette in the leg and put him in the hospital for a few days. No charges were filed in the case—but it was a sorely trying blow to his prestige as a man of peace.

It was understandable that Father DuKette grew to dislike Detroit after that incident. Next year, when the bishop sent him to Flint to help out in the apostolate among the colored workers of that automobile manufacturing town, Father Norman found a new place for himself. He saw the opportunity for opening a quiet and secluded mission, far from Detroit's megalopolitan maelstrom. He prevailed on Bishop Gallagher to assign him full-time to the colored neighborhood of Flint, and there he has remained ever since.

In Flint he first took a room in a small house on Clifford Street, and began to form his parish by saying Mass in the private homes of Negro Catholic residents of the neighborhood until he had contacted enough families to create the nucleus of his new flock. He took over a former Methodist parsonage and used it as temporary quarters for his church until he was able to build his first mission chapel. In time he gathered more than a hundred families, shepherding them through the depression, baptizing their children, arranging for the education of the children at the many Catholic schools in Flint, and forming his Christ the King Mission into a center of Catholic life in the southeastern part of the city.

Meanwhile, with the death of Fathers Uncles and Theobald, and with the departure of Father Joseph John for the missions, Father DuKette became the dean of the living colored priests in the country.

He carries his dignity without ostentation. He patiently pursues the routine life of the neighborhood mission in Flint, conducting the instruction classes on weekday evenings to add to the number of the more than two hundred families he has won as converts to the faith in his quarter-century as a priest.

One of his admirers, writing in *The Torch* magazine for January, 1947, limned this portrait of Father DuKette:

> He is a plain man, delicately formed, slight in stature, modestly reserved, quiet and dignified. To see him in his long, black cassock, his close-cropped head bent slightly forward as he talks, his gentle eyes beaming behind his shell-rimmed glasses, is to take with you a picture you cherish forever; an impression that you have touched something a little holier than common things. Thus we like to think—who knows?—Blessed Martin may have been placing God on the spot again—and here we have something of our own, that is a little beyond our vision. It is there, shining through his dark face—majesty; shining through his gentle eyes—serenity. There is more than that, there is piety, prayer.

Characteristic of his devotion to his flock is the story of how a white man called upon Father DuKette one wintry night when the blizzards of eastern Michigan were whipping snow and sleet against the windowpanes of the Flint homes. The visitor found Father DuKette shivering in his greatcoat as he endeavored to read his prayers in his unheated house. His hands were almost stiff with cold, and he had difficulty turning the pages of his breviary book. His visitor asked if the priest had any coal left for heating.

"Oh yes," he replied humbly; "I have a little coal left, but I want to save it for Sunday Mass tomorrow so the people will be warm and comfortable."

Within a few hours, the visitor had secured the delivery of a truckload of coal to replenish the impoverished priest's coal bin.

It was not until the time of his silver jubilee as a priest that his little congregation could raise enough money to build a permanent church. In 1951 an unimposing frame structure with a colonnaded brick front was constructed on Clifford Street in Flint. It was the scene of his solemn Mass of Thanksgiving on September 18, 1951, with Bishop Joseph Albers of Lansing presiding in the sanctuary.

Detroit also welcomed him back for a jubilee Mass in the Sacred Heart Church at Eliot and Rivard streets, the scene of his youthful contacts with the Church as a boy in Detroit. Father Wade came up from Louisiana and Father Ball from Washington to serve as deacon and subdeacon of his Mass, September 16. Father Leonard Cunningham, C.S.Sp., as master of ceremonies, made the liturgical function the first to be staffed by four Negro priests in Michigan.

After the jubilee luncheon at the Gotham Hotel, there was a public reception to honor the jubilarian at the Knights of Columbus Hall on Woodward Avenue in Detroit. The tributes paid him by the speakers and by the many hundreds of guests who filed in were an *amende honorable* for the humiliating experience that Father Norman had met with in Detroit more than twenty years before. Gifts, messages, and personal expressions of congratulations flooded in to Father DuKette for his jubilee. He cherished above all of them the special blessing sent by Pope Pius XII from Rome for the happy occasion.

It will remain for a future historian to assess the achievements of Father DuKette and the other living colored priests. This interim estimate will close with another excerpt from Elizabeth Madden's tribute to him:

> No one would be quite as surprised as Father DuKette to hear himself called a great man. But he is great. The secret of his greatness lies within, far within. His profound spirituality explains it all. If we ever stop to wonder why the Son of God should have spent so much time on wayfarers and derelicts, wayside beggars and lepers, we will remember it was because He loved all men and sought to save the lowest and the vilest. So—we have found the answer to Father DuKette's power. He has that same Christlike heart. . . . For the little Negro Mission and the humble Negro priest are slowly rising to the top of the long Mount—slowly, still struggling, but with a regenerating warmth and brightness, as the slowly rising sun disperses its rays into the shadowed places, into the clefts of the rocks and the mountains and caves; so slowly, in the hard way, Father DuKette has brought into his fold at the present day, some two hundred families. . . . His gentleness, his solicitude for all people, have brought the white people and the Negro together, working side by side, planning, building, still struggling, but struggling together for the colored Mission of Christ the King.

*   *   *   *   *

After Father Derricks' ordination in 1927, there was a gap of six years before another colored priest was ordained.

On June 10, 1933, one of the eight raised to the honor of the priesthood by Archbishop John J. Cantwell of Los Angeles and San Diego was Father Charles A. Logan. A native of Prescott, Arizona, he had been brought by his parents to Los Angeles at the age of five. He received his primary education from the Sisters of the Holy Cross in St. Agnes parish in Los Angeles.

In 1925 he entered the preparatory seminary of St. Joseph College at Mount View, California. In 1927 he transferred to the major seminary at Menlo Park, California.

He offered his first Mass in Holy Name parish in Los Angeles, where he served some time as assistant. He was also attached to other churches in the archdiocese both in Los Angeles and in Santa Barbara, and elsewhere. As of this writing, he is assistant pastor at Pico, California, a suburb of Los Angeles. He is in charge of St. Francis Xavier "mission" for Spanish-American Catholics.

When I interviewed him there in the summer of 1953, his eyes lighted up only when he spoke of the classes of children he had prepared for their first Holy Communion.

Otherwise, they were sad as he recounted the story of his life and his experience with the anomalies of the color problem. He forbade publication of the story, though it was one of the more dramatic and tragic of the sagas I have listened to in the course of this study.

CHAPTER XIII

First Fruits of St. Augustine's

MAURICE ROUSSEVE, S.V.D.

1906—

On November 1, 1920, Father Matthew Christman, S.V.D., the founder of the recently organized minor seminary known as Sacred Heart College in Greenville, Mississippi, arrived in New Orleans to take back to the seminary some prospective candidates, among them Louis Schuman, an orphan at the Lafon Home, and Auguste Legier, a young boy of the Holy Redeemer parish.

Father Christman said Mass next day in the new Church of the Holy Redeemer. Serving his Mass was a quiet and devout boy who had been writing to him about his vocation since the middle of the summer. After Mass, Father Christman questioned young Maurice Rousseve at length to sound him out on why he wished to become a priest. Together they went to the Rousseve family home. There Father Christman explained to his father, Barthelemy Rousseve, and to his mother, Valentine Mansion Rousseve, his hopes of establishing a seminary to train colored lads for the priesthood. He urged that they allow Maurice to transfer from Xavier High School to the new Sacred Heart College up the Mississippi at Greenville. Before the day was over the decision was reached. Maurice joined the two other boys in the little band that accompanied Father Christman back to his hopeful project in the Delta country.

It was Maurice's first long trip away from New Orleans. He had been born there on September 22, 1906, of a distinguished Creole family that traced its free ancestry far back into the period of Spanish rule in the Crescent City. One of his great-great-grandfathers had been Dominique Foster, a veteran of Andrew Jackson's army in the Battle of New Orleans.

Maurice's family, like Father Esnard's, lived in old St. Augustine's parish on the northeast edge of the French Quarter. Like his many brothers and sisters, Maurice was baptized in the parish church, attended Mass there with his family in the colored section of the church, received his first Communion and Confirmation there, and lived in awe of Father Subileau's beard and thunderous sermons.

Though St. Augustine's parish had provided a school for colored children on the site of the old College de Orléans as far back as 1838, young Rousseve began his grammer school at the Institution Catholique, a private school at Dauphine and Touro streets. It had been founded by a bequest of the rich Creole widow, Mrs. Bernard Couvent, who died in 1837, leaving a large sum of money for the establishment of a school for free colored children in the Cathedral parish. Maurice's father was a member of the board of laymen who administered properties for the endowment of the school and had charge of the appointment of lay teachers.

Under their guidance, Maurice spent his first three years of elementary education learning both French and English, and acquiring skill in reading, writing, and spelling. About half of the students were from the Lafon Orphan Home, but there were also many from the respected and well-placed Creole families of the neighborhood.

The school came to an abrupt and sorry end in the hurricane of 1915. The building was destroyed completely. The pupils were dispersed to other schools. Young Maurice was enrolled in the school just erected by the Sisters of the Holy Family alongside their historic motherhouse on Orléans Street. For three more years Maurice studied under the Holy Family nuns. But he was not prepared by them for his first Communion. Nor could he serve Mass in their chapel—that privilege was then reserved to white altar boys. It was in St. Augustine's Church that Maurice attended Communion preparation classes, sitting in a segregated corner while the priest taught both white and colored children of the parish and readied them for receiving Holy Communion together.

In 1917 the archbishop purchased a former non-Catholic church building near the corner of Royal and Frenchman streets. He turned the church over to the Josephite Fathers to conduct services for the colored

Catholics who had formerly attended St. Augustine's and other neighboring churches. The new church was named Holy Redeemer, and Maurice became one of the first altar boys when it was opened. He soon grew attached to the church, working in the parish office, running errands for the pastor, Father Joseph Lally, and taking great pride in the impressive new center of colored Catholic life, just a block from the demolished Institution Catholique which was slow in rising from its ruins.

Father Lally encouraged young Maurice in his aspirations toward the priesthood. He kept in close touch with the lad even after he transferred to Xavier Preparatory School to begin his high-school work in 1918. Maurice regularly served Mass at Holy Redeemer before making the long trip uptown to the Blessed Sacrament Sisters' School fifty blocks above Canal Street in the former buildings of the old Southern University.

Thus when Father Christman wrote in July, 1920, to ask Father Lally whether there were any likely candidates for the new seminary from his parish, the Josephite Father was able to assure him that a trip down to the city to recruit subjects for the new venture would not be fruitless.

Maurice willingly returned to Greenville with Father Christman in the fall of that year. It was the beginning of a great adventure, and Father Christman's optimistic enthusiasm for the seminary was soon communicated to the three new boys he took with him by train. He told them of the years of planning and discussion that had gone into the opening of the school. He gave full credit to Father James Wendel, who had died just a few months before, for his persevering insistence on the need for a special seminary and his energetic championing of the cause of colored priests in the United States.

It was a humble enough Nazareth to which Father Christman introduced the new boys next day, November 5. On the outskirts of Greenville, the enterprising missionary had built during the past summer a plain, boxlike, two-story frame building. It stood in the churchyard to the rear of the rectory of the Sacred Heart Mission, founded just seven years before by Father John Hoenderop, S.V.D. There had been some bitter colored Protestant opposition to the new mission, especially after the erection of the grammar school building in 1913. Of the six thousand Negroes in the town, only a dozen and a half were Catholics. Yet by the end of the first year, the school enrolled 120 children. The non-Catholics decided to establish a private school of their own to combat the influence of the Catholic school. However, the work had prospered and both church and school had grown each year.

The top floor of the parochial high school had been fitted out as a dormitory for the prospective seminarians. At the time that Maurice and his two companions arrived, they almost doubled the student body. There were only four other candidates for the new seminary, one of whom was Archibald Derricks, who had already graduated from the academic department of Howard University, and was soon to leave to seeks orders in the Trinitarians.

For a while during the first year, the school looked like a *petite seminaire* on the European style—a few sacerdotal hopefuls gathered together by a zealous curé in his own home and taught their seminary studies by the pastor between the regular routine of parochial duties. Father Christman was practically alone on the mission at the time, assisted only by Father Anthony Jacobs who was just learning English. He managed all the affairs of the church and school, and he taught all of the classes in the inchoate seminary. From him the students learned algebra, history, Latin and Greek. Because there were so few (only fourteen by the end of the first term), the boys also attended some of the classes in the high school taught by the Blue Sisters of the Holy Ghost.

Maurice found seminary life congenial. He liked the regular round of devotions that Father Christman prescribed for the boys: prayers and hymns in the morning and evening, and special sermons and conferences for them only at stated times during the week and on Sunday. The seminarians engaged in their recreations together, a wooden fence down the middle of a yard separating them from the boys and girls of the mission school. Occasionally, however, they played tennis and other games with the school boys and engaged in competitive sports with their teams.

In 1921 Fathers Xavier Baltes and Cosmas Schneider were added to the staff of the seminary, and Father Jacobs was made assistant in the parish. Thirty-one boys were on hand for the beginning of the momentous year, full of excitement for Maurice and all of the other seminarians.

Opposition to the seminary was stirred up by the Ku Klux Klan, not only in Greenville itself, but as far away as west Texas. A KKK newspaper in Texas attacked the seminary on the charge that white and colored were mingled, and that white Sisters were being forced to serve colored students at table. Other KKK papers also pressed the charges, trying to inflame Catholic and Protestant opposition to the new seminary on the grounds that it would soon mean that white women would be forced to kneel down and confess their sins to a colored priest.

Rumors began to fly in Greenville. Some of the Negro citizens warned the Fathers that the KKK was planning to burn down the seminary. To avoid a panic among them, the students were left in ignorance of the threat. The superiors called on the mayor and on Senator Percy to request that a committee be appointed to examine the seminary and refute the KKK charges. The Knights of Columbus of San Antonio (where the original charges were invented) also sent a telegram to the mayor of Greenville asking him to investigate.

Maurice and the other seminarians were thus subjected to careful scrutiny by a civic committee made up of the mayor, Judge Emmett Harty, an Episcopalian minister, and a non-Catholic lawyer. These four men issued a favorable report. They pointed out how similar were the practices of the Catholic seminary to those of non-Catholic Bible institutes run for the training of colored ministers. Like these, the Catholic boys were being trained to spread the Gospel among the colored folk of the South. The committee rectified all of the misrepresentations, even those appearing in the Catholic press at the time. Both the lawyer and the judge, though non-Catholics, wrote letters in refutation of the bizarre charges that were repeated in the Catholic magazines.

Other precautions were also taken to ward off possible outbreaks in the tense situation. One of the Catholic Negro parishioners always made it a practice to accompany the seminarians whenever they went out for a picnic in the woods or to the nearby creeks and bayous. He carried guns to let the local KKK know that he was ready and willing to defend the seminarians against their pranks and ambushes. The youngsters were therefore not molested. But neither were they bothering their heads about the tensions between the older men. They felt at ease as they went on hikes around Greenville, and they even walked down the city streets with cheerful unconcern.

At times, some of the townsfolk shouted insults at them, referring to them as the "little nigger priests." The neophytes took this as a compliment. Once they were actually threatened. On a botany field trip with Father Cosmas Schneider one day, the little band of seminarians strayed inadvertently into a cultivated patch kept by one of the local colored farmers. In defense of his private property and his crops, the farmer came out of his house shouting, "Get out! Get out, or I'll shoot. If you don't hear me talk, you'll hear me shoot!" The lads made it back to the road on the double. They did not stop until they were well out of sight of the farmhouse. None of them dreamed that he would carry out his threat, but they just wanted to be a safe distance away in case his gun went off.

Thus the hostility of some people in Greenville became evident to the seminarians. And it was especially manifest to Father Christman when he tried to buy provisions for the boys and the mission. There was not much money for their support, and prices always seemed to be higher whenever they needed supplies. The result was a Spartan regime for the boys months on end. Breakfast often consisted of nothing more than weak coffee, peanut butter, and a slice of bread. Dinner was beans, cornbread, and soup. Meat was a rare item on the table. Vegetables appeared in adequate quantities only when the little vegetable garden on the property was producing its cabbages and beans.

It was a hard life for the young levites. The dirty, dusty section of town, the unpaved roads around the mission, the lack of drainage for the rain water, and the general poverty of the neighborhood all contributed to the hampering of the perseverance of the ambitious lads. It was a great relief to them to return home for vacation in summer and fatten up on home cooking against the day of their return in the fall.

Though relations between the seminary and the few Catholic people were generally good in Greenville, the Divine Word Fathers decided to move it to Bay St. Louis for its permanent location. The two years at Greenville had proved that the institution was feasible. But it was thought best to move the seminary closer to New Orleans and Catholic Louisiana, which were regarded as the best seed beds for future vocations. It would help the present seminarians like Maurice to be closer to their homes, and thus able to be visited by their parents and relatives—a good antidote to homesickness and a stimulus to morale.

Besides, it was imperative to have a self-sufficient seminary, not connected with or dependent on a coeducational school such as the Sacred Heart Mission high school. The seminarians did not mix with the girls of the mission school, but the atmosphere of a coeducational school was not conducive to the cultivation of serious prayer and study habits.

In 1921 the boys were informed that negotiations were under way for the purchase of a suitable piece of property in Bay St. Louis. The local pastor, Father A. J. Gmelch, was in favor of the move. He agreed to the division of his parish, and signified his willingness to turn over to the Divine Word Fathers the colored school then operating in Bay St. Louis. He wrote to the Bishop of Natchez, John E. Gunn, D.D.:

> I believe that true vocations to the priesthood can be found among the colored. I admire the Fathers of the Divine Word for their courage in giving the colored the advantages of a seminary. As members of the Society of the Divine Word, the future colored priests will be directed wisely and strongly supported. In my opinion your Lordship is doing a great service to the Church by the encouragement and active support you are giving the Fathers of the Divine Word in this undertaking. I shall be very glad to have the seminary located in Bay St. Louis.

This favorable attitude on the part of the leader of the local clergy paved the way for acquiring the seminary property and for the transfer of the institution to the Gulf Coast city.

By October, 1921, the site was purchased. The Divine Word provincial, Father Peter Janser, who had been the ardent supporter of Father Wendel and Father Christman, concluded all of the negotiations with the bishop and the superiors in Holland, and finally wrote a circular letter to all the cardinals, bishops, and archbishops of the United

States, explaining the purpose of the new St. Augustine's Mission House to be located in Bay St. Louis, Mississippi.

The boys in Greenville meanwhile eagerly awaited news of the proposed new building down at the Bay. The raising of funds was a slow and tedious process. Cardinal O'Connell of Boston sent a thousand dollars, other bishops contributed like amounts, and donations were forthcoming from Mother Katherine Drexel and Monsignor John E. Burke of the Catholic Board for Mission Work among the Colored People. Cardinal Dougherty promised to support the venture with the last farthing of the funds collected by the Bureau of Indian and Negro Missions, of whose board he was a member. The Bureau did contribute $20,000 toward the first building, and later added another $10,000.

Finally in the summer of 1922, after a change of architects, the plans were drawn and approved for a large brick building to house the minor seminary. A New Orleans contractor agreed to erect the building. By September construction had begun. The cornerstone was laid on November 23. By July of the following year the three-story building was completed and ready for occupancy.

A firmer foundation than the bricks and mortar was given to the young seminary in April of the year 1923. It was a special Apostolic Brief on the seminary by the new Pope, Pius XI, and dated at St. Peter's April 5. Addressed to Father William Gier, Superior General of the Society of the Divine Word, the official Brief gave the Pontiff's highest approval to the proposed new Mission House of St. Augustine at Bay St. Louis. It was a new confirmation of their priestly vocations for Maurice and all of the other seminarians at Greenville when they read the confident and inspiring words of the Holy Father:

> It is to us a source of deep joy to learn that the college for the education of Negroes which you had established temporarily at Greenville, in the Diocese of Natchez, will shortly be transferred to Bay St. Louis in the same diocese, and converted into a mission house for the training of Negro youth according to the Rule of your Order. . . . In your new undertaking you are following the very principle which, in so far as circumstances allowed, has always guided the Catholic Church. To this mother has arisen, especially in recent times, a numerous progeny among the black races—a host of children who have

frequently displayed virtues so splendid that they sealed their
faith with their blood as in the most glorious epochs of
Christian history. The Negroes occupy enormous areas of the
earth, and it is undoubted that these races, which the Church
takes so loving and maternal an interest in gladdening with the
knowledge of her joyful message, will in the course of time be
trained in all branches of human civilization, and will thus
arise from their present lowly stages of culture, and attain a
high level in their mode of life and moral training. If therefore we wish to accomplish useful and solid work in this field,
it is indispensable that priests of the same race shall make it
their life-task to lead these peoples to the Christian faith and
to a higher cultural level.

The Holy Father made a strong plea for the creation of a colored
clergy "as soon as possible." He pledged himself to do everything to
promote the salutary undertaking. It was thus with the special blessing
of the sovereign Pontiff that the new seminary was launched in the
summer of 1923. Maurice and the other seminarians gathered at Bay
St. Louis in September, enthusiastic over the prospect of another pioneer
venture. Twenty-two boys in the first class took possession of the still
unfinished building on the unlandscaped plantation. With Father
Christman in the van, they tackled the dual task of setting up the
interior order of the seminary and conquering the thickets of jungle
underbrush and draining the swamplands of the extensive estate.

By the time the formal dedication took place in September, the
seminarians had transformed the rugged terrain into what looked like
the beginnings of a religious house and a monastery garden. Maurice's
relatives journeyed from New Orleans with many other colored Catholics who crowded the excursion train for the big event. Bishop Gunn
officially blessed the building and its temporary chapel. It was solemnly
dedicated under the patronage of St. Augustine to the holy purposes of
a seminary for future priests.

After the celebration was over and the crowds had departed, the boys
settled down to the full religious routine of prayer and study, of work
and recreation that made the months speed by rapidly. Maurice advanced with his class each year, maturing into a quiet, deep-praying,
and religious seminarian. By 1926 he and his fellow students Vincent

Smith and Ernest Casacalvo had completed their preparatory seminary work. They were sent North for their year of novitiate at East Troy, Wisconsin, where they joined the prep students from Techny, Illinois, and Girard, Pennsylvania, for the intensive spiritual training under Father Herman Joseph Richarz, the gentle and holy novicemaster.

The year passed quickly. For their second year of special training, Maurice and Vincent Smith were missioned to Bay St. Louis to teach the minor seminarians in accordance with Father Christman's plan, which he modeled on the Jesuit seminary training program. Maurice taught ancient history, English, and Greek. At the beginning of the next year, he and Vincent Smith pronounced their first vows on September 8, 1928.

The question of starting a major seminary at Bay St. Louis had been discussed for many years. Maurice and the other seminarians were given their choice of going to Rome for their philosophical and theological studies. It was also proposed to send them to St. Gabriel's Mission House in Austria, or to the American Mission House at Techny. But Maurice and his fellow students felt that more boys would be attracted to the priesthood if a fully equipped seminary were established at Bay St. Louis, and more of the minor seminarians would be inspired to persevere if they saw their older brothers going through the course to the priesthood and being ordained right there in the seminary. They felt they were pioneers, and they began their higher studies in pioneer style in a small frame cottage near the highway.

Maurice and Vincent Smith were joined that year by two other American seminarians from the novitiate, Anthony Bourges and Francis Wade, and two from Central America, Philip Marin and Alban Velasquez. Together the six seminarians undertook their two years of philosophical studies under Father Christman, who was also the rector of the whole seminary, indefatigable fund-raiser, master architect and planner, and spiritual father of the thirty-nine minor seminarians.

One of the best rooms in the minor seminary building was turned over to the major seminarians for their library, study hall, music room, recreation room, and lecture hall—all in one. A portion of the students' dining room was partitioned for the philosophy students' refectory. All these temporary arrangements were endured in the hope of the new building soon to be erected as a major seminary. The site was chosen in 1928, about a block to the east of the junior seminary. The superiors purchased an adjoining property for six thousand dollars to give the theologians sufficient room for privacy and activities. Under the giant spreading oaks a building in Spanish style was planned, with large airy rooms and spacious verandas. Father Christman threw himself into the work of raising money for the proposed building. It proved too much for him. He overworked himself for his boys. "The seminary *has* to be a success," he said. "If we fail, there will never be a second attempt to found a seminary for colored boys." He drove himself mercilessly on his appointed mission.

In February, 1929, in the midst of his labors, Father Christman suddenly died of a heart attack. One of the other Fathers called all of the seminarians together in the chapel. He told them all to kneel and pray for the repose of the soul of their spiritual father, now gone home to God. The younger boys all broke down and sobbed. Even the older seminarians had difficulty controlling their tears. Maurice felt numbed at the loss of the spiritual shepherd of his soul, the guardian of his vocation.

For a while it looked as though the major seminary would be buried with Father Christman. Things had so centered around him that seminary life came to a standstill at his death. For a whole month there was only waiting and watching. Some proposed that the idea be abandoned and that the seminarians be sent away to larger and better established seminaries. But after a delay of more than thirty days, Father John Thilges was sent down from Techny to continue teaching where Father Christman left off.

Finishing their philosophy studies that year, the students launched out into the depths of theology under the guidance of a hastily assembled theological faculty. Father Joseph Murphy, S.V.D., one of the first American members of the Society, and a brilliant graduate from the Angelicum in Rome, volunteered to devote his life to the seminary at the Bay. He taught church history, dogma, and Scripture. Father John Kemper assumed charge of moral theology classes. A diocesan priest, Father J. V. Hoffman from Nebraska, was secured to teach apologetics.

Under these teachers Maurice and his companions quickly made progress in the sacred sciences. The standards of the school were set and kept high. All of the classes were strictly conducted in Latin, and the regular examinations administered. Indeed, the requirements were even higher than in the larger seminaries, and the students were specially tutored to achieve their proficiency in the divinity courses.

Bishop Gerow of Natchez was satisfied with their progress. He journeyed to the Bay in November, 1930, to administer the tonsure to Maurice and his fellow candidates. In December of 1931 and again in 1932 he returned for minor orders. In March of 1933, the bishop administered the oath of the subdeaconate and conferred that order on the class. In November of the same year they were made deacons. All eyes were then turned to the great day of ordination to the priesthood.

It was an historic day—May 23, 1934. As the first in seniority, Maurice Rousseve approached the ordination ceremony at the head of the little band of four ordinands who filed into the huge outdoor tent that had been rented and set up as a tabernacle for the occasion. The little chapel of the seminary was too small to accommodate the large gathering of people who came from Louisiana, Kentucky, and Illinois, and even from the District of Columbia for the sacred ceremony.

Under the oak trees that shielded the tent from the sun's heat, the bishop spread his hands over the ordinands, and they rose as the first ordained colored priests of the South, the first to be so anointed in Mississippi, the first Divine Word Fathers to have the Holy Spirit breathe upon them at St. Augustine's.

Father Rousseve had the happiness of giving his blessing first to his widowed mother, and then to his brothers and sisters, one of whom was Sister Mary Theresa Vincent, a religious of the Holy Family congregation. His brother Charles was there too, taking leave from the historical and literary work that was soon to gain him national recognition, when his well-developed book *The Negro in Louisiana* would be published. His other brothers also shared the happiness of the occasion: Ferdinand, educated at M.I.T., Chicago, and Harvard, later to achieve renown as an architect, a teacher at Harvard, Southern University, and Boston College; Numa, an artist of parts, instructor in fine arts at Xavier; and Rene, a social worker-to-be. His twin sisters,

Leona and Leonie, both destined to be schoolteachers and administrators, were also in the family party.

Next day, Father Maurice celebrated his first private Mass in the parish Church of St. Rose de Lima in Bay St. Louis. It was there that he first gave Holy Communion to his mother and to all of his family and friends. There was great happiness for his mother that day, as there would be a few years later when she would be chosen Catholic Mother of 1942 by the Catholic Committee of the South, and given an award in recognition of her successful mothering of her model family.

In contrast to Father Plantevigne's tragedy, the home parish of Holy Redeemer welcomed Father Rousseve back to New Orleans for his first solemn High Mass the next Sunday. It was a happy and holy experience for the new priest and for his family. Old familiar faces were at the altar rail to receive the blessing of the former altar boy now returned as an altar man of God. Father John Lundrigan, who was later to lose his life in saving a drowning colored boy, preached a glowing sermon.

For the next weeks Father Rousseve was the honored guest at each of the colored churches and convents in New Orleans. He participated in the celebration of the solemn High Mass in the St. Louis Cathedral in the Crescent City for the opening of the national convention of the Knights of Peter Claver. His three fellow ordinands, Father Vincent Smith, Anthony Bourges, and Francis Wade, were also on the altar with him on that long-awaited occasion.

Xavier University honored its former scholar by inviting him to open their first summer school that year with a Mass and sermon. He returned to Xavier Preparatory School to offer Mass in the convent and in the nearby Church of the Blessed Sacrament.

The rest of that first summer was spent in giving missions. Paired with Father Wade, the young priest traveled to Pointe-a-la-Hache, Louisiana, to Port Arthur, Texas, and elsewhere, to continue his work.

Back at the seminary, Maurice awaited his assignment for the coming year. Bishop Desmond of Alexandria, Louisiana, had interviewed the young priests and intimated that he had bid for their services in Marksville, but that some of the diocesan clergy were objecting to their assignment in the non-Catholic section of Louisiana. Bishop

Jeanmard, whose diocese embraced most of French Acadian Louisiana, then requested that they be assigned to a new colored parish that he was opening in Lafayette, Louisiana.

When the missions were over, Father Maurice and Father Wade joined their other two newly ordained companions as assistant pastors in the Immaculate Heart of Mary parish in Lafayette. The tasks of building the parish occupied all four priests in a regular round of parish duties. Father Maurice made that his main work for the next four years.

In the meantime, he was in constant demand as a retreat master, missionary, and occasional speaker, and a substitute in other parishes and institutions around the South. In New Orleans, he gave a mission at the Holy Ghost Church. In Cassard Lane, near Donaldsonville, he labored for a whole month, preaching, teaching catechism, and doing rural mission work in the environs. Whites as well as colored came to hear him, and in places like Maurice and Coulee Croche, Louisiana, where he gave missions and triduums for the Negroes in the "white" church, even the regular white parishioners attended.

In 1939 Father Rousseve was transferred to the Notre Dame Church in St. Martinville, Louisiana, the city that closely associates itself with the Evangeline tradition. The grave of Longfellow's heroine is proudly pointed out in the old graveyard beside St. Martin's Church. Across town, the Divine Word Fathers had built in the previous year a new church for the colored Catholics of the city. Within two years Father Maurice was made pastor, the first colored priest to be put in full charge of a Louisiana parish.

The great need of the parish at the time was an addition to the small schoolhouse built by Mother Katherine Drexel's donations almost twenty years before. Father Rousseve energetically pushed the building of the larger school and the new convent. The Sisters of the Blessed Sacrament, who had for three years been commuting daily from New Iberia to teach in St. Martinville, were thus housed in their own convent. There was some gossip about town when the novel idea of having white Sisters teach in a parish under a colored pastor was first broached. But Father Rousseve smoothed the way for the new departure by his quiet and diplomatic handling of the situation.

Not long after, the Divine Word superiors appointed a white priest to be an assistant in the parish. That too was taken in stride, where before it might have caused a major disturbance in the race-split community.

The ultimate was achieved when one Sunday the acting pastor of the white church, Father LeGros, came to invite Father Rousseve to say an extra Mass in St. Martin's Church for the white men's quarterly communion. Father LeGros overrode Maurice's objections by saying, "Listen, Father, you're a priest and I'm a priest. You come and say Mass." One of the Knights of Columbus served the Mass. He afterwards thanked Father Rousseve for coming, and shook hands with him.

Father Rousseve gradually won the confidence of the white priests and the townspeople of St. Martinville while efficiently ministering to the spiritual needs of his colored parishioners. He extended the reach of his zeal to include many hundreds of rural Negroes living in the environs of St. Martinville, incorporating subsidiary missions for them at Cade and St. John. Up and down the Teche Bayou he rode the lanes of the rural districts in quest of his scattered flock. His mastery of French, and his quiet subdued manner of speaking made him a welcome guest and a trusted spiritual guide for his people.

After almost ten years of this pastoral life, Father Rousseve was transferred to the seminary in Bay St. Louis. He was made prefect and teacher of the major seminarians and also appointed vice-provincial of the Divine Word Fathers of the Southern Province. In these offices of responsibility and trust, Father Maurice carried out, in his modest, retiring, and self-effacing way, the many exacting duties of his daily routine.

Before the young seminarians Father Maurice was an example of everything the Church expects of its priests. As the first fruits of St. Augustine's Seminary, he was living proof that the ideals to which it is dedicated can be realized. It was not founded in vain if it can still produce more strong men of God like Father Maurice Rousseve, priest of the Society of the Divine Word.

However, the demands of the mission work in south Louisiana soon resulted in his return to a pastorate there. He was assigned to St. Benedict the Moor Church in Duson, Louisiana, in the fall of 1952.

CHAPTER XIV

Trappist Novicemaster

FATHER MARY SIMON (VINCENT, S.V.D.) SMITH, O.C.S.O.

1894 – 1952

He long wanted to give his life to God in the stark austerity of the Trappists. He wanted to die as a spiritual son of Our Lady of La Trappe and be buried in the simple Trappist habit. In March, 1952, he achieved this desire of his long years. The colored man who had been born as plain Vincent Smith died as Father Mary Simon, a novice-master in the Order of the Cistercians of the Strict Observance in their new foundation of Our Lady of the Genessee at Piffard, near Rochester, New York.

As far back as he could remember, the Trappists had been in his mind and in his life. Vincent was brought into the world not many miles from their famed monastery of Gethsemani in Kentucky. Born in Lebanon, Kentucky, on August 2, 1894, Vincent was the son of a man who lived up to his name, Pious Smith, and of a mother, Mary Eliza Spalding, who was connected with the family of Bishop John Lancaster Spalding. Pious Smith's folks had come to Kentucky from Creole Louisiana. His wife's family were originally from Catholic Maryland as were many of the pioneer Catholic families of Kentucky's Blue Grass region.

In his trade as a plasterer, Pious Smith was employed by the Trappists to help in the construction of their monastery at Gethsemani. There he often took his sons as helpers. When Vincent was a boy he too made the trip to Gethsemani. He was deeply impressed by the atmosphere of holiness he sensed there. In later years he told how the determination had first shaped itself in his mind.

"Some day I am going to go in Gethsemani as a Trappist," he said to himself. He nurtured this ambition to join the ranks of the monks who spent themselves in prayer and silent labor for God. But the dream seemed far away when he faced the realities of life in the Kentucky of the period before the first World War.

As the twelfth of thirteen children, he had to go to work by the time he was seventeen to support himself and help care for the rest of the children.

Fortunately for his future vocation, young Vincent got a job as chauffeur and valet of Bishop Ferdinand Brossart of Covington, Kentucky. The bishop took a personal interest in the smiling, happy and devout lad. He had a special uniform made for Vincent so that he could accompany the bishop anywhere he went, even up the aisle of the Cathedral for solemn pontifical Masses.

The German Sisters who kept house for the bishop in Covington appointed themselves as chaperones of the young chauffeur, knowing his desire to become a priest. But he needed very little watching. He had no interest in girls, even in one who was enamored of him. He preferred to take his sister Priscilla to parties when he went to them. And he preferred the company of priests and Sisters to that of his contemporaries who noised up the town after hours.

During the first World War, the national emergency pushed Vincent's hopes for a priestly career into the background. He enlisted as a private in the United States Army and served for eighteen months, during which time he was stationed in France with a service battalion.

In 1919, upon his discharge from the Army, Vincent felt even more convinced that he had a vocation to the priesthood. The Bishop of Louisville gave him no encouragement whatsoever. But Bishop Brossart of Covington enthusiastically supported him. He did not have a seminary of his own and could not promise him admission into any major seminary because Vincent had not finished high school. But the bishop was instrumental in sending him to St. Emma's Military Institute in Rock Castle, Virginia, for high-school work.

Application was also sent to the one seminary that had admitted and ordained colored priests in the United States: St. Joseph's in Baltimore. The Josephite Fathers were willing to admit Vincent. But they could not guarantee that Cardinal Gibbons would ordain him. At that time the aged prelate, who had personally ordained two colored priests, was reluctant to ordain any more because of the difficulty of securing pastorates for them.

Vincent did not give up hope. He worked summers in the steel mills of Gary, Indiana, and kept saving his money and praying for a chance to study for the priesthood. As though in answer to his own and his devout parents' prayers, news came of the opening of Sacred Heart College as a minor seminary for colored boys in Greenville, Missisippi, in November, 1920. Vincent transferred on March 31, 1921, and continued his high-school studies with the first dozen aspirants to the priesthood there.

He later pursued his studies at Bay St. Louis when the seminary was moved to its present site in 1923 and renamed St. Augustine's.

As an older lad (Vincent was twenty-seven when he entered), he was a stabilizing influence in the seminary. More than anyone else, Vincent swept the younger seminarians along with his contagious spirit of optimism and joy, especially when the life of the institution was grim and austere. In the poverty of the early days, there was much to test the genuineness of the seminarians' will-to-stay. Even after the Holy Father's personal representative in the United States, Monsignor Fumasoni-Biondi, visited the seminary and devoted his resources to the betterment of its financial condition, there were many instances where Vincent's buoyant jollity and trusted leadership made the difference between discouragement and the acceptance of the hard things in life for the sake of the *Introibo,* the entry to the altar of God.

Graduating in 1926 with the pioneer group of seminarians, Vincent shared with them all of the "firsts" they achieved in the course of the next few years. He was with the first group of colored seminarians to matriculate at East Troy, Wisconsin, for their novitiate. He took his first vows with them in 1928. He advanced through the years of the major seminary training at Bay St. Louis. He was in the first class for tonsure in 1930, for minor orders in 1931 and 1932, for subdiaconate in 1933, diaconate later the same year, and finally for ordination to the priesthood by Bishop Gerow in May, 1934.

Shortly before his ordination, his aged mother, now living a life that was all prayer in expectation of her son's coming as a priest, was out walking in her garden at the old home in Lebanon. Deep in prayer, she heard a heavenly voice of greeting, saying words much like those of the Christmas angel to the shepherds, announcing good tidings of great joy. She knew then that her life-long prayers to have her son become a priest were realized.

Her happiness was full when Father Vincent Smith was welcomed back to Lebanon as Kentucky's first colored priest. In Lebanon's St. Augustine Church, where he had been baptized, had received his first Communion, had served as an altar boy, and had been confirmed, he chanted his first solemn High Mass on June 10. The places of honor in the congregation were occupied by his venerable parents, both over eighty years old. Thirty priests gathered for the occasion, many of them friends from the days when he had worked for Bishop Brossart. Two of his five cousins who were nuns also came for the memorable event.

"I remember going home to celebrate my first solemn Mass," Father Vincent said later. "It seemed that the whole population turned out. I think they did. The Church had been restricted to colored for my Mass, but the white parishioners crowded in too."

It was the "Nunc Dimittis" for his parents. Within a few months, Vincent was back to celebrate the requiem for his father, who died on October 31 that year. His mother went home to God a year after her son's ordination, dying on May 27, 1935.

Meanwhile, Father Vincent, like the other newly ordained colored priests of the Divine Word Society, had received his first appointment. They had expected to be assigned to teach at a projected college for colored youth in Marksville or Mansura, in the diocese of Alexandria, Louisiana. Plans for this and for them fell through during the summer after their ordination. Bishop Jeanmard of Lafayette, Louisiana, secured the services of the new priests for a colored parish in his see city. There a community house for the religious priests was erected, and Father Patzelt was made superior of the community and pastor of the new Church of the Immaculate Heart of Mary.

Father Smith and Father Bourges drove up to Lafayette in style in September, 1934. They had acquired an old Studebaker from Father Edward Kramer of the Catholic Board for Mission Work among

Colored People in New York. In the gift car they made their triumphant entry into their pioneer parish—the first ever to be staffed by colored priests in the Deep South.

With the unction of his new priesthood still upon him, Father Vincent plunged into the work of building the living Church while the carpenters and brickmasons erected the edifice to house the presence of Christ's Body, eucharistic and mystical. Holy Mass for the prospective parishioners was held each Sunday in the Holy Rosary Institute Hall throughout the fall months. It was not until the Sunday before Christmas that the new church was dedicated. There Father Smith was able to begin that long career of pulpit oratory that distinguished him as the outstanding colored missioner he became.

The routine of parish life consumed all of his other time in those first years. Reclaiming the indifferent, teaching catechism to the young and old alike, hearing endless confessions, going on sick calls and on parish visits, and observing the full cycle of the parish feasts as the years' seasons came and went, Father Smith was kept close to his parish boundaries, save for a few weeks each year.

There was an annual series of lectures, sermons, missions, and talks that took him off on his journeyings each fall. On his visits back home, he often took time out to spend some days with the Trappists at Gethsemani in a spiritual retreat, drinking in the prayerfulness and holiness of the monastery as spiritual refreshment for the toil ahead. Each time he renewed his boyhood determination to enter the monastery if he could possibly make the grade.

Back in Lafayette, the devoted parishioners grew to love their jolly, cheerful, ever-pleasant *le père Smeeth*. To the French-speaking colored Catholics of the neighborhood he became a deeply revered spiritual father. They liked his roaring oratory, his generous compassion, his serenity, and his mature spiritual solidity.

Nonetheless, Father Vincent found it difficult to adjust to the artificialities that the segregation system imposed on him even in his relationships with fellow priests. He was warned not to offer his hand, though anointed with the same oils, to his fellow white priests for a friendly handclasp if he met them on the street. He was not allowed to accept invitations to dine with them lest it violate the accepted social codes of the community. Still he bore the extra cross with patience. He submitted his judgment to the decision of those who prudently counseled against innovations.

After four years of ministry in the Deep South, Father Smith asked for a transfer to a border city parish or to a northern one. His superiors offered his services as an assistant in one of the Divine Word parishes in a border city. But the ecclesiastical authorities did not take any action on the offer.

Father Smith was therefore assigned to the traveling mission band and was given St. Nicholas' rectory in St. Louis as his home and headquarters. From 1938 to 1940 he was associated with his close friend, Father Charles Reinelt, S.V.D., the well-liked pastor of St. Nicholas. In the fall of 1940 he was appointed assistant at St. Elizabeth's Church in South Side Chicago.

His years of giving missions and retreats made him a familiar figure in Aframerica. He was in constant demand as a speaker and missionary. A sample of his busy itinerary is given us in his fall schedule for 1940. In September he was in Pittsburgh for the opening of the eleventh annual convention of the National Catholic Interracial Federation. He also gave a week's mission at the local St. Benedict's Church. Then he entrained for Memphis and another mission at St. Anthony's Church there.

In October he was a participant in the Midwest Clergy Conference on Negro Welfare in Milwaukee. He gave papers at the semi-annual meetings of the conference and eventually served as a vice-president of the conference from 1943 to 1945.

Later in October, 1940, Father Smith was in Madison, Wisconsin, for an address to the white St. Francis Xavier retreat club. Next month, in Chicago, he was a guest of the Monday Evening Club, a group of prominent white Catholic Chicagoans whom he addressed on the subject of the Negro missions. Later he hurried South to Little Rock and Tulsa to give three-day revivals and two-week missions at the Catholic churches for the colored in those localities.

Summers found him engaged in outdoor missions at newly established parishes throughout the Midwest and the South. For a number of years he preached on the spacious lawns of St. Rita's Mission in Indianapolis.

Upon the outbreak of World War II, Father Vincent plunged into USO work. He toured the army camps where colored soldiers were stationed, acting in an advisory capacity for the USO officials, and serving as an auxiliary chaplain at a number of military installations throughout the country.

His popularity with colored Catholics across the land and especially in Chicago did not keep him immune from carping criticism and personal attacks on the part of some people in Bronzeville who seemed to trade in calumny and slander. Rumors were spread about the colored neighborhoods of the South Side slums that did great damage to Father Smith's reputation. He keenly felt these desperate attempts to undercut his apostolate and put an end to his effective influence in that area. Things reached such an impasse in 1943 that Father Smith decided to try to secure admission to the Trappists. He packed up and departed for a leave of absence in Lebanon and Gethsemani where he could seek admittance to the Abbey in person.

On this first try, however, Father Smith was not accepted by the abbot at Gethsemani. Father Hunter, provincial of the eastern province of the Divine Word Society, visiting at Gethsemani, prevailed upon Father Vincent to continue his active apostolate for a few more years. He accepted the post of assistant pastor at St. Peter's Church in Asbury Park, New Jersey. Next year he was promoted to his first full pastorate, Our Lady of the Divine Shepherd Church on Pennington Avenue in Trenton. There he remained for five years as pastor of the small mission for colored Catholics. Most of the time he had a white priest as his assistant pastor.

In both these churches, Father Smith bravely battled against the world, the flesh, and the devil, often in a manner that was reminiscent of Bruce Marshall's priest in *The World, the Flesh, and Father Smith.* Perhaps someday someone with a pen of a novelist will recount the episodes of Father Smith's slum apostolate in Chicago and in New Jersey, his work with the juvenile delinquents and the gangs of Bronzeville, his experiences in dealing with broken homes and shattered lives, and his patient struggling with the tangled dilemmas of the color line.

The endless demands of the ministry and the ceaseless drain on his spiritual life that resulted from his fame and uniqueness served but to deepen his desire to spend his last years closer to God.

Each year his Father Provincial visited the missions on his annual tour of inspection. He asked Father Vincent, "What can I give you?" The reply was always the same: "Only one thing I want. Let me go to the Trappists."

In 1948 his wish was finally granted. He was given leave to apply for admission to the Trappist Monastery in Gethsemani, then riding the crest of its fame as the haven of *The Man Who Got Even with God,* and of the poet who ascended *The Seven Storey Mountain.* Father Vincent still did not know whether he would be accepted. He knew that the monks were reluctant to accept transfers from other religious orders.

During the summer, Father Vincent paid one last visit to St. Augustine's Seminary in Bay St. Louis to make the community retreat. He bade farewell to the friends who had pioneered with him there. Two months later he sent his books as a parting gift to Father Anthony Bourges. On Columbus Day, he passed under the arch at Gethsemani that announced *Pax Intrantibus,* peace to those who enter.

A month later, he received the habit of an Oblate, pending the arrival of authorization from Rome for his admission to the novitiate. Permission for this reached Father Vincent in the following spring. He was given the habit of the Trappist novice on May 15, 1949.

The friends he had left behind had a hard time visualizing Father Vincent as a Trappist. He had always been vivacious, genial, talkative, and extroverted. They could not picture him as a cowled, silent, and subdued monk. But to the priest-novice, it was a real spiritual homecoming to be received back into Gethsemani. Five years before when his sister had asked him why he had gone to the Trappists, he had answered simply, "Sis, I expect I'll be in there for good one of these days."

His novicemaster, Father Urban, found him a quiet, jolly, and well-liked member of the novitiate community. At fifty-five, he was unable to do the hard manual labor about the farm with the other novices. But he returned to the hobby of his seminary days by taking charge of the beehives on the grounds. He had learned the apiarist's art when he was a boy, and had kept it up at Bay St. Louis. With his experience, he improved the yield of the hives to about fifty pounds of honey per year each, which was twenty pounds over the average for Kentucky.

He sought his penance and mortification in the routine bee stings that accompanied his work. He seldom bothered with the bee keeper's usual gear of mask, gloves, and smoke pot. One day when a wind storm blew over one of the hives, he rushed to the rescue and put it back in place, even remaining to weight it down with a stone for safety. He was peppered with dozens of stings. A chuckle was his only answer to queries about the number of stings he had received.

Otherwise, his two years of Trappist novitiate were routine. He kept at the serious task of preparing for death with almost a premonition of its closeness. Whenever his novicemaster would remark that he probably had a good many years ahead of him as a Trappist, Father Vincent would shake his head in vigorous denial, asserting that he wouldn't be around much longer.

As the day of his solemn profession drew near, Father Urban asked him how many of his relatives would be likely to come over from Lebanon. He answered that he did not expect any visitors that day at all, save his former provincial who was to deliver the sermon for the occasion. But on the Feast of the Holy Trinity, May 20, 1951, when Vincent sang his solemn vows as Father Mary Simon, O.C.S.O., there was a great turnout of his sisters and brothers, cousins and nephews and nieces. Father Simon spent the day with them, posing for group pictures and exchanging news about the family. It was their last glimpse of him.

A few days later, Father Simon was, in a surprising move, appointed novicemaster for the new Monastery of Christ the King at Piffard in the Genesee Valley in western New York. Father Simon chuckled when he learned that he was to be stationed there. In his time as a Divine Word Father, he had stayed at St. Michael's Mission House at Conesus, New York. It was near Lake Erie and he had suffered so much from the cold there that he said, even to God in prayer, that he would rather die than have to go back there. It was rather ironical that he was immediately sent to the new foundation not far from Conesus as his first assignment in the Trappist life.

His silent months there were short. It is a tribute to the thoroughness of his spiritual training and to his unerring grasp of the spiritual life that he was straightway appointed as novicemaster. The Cistercians are rightly slow in intrusting this vital role to transfer religious from other orders. They fear that these religious might fail to transmit the true Cistercian spirit to the newer incoming generations of postulants and novices. Father Simon, who had for years been a Trappist in the deeper cloisters of his heart, was confidently elevated to that responsible office at Christ the King Monastery.

Father Simon gave himself unsparingly to the spiritual work of the Trappists on behalf not only of his novices but also of the thousands who came for confession, retreats, and spiritual counsel. He knew he had heart trouble. But he did not make that an excuse for retirement or rest. Within a year, his tired heart gave way. He was stricken on Saturday, March 22, 1952, with a coronary thrombosis. Taken to the hospital of St. Mary's in Rochester, he was accorded all that medical attention could provide. On Tuesday, March 25, the feast of the Annunciation of the Blessed Virgin, he breathed his last. His novices at Piffard and his former fellow novices back in Gethsemani mourned his passing. One of his devoted assistants wrote a "requiescat" for him on the day of his death:

> He gave his heart to little things
> Like mending socks or novice wings,
> To blessings, smiles, and friendly nods,
> Tending souls—or minor chores of God's.

> He gave his heart to Nature's smaller fry,
> To crickets, ferns, a June-bug gone awry;
> Sparrows, harebells, centipedes,
> Minnows, moths and clover seeds.

> To honey-bees—swarming, nectar-full bands
> That always knew his careful, calming hands.
> And once they say by using just a pocket knife,
> He brought a dying puppy back to life.

> He gave his heart to things like mixing paint,
> Saying beads, or merely dusting off a Saint.
> The Angel who came to take him home today
> Found he had given his entire heart away.

CHAPTER XV

Pioneers in South Louisiana

ANTHONY BOURGES, S.V.D.
FRANCIS WADE, S.V.D.

The reception that south Louisiana accorded young Father Anthony Bourges in 1934 was much more public and official than that which Father Plantevigne had experienced almost thirty years before. A whole generation had passed. With it the immediate memories of the Civil War had faded more into the dimness of oblivion. True, the Vermillion River country, like the Delta country of Pointe Coupee, had been visited by the fire and sword of Yankee plunderers. But the scars of the war had not been left so deep in the souls of the Vermillionaires.

One of the major causes of the friction between white and colored had been removed from the Lafayette scene in 1911 when the French Congregation of the Holy Ghost, to which Father Burgess belonged, founded a separate parish for the colored Catholics of St. John the Evangelist Church (later Cathedral) in Lafayette. At the invitation of the pastor, Monsignor W. J. Teurlings, and on the approval of the Archbishop of New Orleans (to whose jurisdiction Lafayette then belonged), the Holy Ghost Fathers opened the new Church of St. Paul in 1912, complete with a grammar school conducted by the Sisters of the Holy Family.

St. Paul's soon became a thriving center of colored Catholic life in Lafayette. Within a few years it had an enrollment in the school of 200 boys and 175 girls. Among the boys, young Anthony Bourges was outstanding for his quickness of mind, his deep piety, and his devoted serving of Mass at the altar. He considered St. Paul's as his native parish, though he had been born in the small town of Scott, Louisiana, just five miles west of the city. He had been baptized at the Church of St. Peter and Paul in Scott within a month after his birth, on January 7, 1904. His family moved to Lafayette while he was still a child. Thus he enrolled in the new St. Paul's School and came to look upon St. Paul's as the home of his soul.

His family belonged to the nucleus of the stable, extended Catholic families which were the backbone of the parish. His father, Arthur Bourges, was a building contractor, having worked his way up through the trades of painting and paperhanging. Through his mother, Louise Mouton Bourges, he was connected with the numerous Mouton clan of Grand Coteau and the neighboring parishes. Many of the Mouton girls had attended the colored school conducted by the Ladies of the Sacred Heart on the grounds of their historic old college at Grand Coteau, founded in the time of Blessed Philippine Duchesne, and favored with a famous miracle performed by St. John Berchmans, the Jesuit patron of youth.

Anthony's grandaunt had been given the name of Sister Berchmans when she left Grand Coteau to join the Holy Family Sisters in New Orleans. She became known in Catholic circles there as the faithful doorkeeper of their French Quarter convent on Orléans Street. For more than fifty years she greeted all visitors with her pleasant smile and with the twinkling holiness of her eyes. She helped pray many a young boy (myself among them) into a vocation for the priesthood. Her part in the genesis of the vocation of young Anthony was the endless litany of prayers she offered for her grandnephew.

Her prayers followed him to Chicago when he went there after his sixth year in St. Paul's School to live with one of his uncles. For his seventh grade he attended St. Sebastian School on Wellington Avenue in Chicago. A year later he returned to Lafayette and completed his schooling at St. Paul.

In 1921, feeling called to the apostolic life of the priesthood, Anthony wrote to Father Christman at Greenville, asking for admittance to the minor seminary. He was immediately accepted. In August of that year he made the three-hundred-mile journey up the Mississippi Delta country to join the little band of students in the pioneer enterprise that was Sacred Heart College.

Where Maurice Rousseve was admittedly the most brilliant student, and Vincent Smith the natural leader and best orator, Anthony Bourges became known about the seminary as the student with the most spontaneous piety. He was the most deeply religious and thoroughly Catholic-spirited of the seminarians, always bubbling with the manifest fruits of the Holy Ghost, charity, joy, peace, patience, and benignity. He took to the seminary life as a natural transition from a holy family to a holy religious order. He contributed much to the seminary's sound religious spirit.

Anthony was by no means a recluse. He played games with the other seminarians all through the year, football in the fall, basketball in the winter, baseball through the summer. He participated with zest in the picnics to the River Jordan, and swam with the swiftest there and in the Bay. He played in the orchestra and sang in the polyphonic choir and in the informal groups that got up the plays and cantatas for the entertainment of the community.

Anthony struck it off well with the students from Central America, especially with Philip Marin of British Honduras. Like the other seminarians, he laughed and sang his way through the difficult years at the Bay. He was duly promoted with his class through each of the stages of preparation for the priesthood there, at East Troy, and in the major seminary.

In 1934 after his ordination, for which a large delegation journeyed from Lafayette, Father Anthony Bourges had the consolation of giving his first blessing to his aging parents. With them he returned to his native parish to offer his first solemn High Mass at St. Paul's Church in Lafayette. The demand for pews was so great that children were not allowed to attend. The church was packed with proud parishioners witnessing the first attainment by one of their parishioners of the high dignity of the priesthood. Father Anthony measured up to their expectations. They found him a happy but serious replica of the Curé d'Ars, and they were doubly proud when he was appointed to the service of the Lafayette colored Catholics in September, 1934.

In the building of the parish of the Immaculate Heart of Mary in Lafayette, and in the awakening of Catholic life in the satellite missions that were served from that central location, Father Anthony played an outstanding and pioneer role. The task that he and his fellow priests set for themselves was much like that of the earlier missionaries among the whites, before the setting up of their churches and the organization of their parish life. Vast areas of the Vermillion River had been without priests for generations after the Acadian French settled in the bayou land of south Louisiana. Early French priests and Jesuit missionaries from New Orleans and Grand Coteau had ridden the bayous and the country roads in search of the rural communities that later became centers for the flourishing parishes that dot the area. Priests were always scarce, and the recruitment of French-speaking clergy from Canada, France, and Belgium never quite matched the needs of the people. The result was that the colored Catholics were somewhat neglected, save for the minimum necessities of their religious life— baptism, Communion, marriage, Mass attendance, and funerals. Their inability to participate in the full parish life, and especially to attend the parochial schools, had resulted in the drifting away from the church of whole families of once-Catholic Negroes. Even the setting up of the many "Mother Drexel" schools, and the experiment with a few all colored parishes like St. Paul's in Lafayette did not control the leakage from the Church.

It was to this apostolate of the spiritually untended Catholic Negroes of south Louisiana that Father Bourges and his fellow colored priests dedicated their lives. The major portion of their work in Lafayette was the reclaiming of souls who had been baptized in infancy, but lost to the Church by moving to the outskirts of town on the other side of the tracks three and four miles from St. Paul's Church. Almost two hundred once-Catholic families were soon discovered who had not been married in church. These and others whose children were in sporadic and desultory attendance at the grubby public schools were the first conquests of the new priests.

The new parish was established within a few blocks of Holy Rosary Institute, an Industrial School for Colored Girls, transferred from Galveston to Lafayette in 1913 by Father Philip Keller. Since 1929 the Divine Word Fathers had been chaplaining and managing the Institute in co-operation with the Holy Family Sisters, who taught the majority of the classes. Father Herman Patzelt, S.V.D., was head of both the Institute and the parish. Under him young Father Bourges and his fellow colored priests worked out from the Institute, holding Sunday Masses there, and using it as the base for parish operations pending the building of the parish church.

Father Bourges' easy fluency in French afforded him a big advantage over both Father Smith and Father Wade. With his command of the Acadian dialects, Father Bourges gained access to the French-speaking homes of the neighborhood while the other two priests concentrated on the English-speaking adults and children. Because French was the predominant language in the rural areas and small towns over the countryside, Father Bourges made good use of a Studebaker touring car to range out for missionary contacts. The Holy Ghost Fathers of Lafayette had laid the foundations for the missions in Father Bourges' birthplace, Scott, and also in Duson and Mouton Switch. These places were now turned over to the care of the staff at Immaculate Heart parish in Lafayette.

At Mouton Switch, to take a typical example of his work, Father Bourges first began holding catechism classes in the home of some Catholic sharecroppers, the Babineaux family. Twice a week, he made the five-mile trip to teach catechism to the children gathered in the Babineaux home. Mrs. Babineaux herded the neighborhood youngsters together, provided them with chairs and benches, or lined them up on boards stretched from box to box or from one small keg to another. For seven years the process of parish-building thus persistently went on. Soon Mass was offered for the little congregation in the Babineaux home. Finally, a chapel was built for the extended spiritual family of the old matriarchal soul.

Elsewhere the same process was duplicated. In the area west of Lafayette, Father Bourges assembled a nucleus of two rural parishes, one in Scott and the other in Duson. After one year of labor in these farming districts, he was able to move to Duson as a resident missionary, while still retaining nominal status as assistant to Father Patzelt in the Lafayette church. Two years of work in the confines of his hundred-square-mile parish resulted in bringing back to the Church more than four families for each square mile. With Father Patzelt's approval, he built the church, school, and rectory at Duson and laid plans for the erection of a subsidiary mission chapel on the outskirts of Scott as well.

In 1939 Father Anthony was appointed administrator of the Lafayette parish of the Immaculate Heart of Mary. He there proved his capabilities by efficient and respected shepherding of the congregation. In due time he was raised to the status of pastor, on a level of equality with the other heads of the local Catholic parishes.

Father Bourges took his place with the white clergy in the Cathedral for the solemn requiem Mass for the deceased Pontiff, Pius XI, in March, 1939. He and his fellow colored priests participated in the deanery conferences held both at Grand Coteau and in Lafayette. He gradually became an accepted figure in the city-wide and diocesan functions. He acted as one of the twelve deacons of honor assisting the bishop in the ceremonies of Holy Thursday at the Cathedral. He accompanied his parish delegation to the annual Christ the King observance at Grand Coteau. In 1943 he was appointed one of the officials of the Diocesan Synod of Lafayette, the assembly of the bishop and all of the clergy of the diocese.

For eleven years he served as pastor of the steadily growing parish of the Immaculate Heart. He built and enlarged the parochial school, founded and encouraged the parish societies and credit union, and capably directed the staff of assistant priests and teaching Sisters who performed the routine work of the smoothly working parish.

In 1949 he was the central figure in the national convention of the Knights of Peter Claver held in Lafayette. Father Bourges was the celebrant of the solemn High Mass at the Cathedral of St. John the Evangelist for the opening of the convention. Assisted by two other colored priests, he made a splendid picture of a dream come true after many long years of striving on the part of colored Catholic organizations like the Knights for the creation of a well-educated, altar-trained colored clergy. He answered in his own person and in the position of esteem he held among them, the query as to whether colored Catholics really wished to have men of their own as priests.

Around the city, the white Catholics also became accustomed to the acceptance of Father Bourges and his fellow colored priests as full-fledged Catholic clergymen. White Catholics living in the vicinity of the Immaculate Heart Church began dropping in for confessions on Saturday afternoons and evenings. They took their places in line and knelt to confess their sins to God and receive absolution from them through the instrumentality of the colored hands raised over them, the hands of true priests of God.

For sick calls and last anointings, the Sisters at the Charity Hospital often called Father Anthony at night for white patients when no other priests were available. He rushed to the bedside to administer the sacraments to the dying, just as any other priest would. Other white Sisters also invited the Immaculate Heart parish Fathers to say Mass and give Holy Communion in their convents—the Carmelites, and the Sisters of the Most Blessed Sacrament.

The laity generally also accorded to Father Bourges and his confreres the customary marks of respect due to the priesthood, the tipping of the hat, the *"bon jour, mon père,"* or the "Good morning, Father" which are standard Catholic practice. Down at the store one day, some white Catholic men were arguing about a marriage case that involved some points of church law and practice. In walked Father Bourges to make some purchases. The men turned to him, presented him their case, and asked, "What about it, Father?" On other occasions, they have consulted him in almost routine fashion about questions of fasting and abstinence and other church obligations. His decisions and opinions are accepted as final, just as with the other curés of the city.

It was owing to the consistent and reliable fulfillment of their clerical duties that Bishop Jeanmard was able to write:

> The advent of the colored priests in the Diocese marks a new step in the work for our colored people. The enthusiasm with which they were received, and the splendid work they are doing in the three parishes now (1943) entirely under their direction, slay, for all time, the groundless and mischievous myth that the colored people did not care to have priests of their own race to minister to them.[1]

In 1950, when Father Rousseve was transferred from St. Martinville to the seminary, the bishop approved the appointment of Father Bourges as pastor of the large parish of Notre Dame in the Evangeline

[1] Letter to the editor of *St. Augustine's Messenger,* 21 (1943), p. 219.

City. The Divine Word Fathers also appointed him as district superior of the missionaries, both white and colored, laboring in Louisiana. There he continues the same unremitting work for the flock committed to his care.

FATHER FRANCIS GUY WADE, S.V.D.

1 8 9 4 –

Like Fathers Rousseve, Smith, and Bourges, Father Francis Guy Wade belonged to the first class to be ordained at St. Augustine's Seminary in 1934. He too has devoted a score of years to the sacred ministry, joining them in their pioneer work in south Louisiana. As of this writing, he is still living the quiet and dedicated life of a country pastor in a small Acadian village named Maurice. There he has built his own church, a small modest frame building, topped with a simple steeple, and distinguished by no ornate architectural features. Nearby, the tiny rectory houses the pastor in the austere style common to the sharecroppers and tenant farmers of the neighborhood who make up most of his congregation.

Avoiding display and publicity has been a major preoccupation of Father Francis Wade. He believes in working quietly and unobtrusively in behalf of the spiritual concerns of his flock, and these rarely take him off on nation-wide jaunts or into much-heralded spotlights. He is content to cultivate the small corner of the vineyard committed to his care. If the rest of the world passes him by unnoticed, he does not seem to mind. He is fulfilling his lifelong ambition to be and to stay a priest of God and of souls.

That ambition was born almost a half-century ago, when the present Father Francis was an altar boy at St. Augustine's Church, along with his cousin, Norman DuKette, in Washington, D.C. He had been born in Washington September 12, 1894, one of the ten sons and fourteen children of Benjamin Z. Wade and Caroline DuKette Wade. His father, originally of Charles County, Maryland, had also been one of ten sons, and his grandfather too came from a family with ten boys. Benjamin Wade had married his wife down in the "counties," and when their young brood was approaching school age, they moved to Washington to give them a chance to attend a Catholic school. Those down in the counties were closed to colored children.

In the 1880's, "T" Street in northwest Washington was almost the boundary line of the old city. Florida Avenue was actually called Boundary Street. It was in this outskirt neighborhood of Florida, "T," and 18th Street that the little family settled. Francis Guy Wade was born there, the ninth of the Wade children, and he was taken downtown to St. Augustine's Church to be baptized by the new pastor, Father Griffiths, who had just assumed the pastorate the year before (1893).

Though his mother was a convert, she reared her children in the atmosphere of a devout Catholic home. She had a special devotion to the Blessed Virgin, and each evening she gathered her children around the family's statue of the Immaculate Conception to say night prayers and the Rosary. And one of her silent prayers was the constantly repeated entreaty that God would call one of her sons to be a priest at the altar.

She was gratified when the first foreshadowings of the priestly life brought her young boys to the altar as Mass-servers. They regularly made the mile-long journey to St. Augustine's early each morning to be able to serve on the altar for Mass before school began. Francis became an altar boy before he was ten years old, while attending the parochial school operated by the Oblates of Providence from Baltimore, to which order one of his aunts, Sister Mary Joseph Wade, already belonged.

Young Francis came to love the altar and the sacristy during his years at grammar school. Whenever he was late in coming home after school, his mother would always say, "I guess he stopped by church." She encouraged this holy way of spending his spare time in doing chores about the old St. Augustine's. For Francis, the worst part of the affliction of being sick was that he missed out on his chances of serving Mass.

As there was no high school connected to the parish, Francis was obliged to enroll in the old "M" Street High School for his secondary training. Despite the coeducational arrangement of the school, Francis persevered in his desire to be a priest. He made no secret of it. On all of the forms he filled in as his future career ambition: "I want to be a priest."

He had no use for the giddy girls who sat close to him in the classroom. One day when the English teacher was explaining letter-writing forms, and was instructing them never to use "respectively yours" instead of "respectfully yours," one of the girls passed him a little note that was signed "respectively yours."

Francis' reaction was characteristic. "What's the matter with these girls?" he said later. "They know I want to be a priest. Why don't they let me alone and pay attention to the lessons?"

All through his high-school years, Francis continued to serve Mass at St. Augustine's Church. He eventually outgrew the cassocks provided for the usually small altar boys, but he continued to serve on the altar with the ill-fitting habits. Finally, the pastor decided that, since no other boy matched him in size, he should be graduated from the altar boys' society. A formal graduation ceremony was arranged, and Francis was given a book as a premium and a memento of his years of faithful service.

It was an appropriate gift. Francis was an insatiable reader and one of the regular customers at the "K" Street Public Library. He had the habit of going to the library, taking out the pair of books allowed him on his public library card, and then reading them as he walked the long distance home. Sometimes, he would finish a book by the time he got home, and so would dash back to the library for another. It was a surprised librarian who checked back in a book that had just been taken out a few hours before.

Browsing around the shelves, Francis spotted many books he would like to read. He used to hide them in inaccessible places in the stacks so that they would be there when he came back to borrow some more books later in the week. The librarian protested this research practice when she discovered it. She told him he could read all the books he wanted. But she warned him not to try to hide any more of them.

As a boy in high school, Francis often made the pilgrimage out to the famous Franciscan shrine in Washington, built by Father Godfrey Schilling, O.F.M. Father Godfrey was a great promoter of vocations to the priesthood, and when he spied young Francis piously making the rounds of the devotional replicas of the Holy Land shrines in the Monastery Church, he talked to him about a possible vocation to the priesthood. Francis was easily convinced. But still he did not know of any seminary which would admit him at the time. Even Father Godfrey could not promise him a free entry into his own order.

Francis, therefore, at the conclusion of his high-school work in 1912, took a position as a teacher in a public school at Hicks Wharf, near Norfolk, Virginia. He also did office work in Philadelphia and in New York, in which latter place he came to learn of the Graymoor Friars, a group of Episcopalian Franciscans who had come en masse into the Catholic Church recently.

Francis wrote to Father Paul, the prior of the Graymoor Monastery, and asked to be admitted as a postulant. He was accepted as a candidate for the order, but in the capacity of a lay brother, not a seminarian preparing for the priesthood.

For seven years he stayed with the Franciscan Friars of the Atonement, all the while yearning to be a priest and to have the privilege of saying Mass. He had become "Brother Benedict" only because it looked as though he would never have the opportunity of entering a seminary.

The golden opportunity did emerge from the clouds in the early 1920's. Francis learned that the Divine Word Fathers had opened a new seminary in Bay St. Louis. He asked for release from his Franciscan vows so that he might be able to pursue studies for the priesthood in St. Augustine's Seminary. Father Paul agreed to the transfer. He wrote a letter of recommendation stating that Francis "was always faithful here, and his conduct above reproach, and I trust he will prove worthy of a place in your missionary congregation."

While negotiations were being completed, Francis worked for a time in the office of Father Purcell's magazine *The Sign,* published at the Passionists' Monastery in Union City, New Jersey. But when the letter of acceptance came, he immediately set out for Bay St. Louis, with only a few days at home to bid farewell anew to his aging parents and his many brothers and sisters.

Francis Wade entered St. Augustine's Seminary on September 13, 1924. In accordance with the custom, he was placed in the first high class, on the assumption that he knew no Latin. However, he had studied Latin assiduously in high school, and so within a few days he had brushed up enough of the Church's language to skip to third high. He finished the high and junior college course at the Bay in May, 1927, ending up with a class that had started three years before he did—the second to graduate from the new school.

With them he went to make his novitiate at East Troy, and returned to the Bay for his major seminary studies. He took his first vows at the Bay on September 8, 1929, and then proceeded apace with the other members of the pioneer class through all the gradual stages toward the priesthood. He was ordained with his three companions on May 23, 1934, and he returned to Washington and to St. Augustine's Church for his first solemn High Mass a week later.

It was as happy a day for his mother as it was for the newly ordained priest himself. Two of his sisters, by now experienced religious in the Sisterhood of the Oblates of Providence, were also in Washington for the homecoming, Sister Mary Angela having been for years the principal of the Immaculate Conception School in Charleston, South Carolina, and Sister Mary Pius, also a teacher and a superior in the Oblate communities.

His cousin, Father Norman DuKette, journeyed down from Detroit to be the deacon of the Mass, and the pastor, Monsignor Olds, delivered the sermon. For the next few weeks, Francis was welcomed at various churches in Washington and Baltimore, and he preached often and effectively from the altar where he had long before been a simple Mass-server.

Paired off with Father Rousseve, he continued his preaching for the missions that the two young priests gave during the next few months in churches in the South. It was All Saints' Day before Father Wade took up his duties as assistant pastor in the Immaculate Heart of Mary Church in Lafayette.

For three years he co-operated in the establishment of the new parish. As an older and more experienced man, he was given charge of finances and of the business end of the parish. He regularly preached and taught catechism in the church and in the many satellite missions around the vicinity.

In his quiet way, he became interested in the rural apostolate and developed the proficiencies that enabled him to adjust from his northern city habits to those of a country pastor in the Evangeline areas of Louisiana.

He mastered the native patois well enough to preach and hear confessions in French. He learned the farm pattern of living and adopted his pastoral practices to the exigencies of life among the sharecroppers and tenant farmers. In 1937 he became resident missionary at Duson to succeed Father Bourges in the wide expanse of that rural parish. In 1947 he built the Church of St. Joseph at Maurice, and in July of the next year was officially named as resident pastor of that sixty-square-mile parish. For the new building he secured a former army camp chapel from Camp Claiborne. He had it dismantled, hauled down to Maurice, and erected on its present location. Alongside it, he constructed a modest rectory and from there he now branches out to visit the scattered scores of families in his parish. He conducts regular catechism classes in the three rural schools of the area, where the teachers accord him great respect. Truancy has been considerably cut down, and attendance is highest on the days when Father Wade's imposing figure is scheduled to be seen at school.

The nine hundred parishioners of his territory look to Father Wade for the quiet spiritual leadership that a country folk expects of its teacher, prophet, and priest. While he is interested in progressive measures such as rural electrification, deeper wells, soil conservation, and public health promotion, Father Wade's primary concern as a rural pastor is with the spiritual welfare of the flock committed to his care. They revere him as a soft-spoken, quiet man, much given to thinking and to prayer, and little enamored of the flashy agitation or bootless protesting against social forces over which he has no control.

A measure of his status in the colored Catholic community was given by the Knights of Peter Claver, who in their national convention held in 1944 elected him to be their national chaplain.

His rare absences from his parish occur only when the Knights are holding their annual assembly. Otherwise, Father Wade stays close to his pastoral charge, well satisfied to teach catechism to the little ones, to preach the Gospel to the poor and the humble, and to share their poverty and their simple country life with them. He was well on his way toward becoming their gray-headed patriarch in their thoroughly Catholic community.

In the summer of 1954, however, his superiors transferred Father Wade back to Immaculate Heart of Mary parish in Lafayette as pastor of the parish in which he had begun his parochial ministry twenty years before.

CHAPTER XVI

Around the Broad Caribbean

FATHER MAX MURPHY
FATHER THELDON JONES
FATHER WILLIAM L. LANE
FATHER PHILIP MARIN

Like Fathers Esnard and Joseph John, a number of other colored priests have followed a missionary call to work outside the United States. Four of those ordained in the early 1930's volunteered for careers in the countries of the Caribbean region. There are many poignant tales woven into the humdrum lives of these missionaries, some of which cannot bear telling in our generation. What can be revealed shows that the dedicated colored missionary is fully capable of measuring up to the spiritual and physical demands of missionary life, and of remaining faithful to his flock for decade after decade.

FATHER MAX E. MURPHY

1902 –

My first contact with Father Max Murphy occurred on the eve of his departure from his church in Trinidad on a special mission for the United States State Department in 1952.

It was a mission of extreme delicacy and of great importance in easing the strained relations between Americans and Germans in Western Germany's critical urban areas. The High Commissioner of

Germany had requested that the State Department send over a youth specialist who was fluent in German, acquainted with the problems of underprivileged and unemployed youth, and able to aid in program-planning for education, recreation, and welfare services to some of the 750,000 wandering and unemployed German youth between the ages of fourteen and twenty-five.

The High Commissioner's specifications called for a survey of some of the 612 homes for refugee youth, as well as a sampling of the 540 training schools for apprentices, many of which were operated by the Catholic organizations especially in Southern Germany. Because of this link with religious groups in Germany, the State Department preferred a priest-sociologist. The National Catholic Welfare Conference in Washington, on consultation, recommended Father Murphy as a likely candidate. His years of study in a German seminary had given him a command of German and a wide acquaintance with church figures and prominent Catholic laity in Germany.

Permissions were expedited early in 1952. Father Murphy secured a six months' leave of absence. He journeyed to Washington for conferences with State Department officials and his NCWC sponsors; he was briefed by experts in New York, and was soon on his way by Air Force transport to Germany.

It was a difficult assignment. Resentment ran high in Germany against America, especially against the American Army of Occupation. There was still much seething indignation over the large preponderance of Negro soldiers in the United States forces, and over the problems of the dark blossoms in the dust that marked their "occupation." Of the 94,000 illegitimate children of army personnel and German women, upward of 3,200 were identifiable as mulattoes. Great antagonism had been stirred up over the German disbelief in the reality of America's practice of democracy, especially as a result of adverse reports of racial incidents in the German press.

Father Murphy's mission was to allay some of these ill feelings, while fulfilling the other formal requirements of his assignments. Bearing in his person the dignity of the Catholic priesthood and the visible proof of the fair opportunity granted to colored youth to achieve their ambitions in the United States, he set out to tour the large and small cities of the Rhineland and of Southern Germany soon after his arrival on March 5 at Frankfurt.

In the course of the next three months, Father Murphy visited Munich, Bayrischzell, Mannheim, Heidelberg, Altenberg, Dortmund, Essen, Aachen, Bendorf on the Rhine, Maria Laach, Wurtzburg, Wiesbaden, Regensburg, Freiburg, and Berlin. The conditions he found among refugees, the workless, and the demoralized youth of the region were appalling. All of the slum problems in the worst sections of American cities were trebled by the destruction of bombed-out cities, the forced migration of fourteen million people from Eastern Germany, and the deep depression of the defeated prostrate nation.

Father Murphy, while studying the situation, spoke to large crowds of German youth and to many adult assemblies as well. He answered many questions about America and the race problem, clearing up many misunderstandings and explaining the many constructive measures taken to ease racial tensions in the United States. On many occasions he pointed up the parallel between interrace conditions in the States, and the intergroup relations in Germany, especially between native and refugee peoples. He took every opportunity to emphasize the good work done in America by German-born priests and Sisters in their educational work among the Negroes in the South.

On the brighter side of the picture, Father Max has written:

In spite of the hatred engendered by the war, I found many evidences of Christian charity and love in many unexpected places: a group of children in the ward of a tuberculosis sanatorium all looking so pleased when they saw me coming into their room, and all trying to tell me at one time how they were saving their pennies to ransom a pagan baby in Africa; an American Negro officer collecting money from his men every month to help support a German orphange; an American lady who lost her first husband in the First World War and her second husband in the Second World War, in both instances fighting against the Germans, organizing a hospital for tubercular German children, and who personally had adopted two German orphan girls; a German lady who had visited the Southern States of the U.S.A. as a German consultant to the U. S. State Department, returning to Germany and adopting a mulatto child . . . All this encouraged and inspired me.

But when he sat down, late in May to draw up his report, it included many distressing parallels between the German youth of today and the American Negro youth of the depression years:

Not alone the wandering youth, but also a part of the indigenous youth still bear the scars and effects of misguidance and personal suffering. There is still in West Germany an astonishingly high number of wandering youth, particularly refugees from the East Zone whose parents and brothers and sisters live as refugees. Besides a good number of the boys and girls on the road have, somewhere in the Federal Republic, a permanent home. They left their homes because of lack of employment opportunities, or because of conflicts between the parents, or because they themselves had been charged with some offense. They try to find work as manual laborers abroad, to join the foreign legion, to get jobs in agriculture or in industrial regions, for example Stuttgart. On the road stand thousands of temptations of which they can withstand only a few. A large number of wandering girls have had catastrophic and character-destroying experiences.

In addition, there is a whole army of youth who had a home but who now live on the streets. Physical and spiritual weaknesses are generated which render such youth apt instruments of black marketeers, thieves, etc. Many of these boys and girls had been previously brought up by welfare institutions. They ran away and are known as "Ausreisser" (truants).

It would be a mistake not to include in this picture, also, youth whose characters might be called normal, and who nevertheless slipped; I mean the political radical elements who could not endure the shock of 1945, and who subsequently fell into a state of lethargy, and who have developed a completely nihilistic attitude.

And then there are the "lone wolves" who failed in their honest and repeated attempts to carve out a decent existence, who have become depressed by their failure to attain success, and who have become cynical and selfish. These are the youth who have been bred up in ruins, in vacant lots adjoining factories, in barracks, and in bunkers, who are unable to withstand the sufferings of the dark areas of life into which they have been plunged and who have come to the conclusion that the fruits of fields, the gardens, the vineyards, and the shop windows belong only to the chosen few. They feel that they have been cheated and are resentful of this.

Father Murphy's report recommended the continuance and stepping up of many measures to meet the exigencies of these German youths: more homes for apprentices, more institutions for the refugee and expelled youth, more employment agencies and centers for recreation. His report and his contacts with the Germans made a very favorable impression in the Rhineland and in Southern Germany, particularly in promoting intergroup co-operation and understanding between German refugees and native-born Germans, and between professional groups and non-professional groups.

In the course of his stay, he renewed acquaintance with the many German priests who had studied with him as a seminarian, with the bishop who had given him minor orders, and with many of the exiled Sudeten Germans among whom he had spent his summers while a seminarian.

Upon the conclusion of his work in Germany, Father Murphy went to Rome for an audience with the Holy Father and a pilgrimage to the shrines of the Holy City. He returned to the United States for a final report to the State Department, before resuming his missionary work in Trinidad.

Those four months of labor had brought back many memories of his four years of study in Europe 1930-34. He had studied the last of his sacred theology at Charles University, a German seminary in Prague. Among his professors was the present Archbishop of Prague, Monsignor Josef Beran. He also officiated with Max at his first Mass after he was ordained by the late Karl Cardinal Kaspar in St. Veits Cathedral on June 24, 1934.

After his ordination, Father Max spent several weeks as the guest of Prince Zdenko Labkowiecz and his family at his castle in Bilin in Bohemia. This family and many others had befriended the young seminarian during his seven-month stay in a Czechoslovakian hospital for tubercular patients. Among his Prague friends was Count Ledochowski, a brother of Rev. Vladimir Ledochowski, the Father General of the Society of Jesus in Rome. So kind and genial was the atmosphere of Catholic Prague that Father Murphy entertained the idea of accepting their invitation to remain among them as a priest. But he decided to return to America.

In 1934 Father Murphy journeyed to his home city of Dallas, Texas, to offer his first solemn High Mass in the parish of his childhood. He bore the distinction of being the first colored Texan to be ordained. Like not a few others, he proudly called Texas his home. He had been born in Dallas, December 14, 1902, the fourth of his parents' six children.

St. Peter's colored Catholic church was founded in Dallas when Max was three years old. He grew up in its shadow. In 1910 the Sisters of the Holy Ghost opened a grammar school in the parish. Max was among its early pupils, intelligent, devout, and an eager Mass-server. At the age of eighteen, feeling called to the priesthood, Max enrolled in the Sacred Heart Seminary in Greenville. He studied his high-school and junior college work under the Divine Word Fathers there and in Bay St. Louis. He even went as far as the novitiate in East Troy. But in 1927, realizing that he had no vocation to the religious order, he left the novitiate to seek admittance to a diocesan seminary.

With the aid of Father Lissner, but still without a sponsoring bishop, Max entered St. Patrick's Seminary, Menlo Park, California. He studied there for three years before embarking for Europe and Prague and theology.

Father Tim Sullivan, his old pastor and a pioneer in the colored apostolate in Texas, welcomed young Father Murphy back for his first solemn Mass. Only one other priest showed up for the occasion. The bishop, who had refused to accept him as a candidate for the diocesan priesthood in Texas, nonetheless accorded him the necessary diocesan faculties upon his return. The thirty other bishops to whom Max wrote for a possible appointment either ignored his letters or sent back the usual "time-is-not-ripe" refusals.

Fortunately, Archbishop Pius Dowling, O.P., of Trinidad, B.W.I., who had secured from Texas the services of Father Joseph John, offered Father Murphy a position in his island diocese. Thither he sailed in

1934 to take up pastoral work at South-Oropouche, in Fyzabad. For two years until May, 1937, he labored in that parish. He was transferred to the Church of St. Philip and James in Chaguanas at this latter date. There he has remained until the present writing.

Father Murphy has built up the mission in Chaguanas into a thriving Catholic center, with four satellite mission stations in the environs, and an annual average of 180 infant baptisms and between ten and twenty adult converts. The parish has grown steadily. The chief hindrance to wider development is the predominance of East Indian Moslems in and around Chaguanas, where less than 20 per cent are Catholic.

The parishioners of St. Philip and James are of all nationalities. There are some Chinese Catholics, along with Syrian, Portuguese, French, Spanish, as well as the central core of Negro and colored natives. In his book *Call for Forty Thousand,* Father John Considine gives a good picture of the mission field of Trinidad and the parish of Chaguanas. Of Trinidad's 600,000 souls, more than 30 per cent are Catholics. Father Murphy takes capable care of the large corner of the island committed to his ministrations.

During the war, in addition to his other duties, Father Murphy served as auxiliary chaplain for the many American soldiers and sailors stationed in and around Chaguanas. They, together with the civilians, showed their appreciation by starting the fund from which was built the new high school. With three hundred pupils, the school has been accredited by the British Government and is partly supported by public funds.

There is not much else to record in the humdrum but faithful life of the foreign missionary. The year-in year-out routine of church life moves at a slower pace in the sultriness of the tropics. A rare crisis, like the burning of his presbytery several years ago, interrupts the smooth flow of mission life for the moment. Even a long excursion, like that to Germany for the State Department, is soon lost in the mists of memory under the heat of the equatorial sun.

Yet the faithful priest, standing guard at his mission post throughout the decades, is the living guy wire that anchors the Church to the good earth and keeps her close to the people who till the soil. Father Murphy ranks with the unspectacular but faithful missionaries who have kept the faith alive in distant and out-of-the-way places around the globe.

FATHER THELDON FRANCIS JONES

1 9 0 5 –

In many respects the career of Father Theldon Jones has paralleled that of Father Max Murphy.

Like Father Murphy, Father Jones is a native Texan, having been born in San Antonio during the first decade of the present century. He was one of five brothers, and was raised in the parish of St. Peter Claver in the Alamo City.

Finishing grammar school in San Antonio, he enrolled in St. Augustine's Seminary in Bay St. Louis for his high-school work. Like Father Murphy, he left the Divine Word Fathers after completing his minor seminary work. Seeking a diocesan seminary, he applied to Archbishop McNicholas' Cincinnati Seminary, Mount St. Mary of the West. At the time, pressure from Rome had obliged a number of bishops and archbishops to give more serious consideration to the development of vocations to the priesthood on the part of colored lads.

However, a few years later some of the hierarchy's enthusiasm for the new venture was somewhat deflated. Theldon Jones was dismissed from the seminary in the middle of his theology, for unstated reasons which were no obstacle to his subsequent ordination.

Through the efforts of Father Edward C. Kramer of the Catholic Board of Colored Missions, Theldon was able to join Father Max Murphy at the Charles University Seminary in Prague in 1933. It was there that Father Theldon Jones was ordained in the seminary church, on April 7, 1935. He sang his first solemn Mass on Easter Sunday in the Church of St. James in the Czechoslovakian capital.

Father Theldon Jones's homecoming later in the year was but a way-

station stop on the road to his final destination, Trinidad, where Archbishop Pius Dowling, O.P., had agreed to admit him to the ranks of his
island clergy.

Before leaving for his mission post, Father Jones offered his first
American solemn High Mass in the Harlem Church of St. Mark,
where more than eighteen hundred people attended. Among them
were his stepmother (his parents had died when he was young), one
of his brothers, a sister, and many of his nieces and nephews.

In San Antonio a few days later, Father Theldon offered Mass for
the rest of his family and for the parishioners of his native parish. He
then departed for Trinidad where, since the summer of 1935, he has
been continually at work in the ministry on that island and neighboring ones as well.

Save for an occasional visit to the United States, Father Jones has not
been away from his missionary archdiocese. In 1947 he returned to
New York for a few months' surcease from the tropics to recover his
health. He served as chaplain for the colored Sisters Handmaids of the
Pure Heart of Mary, an order established by the famous apostle of the
Negroes, Father Ignatius Lissner, S.M.A.

Father Jones also gave a number of speeches in the East and the Midwest during his stay in the country in 1947. He spoke at the Catholic
Interracial Council breakfast in the Hotel Sherman in Chicago, May
25, after celebrating High Mass in the Holy Name Cathedral there.
He also visited Rosary College in River Forest for informal discussions
with the Sisters and the students. There he impressed everyone with
his sincere missionary zeal. He told of the three mission stations he
cared for, of the fire that had threatened his presbytery and destroyed
some of his papers, of the necessity of hearing confessions in Spanish as
well as English, and of his main desire—to recover his strength sufficiently to return to his mission as soon as possible.

When questioned as to whether he was a religious order priest or a
diocesan one, Father Jones jokingly replied, "I belong to the Order of
St. Peter!" He conducted himself simply as a Catholic priest among
Catholics, impressing all with the apostolic seriousness of his zeal, his
humble priestliness, his superior but unaffected intellectual attainments
and culture, his earnestness, piety, and sincerity.

Freed from the racial tensions of the United States, Father Jones seemed to feel that it was inappropriate and even alien to suggest among Catholics that his color made any difference to his priesthood. He was far from embittered by his so-called "exile" to the islands. As a missionary, he had gone out of his father's home and his fatherland in quest of souls for Christ. In fulfilling that vocation, he achieved his full stature as a priest. He later wrote to Sister Mary Ellen O'Hanlon, who had invited him to the college:

> Now I want to tell you how much joy it was to have visited your beautiful place and to have been able to meet the good sisters, the fathers, and some of your students. It was an experience not to be soon forgotten, and I take the memory of the beautiful buildings and the surroundings back to my beautiful, small country mission district of Erin. I do hope that you will not forget me and the work down there. . . . Our dear Lord love and keep you, Sister.

FATHER WILLIAM L. LANE

1 8 9 7 –

Not all of the colored priests are cast in the same mold. Some are quiet, retiring, soft-spoken, and imperturbable. Others have the fire of crusaders, the bold, blunt speech of excited men, appalled by the inequities of the social system under which they were obliged to live.

In this latter class, for weal or woe, Father William Leroy Lane has ranged himself. Thereby hangs the tale of the nomadic life he has led, and the strange odyssey of his vocation.

The first event that set Leroy Lane at odds with the South's segregation system was his birth in New York City, on November 27, 1897. His first thirteen years were spent there, but in 1910 he traveled to Bellmead, Virginia, to enroll in St. Emma's Military Industrial and Agricultural School, one of the two rural schools founded there by the Drexel-Morrell family of Philadelphia.

While pursuing his junior high-school studies there, William began to feel that he would like to become a priest. He spoke of this to the Holy Ghost Father who was chaplain at the time. But notwithstanding the fact that Father Burgess was already pursuing a successful career with the Holy Ghost Fathers in Pennsylvania, the chaplain kept putting off the venturesome aspirant. Young Lane could not get a satisfactory answer to the problem of his vocation even up to the time of his graduation in 1914.

Back home in New York, William spoke to his local pastor about his desire to be a priest. He was told to forget about it, because "the time was not ripe" for a colored boy to become a priest. Disappointed, William turned to the trade he had learned at the industrial school. Later, he took up stenography and secured a job in an office in New York.

In 1917, with the entry of the United States into the war, William signed up as a camp secretary with the Knights of Columbus. Overseas, the sight of so many soldiers dying without the Sacraments turned William's mind again toward the early desires he had as a boy to become a priest. Back in the States, the terrible toll of persons dying in the influenza epidemic of 1919 without the consolations of religion further stoutened his determination to find a seminary where he could study for the priesthood.

In 1920, when Father Christman opened his little seminary in Greenville, William Lane was among the first applicants. He enrolled with the first class, and found himself the oldest seminarian in the group, next to Vincent Smith. He was well liked among the seminarians, towering above all of the youngsters as a tall six-footer. He stood erect and straight, save for the slight hump on his right shoulder. His light-olive skin and his jet-black hair and eyebrows made him conspicuous as a distinct personality.

But like Father Augustine Derricks, William found Greenville's first-high program too elementary. He left to return North in the spring of 1923. In Cleveland, he sought admission to a high school where he could learn the rudiments of Latin and prepare for college work. He entered John Carroll College there, but could stay only one year.

Returning to New York, William attended college classes both in

Brooklyn and at Fordham University. He continued to apply to various bishops for admission to a seminary as a candidate for their diocese. Refusals came in literally by the scores, until finally Bishop Schrembs of Cleveland agreed to adopt him. Under his sponsorship, William was admitted to St. Vincent's Seminary operated by the Benedictine Fathers in Latrobe, Pennsylvania.

By 1930, after two years of seminary training, William was ready for the call to minor orders. Bishop Schrembs, however, had been disturbed both by unfavorable reports concerning him and by Lane's outspokenness on the race question. The bishop wavered in his determination to pioneer in the admission of Negro priests to his diocese. He withdrew his sponsorship both of William Lane and of another colored seminarian then studying for the diocese. One report attributes this change of heart to Bishop Schremb's alarm at the shooting of Father DuKette in Detroit the previous year.

William continued his studies at Latrobe in the hope of eventually enlisting the sponsorship of a bishop. At the end of his third year of theology, he was still unsponsored. He was accordingly obliged to leave the seminary.

One ray of hope broke through the gloom. A missionary priest in Trinidad interceded for William with the bishop of that island mission territory—which was in great need of more priests. The bishop agreed to allow William to be ordained for his neglected territory.

Returning to Latrobe, William completed his studies. He was ordained by Bishop Swint of Wheeling, West Virginia, on December 23, 1933. He journeyed to his home parish of St. Charles Borromeo in New York City, for his first solemn High Mass, December 30, 1933.

From 1933 to 1936, Father William Lane labored as a missionary in Trinidad. A native American, he found it extremely difficult to adjust to the British colonial practices toward the islanders. Father Lane espoused their cause and was forthright in his denunciation of the racial injustices there. Though reprimanded by the bishop, he spared no words in denouncing supporters of the colonial administration and its unpalatable racial practices. These and other incidents resulted in his dismissal from the mission and his return to the United States.

Father Lane was so demoralized by the experiences in Trinidad that he did not bother to get his papers in order before leaving. The old bishop died not long afterwards. The new bishop was willing to straighten things out if he would return. But Father Lane would not go back, even to secure a formal release from the diocese to which he was officially connected.

Because of this irregularity and other incidents, Father Lane has had great difficulty in securing incardination into any of the United States' dioceses. He worked for a while in Atlantic City. Later in Washington, Archbishop Curley allowed him to do substitute work in some of the colored churches.

Father Edward Kramer, who had been one of his early encouragers and promoters, prevailed on other bishops to allow Father Lane to do similar work in their dioceses. Bishop Molloy of Covington, Kentucky, accepted him on probation for two years while he served as temporary pastor of Our Saviour's Church. His outspokenness on the race question and other personality difficulties obliged him to move on when that period was over.

In the Youngstown diocese for a while, and in the diocese of Leavenworth (now in Kansas City), Kansas, Father Lane also secured temporary assignments. He was a missionary for a short period in Wisconsin and Minnesota. He was an able, intelligent, even brilliant preacher. But, one after another, the conservative bishops refused to take the risk of adopting in their dioceses a man known for his agitation on the race question.

Of recent years, Father Lane has been seeking incardination in the diocese of Dallas, Texas, after a two-year tour of duty as assistant in Holy Cross Church, Austin, Texas. Located, as of this writing, in Gainesville, Texas, Father Lane has been in charge of the colored mission of St. Charles.

"I have no hard feelings toward anyone," he writes; "and I feel that it is God's Will that I, a pioneer, should have this trouble."

FATHER PHILIP MARIN

1 9 0 4 –

You do not know the quiet, patient heroism of the colored priest until you have sat at the bedside of one in danger of slowly dying of an illness contracted while heroically cleaving to the line of duty to which he has dedicated his life.

That was my experience as I sat beside Father Philip Marin in his top-floor room in Mount St. Rose Sanitarium for Tuberculosis in St. Louis last year. He had been at the point of death a number of times, anointed for his last hours. But he had survived the hemorrhages, to linger longer between death and life. As he spoke in all simplicity about his years of missionary life, one could see the deep inner light shining in his countenance. One could sense an inward peace that marked the presence of the Holy Spirit within his soul.

Father Marin's is the story of a boy who came to the United States to study for the priesthood, and of a worn-out missionary who returned to die in the country of his ordination.

He enrolled with the second band of valiant seminarians at the newly inaugurated Sacred Heart Seminary in Greenville in 1921. The only child of his parents, Philip was born August 23, 1904, in the parish of Stann Creek, British Honduras. As he grew up near the Jesuit Mission there, he became the Fathers' houseboy, running errands, doing the chores about the house and the yard, setting and serving table, and living in a little room in the rectory. Bred in piety and raised in holiness, Philip felt the Holy Spirit calling him to be a priest. He told the good Fathers at the mission about his desire. They tried to secure his admission to Epiphany Apostolic College in Baltimore, but with no success.

Philip secretly wanted to be a Jesuit. But he knew that "the Fathers" had not as yet taken any colored novices at their novitiate at Florissant,

Missouri, the motherhouse of the Missouri Province. (They have since admitted two.)

As second choice, Philip enrolled in Greenville with the Divine Word Fathers. His career there followed the pattern of the second class to go through. Along with Anthony Bourges, Francis Wade, Max Murphy, Eugene Martin, and Alban Velasquez (also from British Honduras), Philip pursued his studies successfully in the minor seminary, in the novitiate at East Troy, Wisconsin (where he took his vows in 1928), and in Bay St. Louis.

All through his seminary days, Philip was hoping that the Jesuit order would open its doors to him. He did not get along with the mission Fathers who conducted the seminary. Once he even told one of them that if "the Fathers" had taken him in their novitiate, he would not have come to St. Augustine's.

On their side, the Divine Word Fathers did not feel that the young seminarian had a special vocation to their religious order. Upon the approach of major orders in 1933, Philip was told that he would have to secure a bishop before he could be ordained. Bishop Murphy of Belize, British Honduras, agreed to adopt the young seminarian. Philip was scheduled to return to Belize to be ordained there in 1934.

Bishop Murphy was absent from his see on his ad limina visit at the time. He therefore issued authorization for Philip's ordination in Bay St. Louis. He was raised to the priesthood by Bishop Gerow on October 21, 1934, five months after his four classmates had received sacred orders.

A few days later, Father Marin sailed for British Honduras. He celebrated his first Mass in the Cathedral at Belize, and a week later, he returned to his home parish for another triumphal celebration at Stann Creek. The whole town turned out to welcome their native priest who had returned to minister in their midst as assistant pastor to "the Fathers" there.

Young Father Marin felt good to be back home again, away from the tensions of race prejudice in the States. He plunged into his job as assistant in the parish at Stann Creek, where for the next sixteen years he endeared himself to the people as an indefatigable shepherd of the widely scattered mission flock.

Stann Creek is an upcountry town deep in the fruit plantation area of British Honduras. The parish numbered more than four thousand baptized Catholics, of every racial and color variety. The ethnic mixture included the whitest type of British and American as well as the darker Caribs, Mayas, Ketchi, and Negroes. The Maya were distinguished by long hair and reddish skin. The Caribs were more brown-skinned, and they predominated in the area, comprising about 70 per cent of the parish.

Father Marin belonged to one of these Carib families. Mostly rural folks, the Caribs frowned upon intermarriage with townspeople, among whom were classed the darker Negroes and the multi-mixture Creoles.

Notwithstanding this racial diversity, the parish worshiped as a unit and all came to revere their young priest as their own padre. They brought more than two thousand children to him for baptism in the course of his ministry.

More than 850 children crowded into the Catholic public school within the parish, jointly supported by the Church and the British Government. Contributing about half the cost of the school, the government exercised some curriculum control and had regular inspections to see that the British standards for this type of school were maintained.

Philip had taught in the school for a few years before entering the seminary. He and other lay teachers had supplemented the work of the devoted Sisters in the training of the young. After a period at the Normal School in Belize, they returned to Stann Creek as "pupil teachers" who were supervised and trained on the job by other teachers.

Father Marin continued to teach in the school even after he returned in 1934. He helped with the catechism classes and with the supervision of the young teachers, and later, when he became pastor, he was officially constituted as the principal of the school.

During his first years, Father Marin took over the missions in the bush. He traveled by boat and mule and bicycle to Hopkins, St. Michael, Little River, and Mullins River to administer the Sacraments to the rural Caribs of the outlying districts. He shared this work with Father Shaeffer until the latter was transferred.

Continuing this itinerant missionary life all through the years of the war, Philip each Sunday would offer three Masses at three widely separated mission chapels, and would return to Stann Creek in time for his weekday work as well.

After the end of the war, the Jesuit missionaries extended their efforts into Spanish Honduras. In 1947 Father Marin was made pastor of the whole Stann Creek district, responsible not only for the outlying missions but also for the management of the central mission church in town. There he said his three Masses each Sunday, straight through the year. A missionary from Belize would usually travel to Stann Creek each weekend to assist him with the outlying chapels.

The burden of the parish fell upon Father Marin's shoulders. Confessions by the hundreds, marriages, baptisms, first Communions, funerals, and all of the details of school management were in his hands. He capably executed all of these duties and thrived under the activity for the first two years of his pastorate. Ministrations to the sick, attendance at the bedside of the dying, visiting in the hospital did not affect his health.

But in 1949 the challenge to his missionary zeal appeared in the form of an "assistant" pastor sent him by the bishop, a Honduras-born Jamaican, who was suffering from an advanced case of consumption. As soon as the local doctor was apprised of the situation, he sent a warning to Father Marin to be careful not to use any of his table utensils and to take other precautionary measures.

Father Philip was not panicked by the warning. "The bishop and the Jesuits have been so good to me; why should I complain?" That was his attitude.

Yet, within a few months, Philip noticed that he himself was beginning to lose weight. He was inevitably thrown into close daily contact with the assistant pastor who lived in the same house, and who rarely went out even for his work as assistant.

The doctor repeated his warning. Finally, Father Marin had to put the case up to the bishop one day when he visited Stann Creek. "Bishop," he said, "I am quite content with where you put me and I will do my best, but if this man stays here, I'll be crippled for life, and I'm not yet an old man." The bishop nevertheless allowed the consumptive to stay on at Stann Creek, even insisting that Father Marin support him out of the parish's meager funds, though he did hardly any parish work.

Within six months, Father Philip broke down with tuberculosis. The doctor ordered him to a sanatorium to attempt recuperation. A position as chaplain was obtained at the Sanatorio San Angelo in Mexico City, operated by the French Sisters of Divine Providence. Father Marin entered the hospital in the early part of 1950. He continued to say daily Mass and to perform the chaplain's duties around the hospital.

In the fall of 1950 the bishop decided to transfer him to St. Louis where he had arranged for Father Marin to be assistant chaplain in St. Mary's Infirmary, a colored hospital. Arriving in St. Louis on the feast of the Immaculate Conception in the biting cold of one of the severest winters, Father Marin immediately became desperately ill. The change of climate from the tropics to the freezing weather of the Midwest was too much. Tests showed positive and active tuberculosis.

Within a fortnight, severe attacks of lung hemorrhages brought him to death's door. He was transferred to Mount St. Rose Sanitarium, where he lingered between life and death all through the rest of the desperately cold winter. He began to mend in the summer, but the marks of his cross and crucifixion are still deep upon him.

One could not help but admire the staunch courage of this good shepherd who stayed at his watch over his flock even when it meant a threat to his health and his life. It gave one a new glimpse into the depths of the soul of the colored priest. It brought back to me personally memories of other great souls whom I have studied and written about, whose kindred spirit I found in the person of this humble, self-sacrificing pastor of souls.

CHAPTER XVII

Army Chaplains

FATHER WILLIAM C. GRAU
FATHER JOHN W. BOWMAN, S.V.D.

Anyone who read the dispatches from the Italian front during the War saw many encomiums of the "Bouncing Buffaloes," the 92nd Division, the only colored combat unit in the United States Army's infantry. Twelve thousand strong, they earned a total of 12,096 decorations for their military achievements in the Rome-Arno River Campaign (they captured the city of Lucca in their first six months of combat), as well as in the Arno-Gothic Line campaign of the following winter, and in the final stages of the Italian campaign in northern Italy.

The "Bouncing Buffaloes" liberated more than 3,000 square miles of enemy territory in their battles. As a price for this, they paid 3,161 casualties in killed, wounded, and missing. They proudly wore more than thirteen hundred Purple Hearts, about six thousand combat badges, upwards of seven hundred bronze stars, ninety-five silver stars, sixteen Legion of Merit awards, one distinguished service medal, and two distinguished service crosses. In the land of mud, mules, and mountains, the 92nd contributed more than its share to the Army's volume of valor.

The head chaplain of the Bouncing Buffaloes at the war's end was Captain William C. Grau, the only Catholic priest among the division's twenty-two chaplains. In a unit that was more than 93 per cent non-Catholic, this appointment was of itself testimony to Padre Grau's intrepid courage and devotion to his men.

Father Grau was a front-line chaplain. His services were in demand on many sectors of the front during combat. He had to travel as much as a hundred miles a day, often under constant German observation and even through enemy fire. The going was hazardous as well from the wretched condition of the road, often negotiable only by mule or jeep. Yet Father Grau kept to his habit of barreling over the rough terrain during daylight. He preferred the hazards of enemy fire to that of black-out driving over unfamiliar roads at night. Carrying the Holy Eucharist within his pyx on these trips to the front in combat time, he always felt that Someone would see him through in his desire to visit the greatest number of troops in danger of death, to hear their confessions, give them Holy Communion, and, where sheltered bunkers made it possible, offer Mass for them in the actual front-line positions.

Unforgettable was one of these Masses, offered in a town not far from the front on Christmas Eve, 1944. It was the first combat Christmas overseas for most of the men. They were feeling mighty homesick, slogging through the Italian mud and fighting the seemingly futile war at a time when folks back home were preparing to celebrate Christmas.

Father Grau took over a ballroom in one of the less damaged hotels for the Midnight Mass services. The Nazis had stripped the place of all ornamentation before they pulled out. The chaplain and his co-workers had to beg, borrow, and liberate all sorts of makeshift equipment to relieve the room of its bareness. Both officers and men cooperated in suggesting possible articles for liberation and loan, even managing to borrow a spare crib and a statue of the Infant of Bethlehem from the local church.

By 23:45 (fifteen minutes before midnight) the place was packed to capacity with the division's top brass, noncoms, and buck privates, both Catholic and Protestants. A group of the soldiers sang the familiar Christmas carols before Mass, to the accompaniment of a field organ, two violins, and a cello. An Italian choir had been engaged by the resourceful padre to sing the High Mass with music by the Italian composer Perosi. Their rendering of the Christmas song of the angels at the Gloria of the Mass reduced the congregation to an awed, hushed silence.

Father Grau delivered a simple, man-to-man sermon on the significance of the Babe of Bethlehem for the man of war. He heard the choked sobs of boys still in their teens, and he saw the swimming eyes of impassive combat veterans, holding back the tears that came in spite of their wills. For a brief moment, they knew the true meaning of the priest as the conscious link between themselves and the Savior of Bethlehem. For weeks afterward they talked about the spirit of that Christmas Mass that gave them a beautiful homelike experience in the midst of the alien ugliness of war.

Father Grau's sixteen months with the 92nd Division in Italy did not represent his first tour of duty overseas. He had been in Rome as a seminarian and a priest from 1930 to 1938, finishing his ecclesiastical education.

All of his years of education had been spent in Catholic schools. He had been born a cradle Catholic in Cleveland, July 17, 1905. As a youth, he had attended Catholic grammar school and high school in his native parish, Holy Name in Cleveland. Under the expert spiritual guidance of the pastor, Father William A. Scullin, formerly the chancellor of the diocese in Bishop Farley's time, the parish continued its tradition of fostering vocations to the priesthood. Archbishop Hurley of St. Augustine, Florida, and Bishop McFadden of Youngstown, Ohio, had both been reared in Holy Name parish. Bishop Michael Ready of Columbus was also connected with the parish in his early years.

Young Grau responded to Father Scullin's incessant preaching about the need of vocations to the priesthood. He made known his desire to serve God as a priest, and Father Scullin encouraged him in his vocation during his high-school years. Upon graduation, William matriculated at John Carroll University in Cleveland in order to prepare for admission into the seminary.

Two years later Bishop Schrembs of Cleveland agreed to enroll William in the class of 1927 at Our Lady of the Lake Seminary. William pursued his church studies successfully for three years there, until a set of adverse circumstances turned Bishop Schrembs against the idea of incorporating colored priests into his diocese.

It seems that Bishop Schrembs was highly disturbed, as was Archbishop McNicholas of Cincinnati, by rumors and misinterpretations connected with the accidental shooting of Father DuKette in Detroit.

He was further disturbed by the truculent behavior of one of the other colored seminarians studying for his diocese. So offensive did this lad become under the admonitions and corrections that must sometimes be given even to the best of seminarians, that Bishop Schrembs wavered in his policy of adopting colored aspirants to the priesthood. After dismissing the insubordinate seminarian, he called in William Grau and informed him that he would not continue sponsorship of his candidacy.

The sudden bombshell rocked young William's vocation. In his distress, he took refuge in the fatherly counsel of his former pastor, Father Scullin. The genial old priest had not lost faith in the genuineness of William's call. He contacted Father Edward C. Kramer, a former classmate of his in Rome, and induced him, as executive secretary of the Catholic Board of Colored Missions, to take William Grau under his wing.

Father Kramer scouted among all of his friends in the episcopate for a possible sponsor. Eventually, Bishop Mahoney of Sioux Falls agreed to stand sponsor for William's admission to a theologate, with the understanding that Father Kramer would secure another bishop in the interim. Moreover, Father Kramer obtained William's admission into the Gregorian University in Rome for the last four years of his studies.

By 1934 William had completed his course. He was ordained in Rome on February 24, 1934, by Cardinal Marchetti. Returning to Cleveland for his first solemn Mass in his native parish, Father Grau spent the summer months performing the functions of his new priesthood there. Father Scullin was greatly pleased with the efficiency and zeal of his temporary curate. But neither he nor Father Kramer had been able to find an opening for him in that or the neighboring dioceses.

In the emergency, Father Kramer proposed to his board of bishops that the new priest be made an assistant of his in the office of the Mission Board in New York. The bishops vetoed this because of Father William's relative youth and inexperience. It was finally agreed that Father Grau would return to Rome to pursue further studies at the Gregorian University. With an eye on a possible career as a seminary professor, the young priest applied himself to his theology. By 1938 he had completed his work for the degree of S.T.L., licentiate in sacred theology.

He used his postgraduate years to broaden his mastery of modern languages, traveling extensively in Europe to attain fluency in German and French as well as in Latin.

Back in the United States, Father Grau finally found a diocesan welcome. Father Kramer had persuaded Bishop Duffy of Buffalo to admit his protégé on probation for five years. He was assigned to the post of assistant at the National Shrine of Our Lady of Victory in Lackawanna, New York, the southern lakeside industrial suburb of Buffalo. Bishop O'Hara later incardinated him into the diocese.

Father Grau has been happy in his work in Lackawanna. Stationed there for twelve years, save for the thirty months of his army career, he has found a congenial apostolate in the areas internationally known as the scene of the labors of Father Nelson Baker, the famed founder of the sprawling set of institutions that surround the giant basilica of Our Lady of Victory.

The appointment to a position at Father Baker's Charities was a logical one. The tolerant spirit of the founder, dead only two years at the time of Father Grau's arrival in 1938, disposed of any petty difficulties that might have arisen elsewhere. Father Baker knew no prejudice. He took children of all races and creeds into his orphan homes and hospital. And when the growth of the giant steel plants rimmed the horizon with their huge smokestacks and drew thousands of Negro workers from the South, Father Baker personally opened a mission for them in their neighborhood. Through the late twenties and the early thirties, he patiently worked for their conversion, bringing more than seven hundred colored adults into the fold. His "All Saints Mission" was the core of his apostolate among the steelworkers.

In 1938 Father Grau took up where Father Baker had left off two years before. While living at the priest's residence alongside the immense shrine of Our Lady of Victory, Father Grau scoured the flatlands around the steel mills in search of converts and fallen-aways. Under the direction of his pastor, the young priest helped gather the remnants of the old parish of St. Charles that had died out with the

building of the many foreign-language churches in Lackawanna—
Polish, Italian, Croatian, Hungarian.

In course of time, the popularity of All Saints Church and its school,
taught by the Felician Sisters, drew scores of these immigrants away
from their churches and blended them with the twenty-two other
nationalities that make up the unique parish. A list of the parish ethnic
backgrounds reads like the roll of all nations—Austrians, Bulgarians,
Bohemian-Slovaks, Czechoslovakians, Dutch, British, French, Greeks,
Germans, Indians, Latvians, Mexicans, Negroes, Puerto Ricans, Rus-
sians, Serbians, Syrians, Spaniards, Scotch-Irish, Roumanians, Ukra-
nians, and Welsh.

One finds him there in the midst of his people, perfectly at ease with
them. No door has ever been slammed in his face. None fears to approach him for confession. Indeed, with his wide range of languages,
he is sought out as confessor by the old folks who still wish to tell their
peccadilloes in Italian, French, German, or the other languages he has
picked up in his dozen years of ministry.

The steelworkers know him as a champion of the laboring man as
well. For years, even since before his army work, he has taught labor
ethics in the Buffalo Diocesan Labor College, a night school conducted
at one of the downtown Catholic school buildings. He has plans for
the opening of another labor school in Lackawanna in the new CIO
union hall. Among the mighty men of steel, the diminutive and aggressive priest-teacher is a revered and respected leader by sheer force of
personality and persuasive eloquence.

His speaking ability has won for him steady invitations to preach in
many of the churches of Buffalo and vicinity. He has talked at civic
luncheons and at Forty Hours' Devotions with equal grace and fluency.
A forthright and unabashed speaker, he has not allowed himself to be
intimidated by any of the possible obstacles one might expect a colored
priest to encounter.

At the rectories around the diocese, he is as welcome as any other
priest might be. As a much-decorated chaplain in the late war, he was
elected over his fellow chaplains to be the padre for the American
Legion Post in Lackawanna.

Father Grau still retains the marks of his experience in the Army.

A man's man, he is proof of the ability of the colored priest to adjust to clerical life if given an even chance to overcome the handicaps which prejudice automatically imposes on him. He takes the ups and downs of his priestly career in stride. He has an army expression to sum up his attitude: "I'm a priest first and foremost; if I am a good Joe, I'll be treated like a good Joe; if I were a heel, I'd be treated like a heel!"

FATHER JOHN WALTER BOWMAN, S.V.D.

1 9 0 8 –

The citation of the Army of the United States by which Chaplain John Walter Bowman was awarded the Bronze Star Medal for meritorious achievement in support of military operations against the enemy in the South Pacific, reads as follows:

> Chaplain Bowman, the only Catholic Chaplain in an Infantry Division, travelled by plane to minister to the moral and spiritual needs of the Catholic men on the widely scattered islands; to wit: Guadalcanal, British Solomon Islands, Sterling Island, Treasury Group, Finschhafen, New Guinea, and Hollandia, Dutch New Guinea. He was unflagging in his zeal and enthusiasm in ministering to the moral and spiritual needs, and bolstering the morale of his troops. He was active in Allied contacts, saying Mass and preaching to Allied Forces. Whenever possible, he ministered to the natives on the islands of Guadalcanal, Sterling Island, and Hollandia. He constructed Chapels for Division Headquarters that served both Catholic and Protestant faiths, and proved an example for other chaplains to follow. During this entire tour of duty, under all circumstances, Chaplain Bowman displayed courage, unusual effectiveness in lifting the moral standards of his men. These achievements reflected honor and esteem on the Chaplains' Corps and were in accordance with the highest tradition of the United States Military Service.

That was the official summary of the dramatic high point of a life that had begun almost forty years before in the Anacostia district of

Washington. The thirteenth of fourteen children of Francis and Cornelia Bowman, John Walter was born on March 16, 1908, and baptized forty days later in St. Teresa's Church in Anacostia. The devout family attended St. Teresa's until Father Franz Schneeweis founded and built Our Lady of Perpetual Help colored church on Morris Road, high up on the hill overlooking southeast Washington, near Fort Stanton Park.

John became Father Schneeweis' faithful altar boy in the little wind-swept church. Shortly after the first World War, when a lad of only eleven years, John conceived the desire to be a priest like his saintly pastor. For seven years he nurtured the ambition. Father Schneeweis, in full sympathy with John's vocation, gave him special catechetical instructions two times a week during his school years, and extended this into the period when the youngster went to work after finishing at Armstrong Technical School in Washington.

In May, 1926, Father Schneeweis wrote in his behalf to Father Christman at St. Augustine's Seminary, with the result that John secured admission to the institution in the fall of the year. By 1931 he had finished his work in the junior college department and transferred to the novitiate of the Divine Word Fathers in East Troy, Wisconsin. Taking his vows on August 15, 1933, he returned to Bay St. Louis to complete his ecclesiastical studies. On January 6, 1939, he was ordained in Bay St. Louis by Bishop Gerow. His provincial appointed him assistant pastor in Duson, Louisiana, in the summer of that year.

While a seminarian, John had plied the trade of journalism writing a number of articles for *St. Augustine's Messenger*. Some of them, like *"Quo Vadis*: Whither Goest Thou?" published in November, 1937, were serious and pensive pieces analyzing the social and religious conditions of the American Negroes. His summary of events and trends in 1937, published in the January issue of 1938, showed the wide acquaintance that the young seminarian had with the spiritual, political, economic, and interracial aspects of Negro life in America. He was especially interested in the problem of relations between whites and Negroes and the role of the interracial councils in bettering these relationships. In May, 1938, in an article entitled "The Spirit of Catholic Youth," John described this Negro-centric phase of Catholic Action, and summarized some practical points and resolutions for the future.

But his main interest was the religious welfare of the colored American. In March, 1938, he wrote a long article discussing the question: "Do Negroes Want Religion?" He cited the fact that more than 50 per cent had no religion whatever, but he nevertheless answered his question in the affirmative, and attributed this to the steady stream of converts that came into the Catholic ranks from all walks of Negro life. In May, 1939, under the title "Lead Kindly Light," he followed up this convert phenomenon with the story of Bishop Duane Hunt of Salt Lake City, a convert from Anglicanism, whose consecration as bishop raised to twelve the number of converts in the ranks of the American hierarchy.

After his assignment to Immaculate Heart of Mary Church in Lafayette in 1941, Father Bowman resumed his journalistic efforts for the *Messenger*. He wrote a vivid account of his two years of missionary work among the people of Duson and Scott under the title, "Where the West Begins," (September, 1941). Describing the wide flat reaches of the parishes in the area where Louisiana begins to look like Texas, he told of the French mannerisms and modes of life of the Creole Negroes who still communicated with each other in the local dialects, though also able to understand and speak English. Their pastor's own deep interest in the religious life of his people is evinced by the intimate portrait he draws of their genuinely Catholic culture, their calm and subdued charity, and their generous spirit of hospitality and co-operation in their peaceful semi-rural communities.

His concern for the social welfare of his parishioners sent him to the Agricultural Conference for Ministers Pastoring Rural Colored Churches in Louisiana, held under U. S. Government auspices at Southern University in Scotlandville, just outside Baton Rouge, in September, 1941. Father Bowman was one of the two Catholic priests in attendance. He made so fine an impression that he was elected treasurer of the forty-five-member conference, whose purpose was to channel information to rural families about the assistance they could receive from various federal agencies and projects.

During the next year, most of his energies were concentrated on the mission at Mouton Switch, one of the outlying missions serviced by the priests of Immaculate Heart Church in Lafayette. Together with the pastor, Father Bourges, Father Bowman undertook the task of building his first rural church. By July, 1942, it was ready for dedication. He wrote two articles describing the growth of the mission and its culmination in the realization of the dreams of Madame Babineaux with the erection of the permanent church.

A month later he received his commission as a chaplain in the United States Army. In early August he reported for training at the chaplains' school at Harvard University where he became the first colored Catholic priest to be inducted into the chaplains' corps.

Upon completion of his course at Harvard, Chaplain Bowman was assigned for a time to the "Bouncing Buffaloes" of the 92nd Division at Fort McClellan, Alabama. He wrote vividly of his first experiences in the Army on maneuvers in an article that appeared in *The Colored Man's Friend,* in July, 1943.

In March of the same year he was transferred to the 93rd Division at Fort Huachuca, Arizona, a division destined for overseas duty in the South Pacific. Chaplain Bowman was raised to the rank of captain before the division embarked for the combat area. From then on, he shared the war fortunes of the 93rd as it beach-headed into the "Canal," the Solomon Islands, New Guinea, and Morotai, Netherlands East Indies. He ministered to Catholics of both the white and Negro units in the division, and found time to care for the spiritual needs of the natives as well.

In January, 1946, he was promoted to the rank of major just before his return to the United States. He was given a hero's welcome by his old parish in Washington and his newer parishes in south Louisiana. Thereafter his chaplain's uniform became a familiar sight up and down the colored missions and churches of the country. For three years he devoted himself to giving missions, sermons, and revivals in the North and South.

His war experiences served him in good stead in these years of missionary life. They were even more valuable in preparing him for the assignment he received in October, 1949—the establishing of a Catholic church in the Protestant stronghold of Mound Bayou, Bolivar County, Mississippi, the unique all-Negro town in the Delta country. The non-Catholic mayor of the small 1,500-person village had continually repeated his request to Bishop Gerow that he open a Catholic school in Mound Bayou. The mayor had seen elsewhere the effective work of the Catholic sisterhoods in their schools. He wanted one for his all-colored town. The bishop of course insisted that a Catholic church would have to be established and staffed before the Sisters would be able to open a school. It was not until the fall of 1949 that Father Bowman was finally appointed to start the mission church and school.

Bolivar County had a long reputation of hostility to Catholics, especially Catholic priests. In the beginning of the century, Father Aloysius Heick, S.V.D., had endeavored to inaugurate some missionary work for the neglected Negroes of the cotton plantations in the county. He built a frame chapel in Marigold, Mississippi, two miles from Mound Bayou. He won a few converts and started plans for the opening of a Catholic mission school for colored children. He mentioned this to the planters of the area, naively hoping for their support. Instead, he was warned that if he ventured on any educational project, he would be run out of the county. A short time later, he was actually chased out. Riding down the road one day, he saw a planter horse-whipping a colored lad. Father Heick rode up and snatched the whip from his hand, scolding him for his cruelty. The man immediately rounded up his fellow Ku Klux Klanners and threatened to tar and feather Father Heick if he stayed overnight. He was forced to leave.

For forty-five years after that, no Catholic priests were welcome in the Mound Bayou area of Bolivar County. The potential hostility of the whites and of the non-Catholic ministers was a challenge to Father Bowman's courage when he first embarked on his new mission in the fall of 1949. The only support that the mayor could guarantee was protection against physical violence and threat. Father Bowman had to start from scratch, secure funds from outside sources, and inch his way gradually into a place in the community.

For Mound Bayou was a proud Protestant community, close-knit and clannish. As one of the oldest and largest colored communities in the South, it was averse to outside and especially to "white" influences, such as the Catholic Church was considered to be in Mississippi Negro circles. The Protestant churches, though disunited among themselves, were united against Catholic infiltration into their areas of influence.

To the community solidarity created and maintained by their clannish churches, the natives of Mound Bayou owed much of their progress. They could point to their threescore years of existence as a unique community and take pride in the fact that they had their own Negro mayor, doctors, lawyers, storekeepers, dentists, and businessmen. The five thousand Negroes in the home-owned farms around the village looked to the Negro Protestant leadership in Mound Bayou for direction and guidance, as well as for marketing and trade.

Father Bowman's progress was understandably slow during his first year. He was able to build a small combination church and rectory, and to win to the Catholic Church about two dozen souls. His parish technically comprised the entire county's 917 square miles, and his potential apostolate was directly concerned with the 5,200 Negroes in the county (more than 74 per cent of the entire population). But obstacles hindered any spectacular advances in convert work.

For a long-range program, Father Bowman saw that a Catholic school was imperative. He secured the assurance of a staff of colored Sisters in 1950 and sent out appeals for funds to build a convent and classroom building.

By 1954 this phase of his mission work was completed. The school was built and put into operation. With that, his roots in the colored community will become deeper and more sturdy, and the fruits of his apostolate more abundant.

CHAPTER XVIII

Missioner on the Move

CLARENCE J. HOWARD, S.V.D.

1907 –

It was a sultry August for southeastern Virginia in 1926. In the vicinity of the Great Dismal Swamp below Norfolk, the Ku Klux Klan was night-riding again. Fiery crosses burning at the crossroads signaled their ominous meetings. Negroes of the coastal section were terrorized. Even whites were not spared. Two young men suspected of fraternizing with the colored were kidnaped by the hooded raiders. They were severely beaten, and dumped unconscious on the front porch of a farmhouse. Another was fearfully branded on the forehead. The Klansmen, after capturing him, held him pinioned to the earth. One of them dipped his finger in gasoline and traced a "K K K" on his forehead. Another put a match to the fluid and seared their brutal trademark upon his head. It was dangerous to be a Negro and a Catholic in those areas. It was even more dangerous to be a Catholic priest or a Yankee.

Yet young Clarence Howard, a bright, energetic, capable colored lad of nineteen who had just graduated first in the first class to finish at the new St. Joseph's High School in Norfolk, was contemplating a future career in the priesthood. He idolized the jolly young pastor of St. Joseph's Church, Father Vincent Warren, S.S.J., who had been assigned to Norfolk soon after his ordination. Father Warren had endeared himself to the colored community by building the church and the school for them and by working zealously both in Norfolk and in its environs.

With the school band Father Warren had been making trips into the rural districts all summer long. By means of its lively music, the band gathered crowds of country folk Negroes for an evening's entertainment. Father Warren always found time to give a little speech about the Church—the friend of the poor and the natural home of aching human souls. Clarence Howard, playing the trumpet in the band on these excursions, saw the kind of useful and godly life to which he wished to dedicate himself. It was during these weeks of the summer's tours that Clarence sent off his application to St. Augustine's Seminary in Bay St. Louis, Mississippi.

His determination was further crystallized one evening when the band played in Princess Anne County for a non-Catholic group gathered at the home of one of the Protestant girls who commuted to Norfolk for school at St. Joseph's during the year. She and her family had invited Father Warren to bring his band down for a concert. He had accepted. But when the news was bruited about, the Klan threatened to hang him if he came down into that Protestant stronghold.

Undismayed, Father Warren went ahead with his plans. In order not to give occasion for the Klan's complaints, Father Warren secured two white men to accompany him in his car, instead of his usual colored driver. Clarence and the rest of the band traveled in the truck as customary.

Things looked ominous as they passed through the county seat, Princess Anne Courthouse, on the way to their destination. There were surprisingly many model-T's and farm trucks parked around the square for a Sunday afternoon. Evidently, there was an assembly somewhere.

As a precaution, Father Warren stopped at the house of a lawyer acquaintance. "I understand there's some feeling against us around here," he said. "Do you think it'll be all right if we go to a colored farmhouse outside of town and have a bit of music for the colored folks around there?"

The lawyer was non-committal. He shrugged his shoulders. "I suppose so," he muttered, "but I don't know . . ."

At the farmhouse the old colored woman, mother of the St. Joseph student, was more alarmed. "Please go back home, Father," she begged; "don't stay here. Those Kluxers is all around. I'm afraid they'll kill you."

Father Warren smiled reassuringly. He told the band to pile out of the truck and set things up for their concert. The bandleader soon struck up some lively music and worries were banished into the sunset.

Sitting in his car on the roadside, Father Warren watched the road and listened to the concert. At dark, as the band played its last piece, they came. A long line of rattletrap cars moving slowly in the haunted dusk, two or three white-hooded figures on each running board. No lights. No license plates. Silvery revolvers pointed from the hands of each of the Klansmen.

Clarence and the other bandsters saw nothing. Their backs were to the road. The bandmaster kept them playing, even though the audience disappeared into the woods and behind the house. Six or seven of the hoodlums came over to Father Warren's car, opened the door, and dragged him out. The two white men tried to resist the Kluxers. One was struck by a blow from the butt of a pistol. He fell stunned into the ditch. In a matter of minutes, the caravan had driven off into the dark with their quarry.

At the end of their last piece, the bandmaster announced, "The K K K got Father!" Like scared rabbits, the youngsters all jumped into the truck and hastened back into town. They drove so fast that, a little more than a mile from town, the motor caught fire. While they stopped to put it out, Clarence and another boy took off on the run to the police station, two miles away. Without stopping for breath, they ran full speed all the way. At the station, they found that the news had already arrived. The alarm had been given. But the police were unable to find any trace of the Klansmen.

Off to the North Carolina border, the Klansmen had sped with the captured pastor. Father Warren had time for fifteen decades of the rosary before the caravan finally turned off the main road and bumped down a rough lane to a clearing in the woods. There they planned to hang and burn him.

At the last minute, one of the guards who had ridden beside Father Warren in the car and had been impressed with his prayerfulness called a conference of the ringleaders. He dissuaded them from stringing up a "holy, prayin' man." The Klansmen decided to turn him loose. They drove him to a crossroads cemetery and deposited him unharmed in the pitch-black night.

It was after midnight before the pastor returned to his flock. They were all assembled and praying in the church, storming heaven for the safety of their priest. When he put in his appearance the congregation swarmed out to welcome him, to smother him with kisses, and to thank God for his safe return.

Father Warren had his little joke about Clarence's two-mile run. He said that the young boy was so frightened by the sight of the Klansmen that he started running and didn't stop until he reached Bay St. Louis.

At any rate, it was within a week after the near-lynching that Clarence did bid farewell to the church in which he had been baptized at the age of twelve, to the school which he had entered at the age of eleven at the behest of a Catholic neighbor, and to the city to which his parents had brought him from his native town of Rocky Mount, North Carolina, where he had been born, January 3, 1907. Clarence left with many happy memories of Norfolk and of the old parish when he set out for the seminary. He cherished the recollection of the good Franciscan Sisters from Baltimore who had taken him into their overcrowded school and had won him to the faith and to the Church, and had prepared him well for his work in the seminary.

At St. Augustine's Seminary, Clarence completed two years of college work before journeying to the Divine Word Novitiate in East Troy, Wisconsin, in 1928. He stood high in the class of twenty that Father Glorius, the novicemaster, trained carefully in the ways of the religious life. On August 15, 1931, Clarence became a religious of the Divine Word Society, by pronouncing his first vows in the chapel at East Troy.

It was a welcome relief from the cold weather of Wisconsin when the young seminarian was assigned to Bay St. Louis for his years of philosophy and theology. His two years in the minor seminary in the quiet coastal town had made it his second home. He liked the seminary life, the teachers, the spirit of the school. Though the Society of the Divine Word also maintained a school of Philosophy and Theology at Techny, Illinois, the Father General in Rome saw to it that St. Augustine's Seminary was staffed with excellent teachers, some of whom were even better than those in Techny and were in constant demand for lecture work in the northern theologate.

By this time, Clarence's mother had also become a Catholic. She was baptized in Norfolk during his seminary days, and as the time for his ordination approached, she traveled down to Bay St. Louis to be present for the solemn event.

On Ascension Thursday, May 6, 1937, Bishop Gerow of Natchez ordained him to the priesthood, together with Father Orin Wells of St. Louis. His old pastor, Father Vincent Warren, was also there. At the first private Mass next day, Father Warren preached the sermon, alluding to the fact that Father Howard was the first Negro priest from both North Carolina and Virginia.

Father Howard considered himself a Virginian, and so returned to Norfolk for his first Mass at St. Joseph's Church. It was no longer housed in the original building erected by Father Warren during the first World War. Prospering in more recent years, the parish had purchased a large church building from a bankrupt Methodist congregation. It was in this converted church that the newly ordained convert celebrated his first solemn High Mass, in June, 1937. Father John Madden, a diocesan priest from Boston, was deacon, and a Trinitarian father was subdeacon. Father James Albert, the Josephite pastor of St. Joseph's Church in Norfolk, preached the sermon.

The first month of his ministry was devoted to his home parish in what was technically a vacation after the hard years of study and preparation for the ordination itself.

In the autumn of 1937 Father Howard received his first appointment for work in the Church of the Immaculate Heart of Mary in Lafayette, Louisiana. There he joined the pioneers of the work in the Evangeline country, under the leadership of Father Patzelt as pastor of the new colored parish. Fathers Rousseve and Wells were also assigned to the new parish. Together they pressed forward in the apostolate among the colored Catholics of French Louisiana.

Father Clarence found that the Negro Catholics at last felt adequately cared for by a sufficient number of priests wholly dedicated to their souls' salvation. The welcome accorded him was uniformly happy and sincere.

In the routine of parish life, Father Clarence took his regular turns at daily and Sunday Mass, at confessions and sermons for the people.

He taught catechism classes in the school, and because of his musical ability, stemming from the old St. Joseph's band in Norfolk, he also taught the music classes and was put in charge of the boys' choir. Under his direction, they were trained into a harmonious and edifying group, and when they appeared in the sanctuary vested in cassocks and surplices for the High Masses on Sundays, the congregation was treated to an inspiring and prayerful service.

For two years the young priest labored consolingly among the devout parishioners of the Immaculate Heart of Mary in Lafayette. In 1939, however, his superiors found a more difficult task for his wide variety of talents. Father Howard was appointed editor of the *St. Augustine's Messenger*. The editorial office was transferred to Techny for a year so that the new editor could learn all of the minutiae of editing and production by working alongside the experienced priests and Brothers who conducted the famous Mission Press there, pouring out the steady stream of books, magazines, pamphlets, catechetical material, church goods, and mission articles in the many languages of the far-flung mission fields engaging the energies of the Fathers and Brothers of the Society of the Divine Word.

During the year of his apprenticeship, Father Howard mastered the difficult art of editing. By the time he was ready to return to the Bay, he had transformed the quarterly magazine into a well-edited, readable, and appealing monthly. It compared very favorably with other mission magazines throughout the country. The bulk of the writing thenceforth also fell to his lot. Each month he produced a large percentage of the copy that went into the publication, rewriting the sketchy reports that busy missionaries sent in to the editorial office, doing the research and field work for hundreds of original articles, and even composing some poetry and verse as fillers for the pages of the *Messenger*. The twelve volumes of the attractive periodical all bear eloquent testimony to Father Howard's dexterity as a writer and zeal as an enthusiast for the missions.

It was during his stay in Illinois in 1939-40 that Father Howard set out on another phase of his busy apostolate. At St. Elizabeth's Church in South Side Chicago in November, 1939, he gave his first "revival," as he called his high-powered missions in the parish churches. Using some of the old-fashioned techniques of the experienced mission priests, Father Howard rapidly established himself as an impressive and moving preacher, an impassioned champion of the Church, and an eloquent and successful pleader for a return to God.

With the passing of the months, his fame spread. Invitations began to pour in from all sections of the country. In the Midwest he gave missions to both colored and white congregations in Minnesota, Iowa, Missouri, and Illinois. After 1940, back in the South, he preached to congregations in all of the southern states, both in the larger cities and in the rural areas, even of Georgia where the recrudescence of the Ku Klux Klan did not interfere with his speaking to mixed congregations.

One by-product of his missions kept him busy as vocation director for the seminary at Bay St. Louis. Always on the lookout for young colored boys who were bright, pious, and ambitious for the priesthood, Father Howard was instrumental in recruiting a large number of seminarians for the Bay. Once in Indianapolis, after a thunderous mission sermon on hell, one of the altar boys came up to him and said, "Father, I think I want to be a priest." In the next class at the seminary, he joined many others that the grace of God had touched through the eloquent and fervent missionary's words.

Despite the desk work in connection with his editing of the *Messenger,* Father Howard continued to be a missioner on the move. He was in constant demand as an occasional speaker for big ceremonies, especially of a mission-oriented nature. The Catholic Student Mission Crusade selected him as one of the main speakers for their annual convention in Cleveland. Catholic colleges and schools in the South and elsewhere engaged him to give special lectures on mission topics. For Communion breakfasts and interracial Masses, for first Masses and for Holy Name rallies, for assemblies of the Knights of Peter Claver, whose regional chaplain he became, Father Howard showed himself a willing and capable speaker. In his vivid and forceful manner, he poured out a torrent of deeply felt, persuasive eloquence, and had little difficulty in holding his audiences spellbound as he discoursed.

As the years went by, Father Clarence became a special favorite among the sisterhoods of the South. He was selected by a large number of communities, mostly white Sisters, to conduct the exercises of their annual retreats. He also returned to give retreats to their school children in places like New Orleans, Mobile, Jackson, Macon, St. Louis, and Chicago. Hearing thousands of confessions in the course of these and other ministries, Father Howard proved himself a patient and sympathetic spiritual father for souls without regard to pigmentation. Only one out of all the thousands of white penitents heard by him felt constrained to confess that she felt some difficulty in approaching the Sacrament when she realized that he was a colored priest.

Wherever he traveled as a missioner on the move, Father Howard found unfailing welcome at the parish rectories of so-called "white" parishes. He graced the cathedral pulpits in a number of dioceses and archdioceses just as any other outstanding priest-orator might have done in the course of a busy career. And in his formal interracial apostolate, he has been active in the Catholic Committee of the South as cochairman of its race relations department. His vigorous championing of the religious rights of his Catholic brethren brought him recognition as the most vocal and forthright Catholic leader in the field. He has constantly emphasized that colored Catholics wish to be treated as full Catholics and full American citizens. They do not condone the compromise solution of the temporary segregated churches, much less the violent type of Jim Crowism and exclusionism practiced by certain parishes, schools, and institutions, which lay claim to being Catholic and universal.

Recognition of his outstanding achievements spread beyond the sea to Rome. In 1951, when a missionary bishop in New Guinea petitioned Rome to send out a missioner to establish a seminary for a native clergy on the island, officials in Rome designated Father Clarence Howard to move to that distant destination. With his staff gathered from among the young priests and Brothers of the Society of the Divine Word, Father Howard had his official departure service in the beautiful chapel of the Holy Spirit at the Mission House in Techny, October 14, 1951. From there he set forth for the new field of his missionary endeavor, leaving behind him a grateful and gratifying harvest of souls gathered in by his zeal.

Reports from the mission field (whose malarial conditions, millions of insects, and sub-tropical weather had been newspaper material during the second World War) show that Father Howard was making slow but steady progress toward establishing his seminary. The bishop had chosen Bagaram on Kairiru Island in New Guinea as the site of the institution. The place had been a flourishing mission before the war. But the Japanese had occupied the town and the buildings during their brief rule over the island. The United States bombers had therefore leveled the whole town and wiped it off the map. Rebuilding promised to be a long and tedious task .

By means of pidgin English, Father Howard has been able to perform some functions of the sacred ministry, like hearing confessions of the native folk in Wewak, Maprik, Kunjingini, and Yakamul as well as Kairiru. His mission jeep, named "Wewak Jack" by the Negro Catholic Michiganders who donated it, has been carrying him around the islands to bear the message and the grace of God to the natives. He looks forward to many years of active mission life in the difficult field.

* * * * *

The year after Father Howard was ordained, Father Francis Marcus Glover was raised to the dignity of the priesthood in an ordination ceremony in Carthage, Tunisia, North Africa, June 29, 1937.

The son of a parochial school janitor, Father Glover had been born in the Yorkville district of New York City in 1911. He attended the St. Francis de Sales parochial school on East 97th Street. With the help of the pastor, Monsignor John F. Brady, young Marcus had attended the minor seminary at Cathedral College High School in New York, but could not secure admission into the major seminary at Dunwoodie.

Instead, he entered the novitiate of the Josephite Fathers in Newburgh, New York. He transferred from their ranks to those of the White Fathers when he enrolled for philosophy studies in Beauport, Quebec. Later, he traveled to their house of theology in Carthage for his studies leading to ordination.

He lived for a number of years in the White Fathers' seminary in Franklin, Pennsylvania, did some pastoral work in Harlem, and as of the present writing, is assisting the work of the Mission Secretariat of the National Catholic Welfare Conference in Washington. Asked to cooperate in this project, he wrote:

> After a careful reading of both your letters and of the title headings of your historical project, I am amazed at your courage. A demonstrated lack of imagination and an elephantine, if jovial, tact are united to a rare degree. That the life-portraits of a few hard-working priests should be daubed in to illustrate this latest and most pathetic exploitation renders it the more oppressive. The fact that serious minded people have been asked to cooperate in this dubious project merely underlines what I have said regarding your courage.

CHAPTER XIX

The Chachere Brothers

FATHERS CARMEN GEORGE and EARL CHACHERE

The third colored family to have more than one priest (after the Healy and Winters families) was that of Ernest Chachere of St. Landry parish, Louisiana. The Chacheres were an old French Creole family with relations on both sides of the color line in and around Opelousas, a railroad and market center in south central Louisiana, on the fringe of the Evangeline country. The colored branch of the family lived in a closed social circle with other free colored families during the pre-Civil War period. Like the French Creoles of New Orleans, they maintained private elementary schools for the young children, sometimes sent the older ones abroad for schooling, and kept a discreet and, of necessity, a distant relationship with the local Catholic church, dominated as it was by the white Catholics.

In 1874 the colored Catholics of Opelousas had induced the Sisters of the Holy Family, a Negro Catholic sisterhood, to open their first school outside of New Orleans, where they had founded their institution thirty years before. The new St. Joseph's Academy devoted itself mainly to the education of colored girls, but young boys were also admitted to the lower grades if their parents wished.

The branch of the Chachere family to which the two priests-to-be were born had in all twelve chidren, the last three of whom were born in the modest little cottage a short distance back of St. Landry Church on Prudhomme Lane. Both Ernest Chachere and his wife, Mary Donatto Chachere, were cradle Catholics and raised a thoroughly religious family.

Their fourth boy was named Carmen George when he was born on January 30, 1909, and baptized in the St. Landry Church on

Washington's Birthday the same year. Two years later, another boy blessed the union. He was named Earl Lawrence upon his birth on July 19, 1911. With their older brothers, Loither, Lancelot, and Carl, the boys grew up in their semi-rural neighborhood on the outskirts of town. By the time they were of school age, four more brothers had joined them—Raymond, Marion, Alton, and Aloysius. These, together with the three sisters, Dorothy, Claudian, and Gertrude, rounded out a full dozen children for *père* and *mère* Chachere.

The boys attended the St. Joseph's School for Boys. This school had been built on land formerly owned by the great-grandparents of the Chacheres. Their descendants sold it to Mother Katharine Drexel so that it could be used for the education of colored children. At the time, the school was conducted by Professor L. D. Lang, a Key West man who had received some of his training at the St. Joseph's College for Negro Catechists in Montgomery. The school was supported by Mother Katherine Drexel's funds. It was dissolved in 1920 when Carmen was still in the fourth grade.

The reason for the closing of the school and the dismantling of the building was simple. A new and separate church for colored Catholics had been established that year in Opelousas by the Holy Ghost Fathers under the able pastorship of Father James A. Hyland, C. S. Sp., later to be the author of *The Dove Flies South*. The new pastor built a temporary church. The bishop persuaded the Holy Family Sisters to consolidate the boys and the girls into one school in an effort to raise standards and attain accreditation. The new Holy Ghost parochial school was the first to be recognized by the state department of education in the whole of rural Louisiana.

Both Carmen and Earl enrolled in the new school. They received a solid rudimentary training at the hands of the Holy Family nuns. Both boys learned Mass-serving and were among the first altar boys at the new church. They soon became known for their piety and faithfulness in serving Father Hyland's Masses.

In 1925, with the encouragement of Father Hyland, Carmen left home to enter the minor seminary at Bay St. Louis. Two years later, Earl, upon completing his grammar school in Opelousas, followed in his brother's steps to enroll at St. Augustine's Seminary. For the next ten years both boys followed the routine course of studies in the minor seminary, at the novitiate in East Troy, and back again in Bay St. Louis for major seminary work.

In 1936, the summer before his reception of minor orders, Carmen spent the customary month's vacation at home in Opelousas. In the course of his weeks in south Louisiana, he made a thorough study of the work of the pioneer colored priests in the Lafayette diocese. Returning to the seminary, he wrote a well-developed article for the *St. Augustine's Messenger,* entitled "Our Colored Priests in the South."[1] He succinctly described the initial experiment of 1934, when Bishop Jeanmard invited the four Divine Word Fathers to Lafayette to initiate the new parish of the Immaculate Heart of Mary. He graphically portrayed their pioneer work, taking the census along every street and lane, gaining the confidence of the people, reclaiming the lost and straying sheep, and gathering in the two thousand souls who formed the nucleus of the parish. One can see the missionary zeal of the writer himself as he eagerly describes the adventures in the apostolate of those he longed to follow.

At the seminary, Carmen was the moving leader of the Catholic Students' Mission Crusade. In November, 1938, he wrote another appealing article captioned "Mission Crusade and Negro Apostolate."[2] In this he cited the CSMC's work for the Negroes in Detroit, Cincinnati, Covington (Ky.), and Kansas City (Mo.).

During his seminary years Carmen served on the executive board of the CSMC and participated in their annual conventions. He gave some stirring addresses on the colored missionary apostolate and the need of the colored priesthood. His oratorical finesse presaged a great career as a missionary in the South.

By 1938 Carmen had reached the eve of ordination. He had been a frail, wiry lad, though he had never been seriously ill as a baby or as a young boy. He had played vigorous sports during his seminary days—baseball, basketball, and handball—and was always on the first team. He had grown to full stature as a handsome young man, with deep-set eyes and wavy black hair. He was a serious and intel-

[1] *St. Augustine's Messenger* (January, 1937).
[2] *St. Augustine's Messenger* (November, 1938), pp. 7, 15-16.

ligent student, ranking with Joseph Bowers as the best theologian in
the 1939 class. From time to time he complained of heart trouble, but
paid little attention to the passing pains.

In the fall of 1938, after Carmen and his brother Earl had presided
over the Divine Word Fathers' mission booth at the National Eucharistic Congress held in New Orleans, Carmen suddenly received orders
from the Superior General in Rome to proceed to the Holy City with
Joseph Bowers for their final year of studies and for ordination in Rome
itself.

The two subdeacons (they had both been raised to that major
order on October 2) left for Rome in November. They received the
diaconate in the Holy City on December 17, and then, with little
more than a month's preparation, were solemnly ordained to the holy
priesthood by the Cardinal Vicar of Rome, on January 22, 1939. For
the rest of the scholastic year they remained at Rome to study theology
and make the pilgrimages to the holy places. By July they had passed
their formal examinations, and also their informal scrutiny beneath
the curious eyes of the Holy Father and the cardinals who were interested in observing the results of the seminary training offered at St.
Augustine's Seminary in Bay St. Louis.

The pair of young priests bade farewell to Very Reverend Joseph
Grendel, S.V.D., their Superior General, and proceeded on a month-
long tour of the Divine Word mission houses in Europe. Reaching
the motherhouse in Steyl, Holland, on July 20, Carmen sat down to
write a letter of appreciation to Father Grendel in Rome. It ran:

Dear Father Superior General:

Before leaving Europe for America, it is only fitting that I
send you a letter of thanks and appreciation for the opportunity
you have given me to visit the larger Houses of the Society in
Europe.

It has been a very great pleasure and a source of edification
and inspiration to have been able to see and spend some time
at St. Gabriel's (Austria), St. Augustine's (Steyl, Holland),
and especially Steyl. We have been warmly received by our
confreres, and have been greatly edified by the conduct of the
Fathers and Brothers whom we have met here. I am very grateful for the opportunity to know and live with those of our

confreres who knew and lived with our holy Founder (Father Arnold Janssen). May a large portion of the good spirit I have seen here go with us to the American Houses.

The Oratory in the former room of our holy Founder is the best in Steyl; and I like most to be there when the older Brothers are present. Their life of prayer and work here has edified me more than all else I have seen in our Houses. Their piety, measured by their labor and self-sacrifice for souls, is indeed very great. I have always esteemed the life of our lay brothers, but now I realize that their material and spiritual help in saving souls is beyond all human estimation.

I had a chance to celebrate holy Mass at the Founder's grave last Wednesday. It was a great joy for me to be able to offer up the holy Sacrifice of the Cross so near the sacred remains of our holy Founder and confreres who have done so much for the Society. Among the latter I thought of Father Peil, who did so much for the American Province and for St. Augustine's Seminary.

We leave Steyl this evening at 8:30 for Bremen and sail in the afternoon of Friday the 21st from there. Once more I wish to thank you, Father Superior General, for all that you have done for me, and I trust that in September I shall be able to begin to work for the Society that takes such good care of me.

> Gratefully and obediently in Christ Jesus
> George Chachere, S.V.D.

There was no forewarning of tragedy ahead. Carmen rather looked forward only to the happiness of offering his first solemn High Mass in his home Church of the Holy Ghost in Opelousas.

His brother Earl, now on terminal leave from the Divine Word Society, was waiting at the station in Mobile, Alabama, when Father Carmen arrived by train from New York in early August. Together the two brothers traveled to Opelousas, anticipating the family reunion and the spiritual celebration in the home parish. Father Carmen stayed at home awaiting the big event scheduled for Sunday, August 5.

The night before the solemn Mass, however, Carmen wished to spend at the rectory close to the Blessed Sacrament for prayer and recollection. His request for this was not granted by the pastor Father William Long, C.S.Sp. Though friendly toward Carmen, Father Long was unaware of the deep spiritual yearnings of Father Carmen's soul. Father Long had already reserved the available rooms in the rectory for the visiting white priests who were coming for the ceremony. He accordingly was obliged to ask Father Carmen to continue residing with his family at their home, just a few blocks from the church on Prudhomme Lane.

It was a greater source of disappointment to Carmen when he learned that the pastor had raised the pew rent for the solemn Mass from a dime to a quarter. The pastor, however, expressly exempted from the charges all of the families of the Chachere relations, whose large number of children made the paying of the pew rent prohibitive.

Nevertheless, on Sunday, August 6, the Holy Ghost Church was crowded for the great event. Father Clarence Howard, S.V.D., was the deacon of the Mass, Earl Chachere was subdeacon. Monsignor Philip Keller, the German-born founder of Holy Rosary Institute in Lafayette, preached the sermon. Unwittingly, he too offended the family and many of the parishioners by stating during the course of the sermon that he wanted to see Father Carmen and the other colored priests depart for Africa's mission work. The people resented this. They wanted their own priests to stay and minister understandingly to their own spiritual needs.

Memories of Father Plantevigne hung heavy in the air after the Mass was over. Father Carmen exhausted himself by giving his individual blessing to hundreds upon hundreds of colored Catholics who had converged on Opelousas from all of the neighboring country, some from as far away as Pointe Coupee parish. Some visitors from north of Opelousas asked Father Carmen to come out to LeBeau, Louisiana, to say Mass for their parish.

Father Carmen requested permission of the pastor to oblige these good parishioners. To his great disappointment, this permission was denied.

Nevertheless, Father Carmen did make the rounds of the other colored Catholic churches in the vicinity. He kept continually on the road during the dog days of August, traveling up and down the county to call on old friends and relatives. He scheduled a Mass for the Nuns

of the Sacred Heart College in Grand Coteau, at their shrine-altar in
the room where St. John Berchmans had appeared to cure a dying
nun not long before his own canonization in 1888.

He also accepted an invitation to say the Mass of the Assumption
on August 15 at the Jesuit Church of Christ the King in Belleview,
not far from Grand Coteau.

The day before the fifteenth was sultry and oppressively hot. Father
Carmen had been out in the heat all day long. He spent himself to
meet the demands of his family and friends that he bless their houses,
their children, their aged, and their farms. He arrived home late in
the still-suffocating heat of the evening. He said his office and night
prayers and bade his mother good night.

In the middle of the night, his mother was awakened by a change
in his breathing in the next room. She heard a few long, heavy sighs,
as though he were struggling to catch his breath. She hurried to his
bedside. By that time, Father Carmen had stopped breathing and
had gone home to God. A sudden heart attack had snatched him away
without warning.

The tragedy was a sad blow to the parents and to the family, as well
as to Father Carmen's many friends in the United States and in Europe.
But the rumors that began to circulate soon afterward were an even
sadder blow. Echoing the case of Father Plantevigne, gossipers began
to build on the facts a whole fabric of imaginary events and explana-
tions. It was declared that he had been rudely refused permission to
say Mass even in the colored church in Opelousas, a patent falsification.
Other rumors exaggerated the conflicts between himself and the pastor.
Still others expanded out of all proportion the implications of the ill-
chosen remarks made during the sermon at the first Mass.

The report was spread that Father Carmen had wasted away from
grief and had died of a broken heart as a result of the mistreatment
he met when he came unto his own and his own received him not.
The rumors had reached such a pitch in the folklore of the people that
when the Myrdal investigators arrived on the scene the next year and
interviewed third- and fourth-hand transmitters of the legends, a
wholly distorted account was transcribed into the official records of the

historic Carnegie study of the Negro in America, much to the discredit of the Catholic Church.[3]

The plain facts, however, as faithfully reported by the eye-witnesses and by the immediate family, including the aged but alert Mrs. Ernest Chachere herself, simply recount a strange tragedy that struck a young priest who gave great promise of a successful career in the much-needed ministry among the Louisiana Creoles.

Some of the promise of that career has been realized in the person of his brother, Earl. He had not returned to St. Augustine's Seminary after his brother's funeral. In fact, he had decided to sever his connections with the Divine Word Society upon the expiration of his temporary vows in the fall. He had long realized that there was an urgent need for a sympathetic and appreciative clergy who would be sensitive and responsive to the special requirements of the ministry to the poor of the South. In the spring of 1939, notices were posted on the bulletin boards of the seminary, asking for volunteers for mission work in Africa. Father Bowers and Father Dauphine were announced as among the first volunteers. It became apparent to Earl that this meant something of a neglect of the missionary needs of the South itself, with its greater concentration of huge potentialities in the Negro apostolate. He saw too that if he took the perpetual vows of the Divine Word order, he would be liable to foreign mission duty without the formality of volunteering.

Consequently, he decided to continue his studies for the priesthood elsewhere. In June he was given leave to seek possible opportunities for seminary work. He unsuccessfully applied to a number of dioceses in the country. For a full year he kept up his efforts at securing admission to a seminary. His quest took him to Cincinnati and Detroit.

[3] The original report on St. Landry parish and Opelousas is such a patently slanted propaganda piece against the Church that no account was taken of it in the Myrdal study, *An American Dilemma* (New York: Harpers, 1942). The glaring inaccuracies and uncorroborated inconsistencies of the piece label it as the product of a diseased and prejudiced mind, bent on vilifying the Church. Father Earl Chachere gave a point-by-point criticism of it when it appeared in the Pittsburgh *Courier* and elsewhere some time later. Father James A. Hyland, C.S.Sp., the former pastor and well-known author also wrote a scholarly evaluation of the falsifications of fact and interpretation in the "report."

At this latter place, through the good offices of Father John Coogan, S.J., of the University of Detroit, Earl secured admission to Father Judge's newly founded home-mission group, the Missionary Servants of the Most Holy Trinity (M.S.S.T.). In 1940 he entered their novitiate at Holy Trinity, Alabama. There, after a year and a half of probation, he again pronounced the religious vows, in December, 1941. For the rest of the scholastic year he acted as prefect of the minor seminarians in the high school at Holy Trinity. Then he matriculated at Catholic University in Washington to complete his theological studies.

Taking classes at the Carmelite College (which was then in the same studies cycle he had left at Bay St. Louis), Frater Austin—Earl's new name—successfully completed his divinity course in the summer of 1944. However, he was obliged to wait another six months before ordination, which in the Trinitarians' order is customarily not conferred until after the pronouncing of the final vows. These Father Austin could not take until the full three years had elapsed since his first vows.

In December of 1944 he was allowed to pronounce the perpetual vows of the Trinitarians. A month later, on February 1, 2, and 3, he was ordained to the subdiaconate, diaconate, and priesthood in the National Shrine of the Immaculate Conception by Bishop McNamara, Auxiliary Bishop of Baltimore and Vicar General of Washington.

Braving the superstitions and fears of the Opelousas folk, Father Austin traveled to Holy Ghost Church for his first solemn High Mass on February 11, 1945. To circumvent the danger of inept remarks at the Mass that might duplicate the resentment created at Father Carmen's ceremony, Father Austin did not have a special preacher for the occasion. He simply spoke a few words himself and dispelled much of the tension of the day by his serene and relaxed calmness.

During his six months of waiting at Catholic University, Father Austin had done some undergraduate and graduate work in sociology, both to fill in his background for an apostolate in the South and to prepare for a possible doctorate in the field. He studied under Bishop Fulton Sheen, Doctors Furfey, Cooper, Parsons, and O'Connor and at length obtained a master's degree.

In the summer of 1945 he was appointed to the staff of the Trinitarians' magazine, *The Missionary Servant,* which had editorial offices at St. Joseph's shrine in Stirling, New Jersey. Besides his routine editorial work, Father Austin gave retreats at the shrine to many bands of pilgrims. He also traveled about the country giving mission talks, collecting donations for the Trinitarians' home mission work, and participating in many interracial activities as well. He gave some interracial retreats, and was even invited to give retreats to all-white groups in Brooklyn. He performed his sacred functions in nearby parishes like Plainfield and Summit, New Jersey, and traveled extensively through the South, visiting Mobile, Lafayette, Galveston, Houston, Port Arthur, and New Orleans in quest of aid for the missions.

Father Austin was very popular as a speaker and missionary. He had a pleasant personality, was mild-mannered in his approach to the thorny aspects of the racial issues, and had the ability to smile while meeting people and talking genially to them in cultured and easy-flowing language.

While he was in Mobile, Alabama, in 1947, I invited him to lecture at Spring Hill College, a 125-year-old Catholic college which had never before admitted a colored speaker to its classrooms or halls. Father Chachere carried the occasion adequately. He gave a well-planned but informal talk to the students on the race problem, and then willingly submitted to cross-questioning by the more aggressive of the college boys. Father Austin handled the prejudiced southerners with aplomb and suavity. He did not show irritation at even the most offensively phrased questions, but deftly responded in such a way as to disarm with his mild answers.

He also participated in our discussions at the Mobile Students' Interracial Council, composed of students from the college and colored veterans from the local Catholic Negro high school. There too he proved himself a genial diplomat in the handling of men and situations, and he successfully outlined a sensible program for betterment of racial relations in the tense Mobile area.

That summer his superiors offered him an opportunity to put some of these recommendations into practice. They assigned him to teach and prefect at the minor seminary of St. Joseph's School, Holy Trinity, Alabama. There was some diffidence about accepting the position on the part of Father Chachere. Some time before, certain church officials had objected to the admission of colored students to the Trinitarians' minor seminary at St. Joseph's, and had succeeded in securing the dismissal of two non-white boys on the grounds of avoiding trouble with the white citizenry and authorities in the county and state.

It was not known what attitude would be assumed toward the operation of St. Joseph's High School with an integrated faculty composed of white and colored priests. However, Father Chachere assumed his duties and was given the routine authorization to function as a Catholic priest in the Alabama parishes.

Parish work was the goal of Father Chachere's aspirations, as it is with many another priest who dedicates his younger years to work in the classroom. Father Chachere for two years performed the regular duties of a teacher of religion, English, and history to the high-school boys. He carried a heavy load of four to five classes daily and put in extra hours as assistant prefect to supervise the students in their recreational activities and study halls.

It became apparent to Father Chachere that he could not hope for parish work while he continued his connections with the Trinitarians. Accordingly, in 1950 he applied for incardination into his home diocese of Lafayette. Bishop Jeanmard accepted him provisionally and assigned him to establish a Catholic parish for the colored folks living in the small town of Port Barré, a score of miles east of Opelousas.

Father Chachere took leave of the Trinitarians and embarked on his new venture in the summer of 1950. By October of the same year a working agreement had been reached with the resident pastor of the Sacred Heart Church in Port Barré, which had been erected as a parish as far back as 1873. It had been a mission center for the smaller churches of the vicinity, such as that at Leonville some miles to the south. The crowding of the church by white parishioners and the exclusion of the colored from the parish school had contributed to the falling off of Negro Catholic attendance at the Port Barré institution.

Father Chachere began his pastorate by rounding up the lost and fallen-away Catholics of his group to attend the special Mass he offered for them in the big church at 7:30 A.M. on Sunday mornings, in between the two Masses for the regular congregation. The convenience of the hour led many white parishioners to attend Father Chachere's Mass as well, to receive Communion from his hands, and to approach him for confession. Within three weeks, more than sixty whites were in regular attendance along with hundreds of colored parishioners, now designated as members of "St. Mary's parish."

In the next spring a fortunate accident hastened the building of the new church for the colored congregation. There was a providential freight train wreck on the Missouri Pacific tracks near Port Barré, and one of the material casualties of the wreck (no persons were hurt) was a carload of cement. When the railroad officials wrote it off as a loss, Father Chachere quickly bought it up. The parishioners hauled the cement to the site purchased for the new church, and soon started the process of fabricating cement blocks for the edifice.

The building was begun in April, 1951, and, by dint of volunteer labor donated by the parishioners in the evenings and over weekends, the structure was roofed in before the fall and ready for Mass at Christmas.

The building of the living stones into the congregation still goes on. With his easy command of local dialects, Father Chachere travels up and down the Teche Bayou contacting the traditionally Catholic and French-speaking farmers of the large parish. He has gathered more than a thousand souls into his congregation, many of whom had begun to frequent the Protestant churches because of the lack of interest in their welfare on the part of the overworked pastors of the larger white congregation.

Some of his relatives had serious misgivings as to whether it was safe for Father Chachere, as a colored priest, to venture out into the rural areas among the prejudiced Acadians. There had been periods of intense racial strife in the area, with a lynching now and then to show the extent of white intransigeance.

The full measure of Father Chachere's acceptance by the community was reached one Saturday night. The pastor of the Sacred Heart Church had been away for a vacation and his substitute had finished his agreed days of service and left. Plans for the pastor's return had miscarried. It became apparent to the lay trustees of the parish that he would not be at the church for Sunday Mass. A committee therefore called on Father Chachere asking him to oblige them by saying Mass and preaching for them the next morning. Even though he could not accept the offer because of previous commitments at a nearby mission church in Randall, Father Chachere was gratified at this recognition that he, as a fully ordained Catholic priest, was acceptable to all of the Catholics of the area, regardless of color and racial differences.

After laying the foundations for St. Mary's parish in this substantial fashion, Father Chachere agreed to accept another similar assignment at Lawtell, Louisiana, where he is pioneering in the new parish of the Holy Family. His place at Port Barré was taken by a newly ordained colored priest, Father Louis LeDoux, whom the bishop appointed to the settled parish soon after his ordination.[4]

[4] Unfortunately, after this had gone to press, reports were received that Father Earl Chachere, as a result of a series of incidents in Lawtell, had been given an extended leave of absence from the Lafayette diocese. His mother and his brothers and sisters as well as his many friends and former parishioners are looking hopefully for his return.

CHAPTER XX

Bishop Bowers and the Africa Men

BISHOP JOSEPH O. BOWERS, S.V.D.
FATHER JOHN DAUPHINE, S.V.D.
FATHER GEORGE G. WILSON, S.V.D.
FATHER CURTIS WASHINGTON, S.V.D.
FATHER RICHARD WINTERS, S.V.D.

It was a historic day for St. Augustine's Seminary. On April 22, 1953, the first of its seminarians to be raised to the episcopate was solemnly consecrated as a Catholic bishop in Bay St. Louis, Mississippi. The presiding pontiff at the pageant-filled ceremony was Cardinal Spellman of New York, assisted by the same Bishop Gerow who had ordained most of the thirty Divine Word Fathers who had finished at St. Augustine's. A number of other bishops and dozens of clergy were also in attendance to witness this first elevation of a colored priest to the bishop's office since the days of Bishop Healy.

Bishop Gerow, however, had not ordained Bishop-elect Bowers to the priesthood. Though the tall, stately, ascetic-looking consecrand had finished most of his studies at Bay St. Louis, he had been sent to Rome in 1938 to finish his last year there. In company with Father Carmen Chachere, whose tragic end we noted above, young Frater Bowers had been ordained in the Eternal City on January 22, 1939.

As a young priest, Bishop Bowers had been missioned to Africa's Gold Coast colony. Thirteen years later, the Holy Father designated him first as Auxiliary Bishop of Accra, Gold Coast, and then just a few weeks later in February, 1953, had appointed him as full and sole occupant of the see of Accra to succeed his good friend Bishop Noser.

It was a meteoric rise for a brilliant young priest who all during his course of studies had given high promise of a bright career as a missionary.

The future bishop was a native of the island of Dominica, British West Indies. He had been born in the City of Mahaut, on March 28, 1910. His father was headmaster of one of the public schools in the city. He saw to it that his young son received an excellent education in the lower forms.

At the age of eighteen, Joseph Bowers entered St. Augustine's Seminary. As was the custom, he was at first tentatively enrolled in first-year high school to learn the rudiments of Latin. But Joseph was promoted a grade each day until he reached his level in fourth high where he really belonged. From that moment he consistently led his class, as he had done in Dominica, and soon received from the strict Fathers of the Divine Word the same sort of commendation he had been given in his report from the tropics. One of his teachers had written of him: "He has achieved wonders in the three years, and has reason to be proud of himself. One of the best scholars for his age in the school. He has made the most of his scholarship."

The humble seminarian was not vain about his achievements. He remained the unassuming, retiring and quiet scholar, somewhat bashful about appearing in public, even to recite his own poems or to play his own or classical music. On one occasion he wrote a well-constructed poem for one of the feast day celebrations. But he persuaded another seminarian to read it for him when the day came.

Young Joseph's mastery of languages, ecclesiastical and others, was sufficient to satisfy the college teachers at the Bay. In 1931 he was recommended for inclusion in the class of novices at East Troy. He returned to the Bay after his vows in 1933.

He sailed smoothly through the intricacies of philosophy. Often the teacher, after having thoroughly confused the class by erudite terminology, would call on young Frater Joseph to explain things. He invariably clarified the matter through his keen intellectual grasp of essentials, his expressive, British-accent diction, and his almost effortless command of the situation.

Some of his professors realized that studies came so easy to Joseph that he was liable to the dangers of laziness. They put extra pressure on him to keep his talents at full stretch. He was made organist of the novitiate choir in East Troy. He was given extra assignments in German composition. He was made available for tutorial work with the other seminarians.

Frater Bowers was also given a large share of the editorial responsibility for *St. Augustine's Messenger*. He did quite a bit of writing and rewriting in the popular mission magazine. In 1938 he wrote a capable overview of the work of the Catholic Church among the American Negroes under the title, "Early Evangelization of the Negro." In it he described the French and Spanish efforts in colonial New Orleans, especially the school established by the Ursuline nuns for colored students even before the Louisiana Purchase. The contributions of the Jesuits in southern Maryland, of Bishop Nerincx and Bishop Flaget in the Midwest, and of Bishop John England in Charleston, were cited as evidence of the paternal interest of the Church in the colored apostolate.

Later in the same year Frater "Joe" wrote "The Papacy and the Negro," a delightful story of Pope Pius IX and a New Orleans slave girl who was given a twenty-minute audience with the Holy Father when taken to Rome by her family, and who evoked from him a strong condemnation of both slavery and racism.

Two other articles appearing in the *Messenger* in 1938 were "Catholic Negro Education" (January), and "Negro Spirituals" (March). Another interesting article appeared two years later as a survey of the Church in the West Indies, "Our Colored Catholic Neighbors" (March, 1940).

Because of his skill as a writer, his high intelligence, and his deep spirituality, the Divine Word superiors had originally intended that the young priest, after his ordination in Rome, would spend some time at the seminary as a teacher. But Father (later Bishop) Adolph Noser, S.V.D., the American vicar-apostolic of the Gold Coast, had sent out an urgent appeal for American priests to aid him in his pioneer enterprise. As the former teacher of Father Joseph, Father Noser was anxious to secure his services in the mission field. Young Father Bowers volunteered for the African apostolate. He left St. Augustine's in the summer of 1939 for his new field of labor.

The mastery of the many native dialects of the Gold Coast was one of Father Joseph's first accomplishments. He moved about from mission to mission as assistant and supervisor before being made head of the Koforidua Church. He left this in March, 1948, to return to Rome for advanced studies in canon law leading to his doctorate in that subject in 1952.

During his Roman years, he had occasion to engage in the Catholic ministry in England and elsewhere on the continent. In 1951 he was assistant in a large white parish in Liverpool, England, conducted by the English Jesuits. He registered that as his most pleasant experience in the mixed ministry, with a special acknowledgment to the Society of Jesus.

It is significant that Bishop Bowers, after many years of experience as religious superior over communities of white priests, should be chosen as a bishop in the same month as another American-trained Negro was made Prime Minister of the Gold Coast colony. His consecration as a bishop on American soil represented not only the coming of age of the colored priesthood, but also the advancing maturity of the Catholic Church and its white hierarchy in the United States. Where twenty-five years ago it was debated whether the risks of ordaining colored priests were too great, it is now an accepted thing that the responsibility of the Catholic bishopric can safely be laid upon the capable shoulders of the well-tested missionary priest.

FATHER JOHN W. DAUPHINE, S.V.D.

1 9 1 0 –

A fellow classmate of Bishop Bowers who ventured out on the mission field of West Africa at the same time as the Bishop in 1939, Father John Dauphine remains there to this day as one of the bishop's most trusted lieutenants. In charge of the upcountry mission of Kwahu Tafo, the Louisiana-born priest has become acclimatized to the mission life. He has already served almost fifteen years on the various mission stations, being located at Nsawam during the war, a village about twenty miles from the capital of Accra.

The awakening of his love for the Church as a boy living in Sacred Heart parish in Port Arthur, Texas (whither his parents had moved from his birthplace, New Iberia, Louisiana), is told in his own words—written recently after an exhausting trek to mission outposts:

> The Rectory and the Church were my hangout places. There I could always be found. My mother often remarked that I should move my belongings there. My good pastor, Rev. J. A. Lally, S.S.J., who while stationed at the Holy Redeemer Church in New Orleans, La., sent several lads to the Seminary, thought he would try his hand here at Sacred Heart Parish, Port Arthur, Texas. So the first week of September, . . . the year being 1925, he told me to go home and inform my parents that he the pastor was sending me to the Seminary. That was startling news indeed. I ran home immediately, and managed to blast out in my excitement the words "St. Augustine Seminary, Bay St. Louis, Mississippi," all in one breath. The packing began immediately. A few days later, I bade farewell to my still bewildered parents, brothers, sisters, relatives and friends.

For the next six hectic years, young John battled his way through the stiff classes of the seminary, and endured the hardship and poverty of the young institution. "Often I felt like throwing in the towel," he wrote, "but God's grace, the prayers of my dear parents and friends, and the ever-encouraging letters of my pastor won out."

He returned home in the summer of 1931 after having received his diploma from St. Augustine's. Before the end of the vacation, he was informed that he had been admitted to the novitiate of the Divine Word at East Troy, Wisconsin. It was in the depths of the economic depression of the thirties. John did not have enough money to make the thousand-mile trip. In his dilemma, a good friend and former classmate came to his rescue. Thanks to his kindness, John was able to take the first step that led to his vows in 1933, to his minor orders in the Bay in 1937, and to his ordination to the priesthood on January 6, 1939.

In June, 1939, he went home to Port Arthur for his first solemn Mass and a vacation. At the end of this month's leave, he was notified that he had received a missionary appointment, along with Father Joseph Bowers, to the Gold Coast of West Africa. After two more weeks of vacation, he joined the superior of the mission, Father Adolph A. Noser, S.V.D., in New York. In his company John sailed from New York on September 5, stopping off at the motherhouse in Steyl, Holland, for six weeks. By December 5 the missionaries had reached Accra, the capital of the Gold Coast colony.

In the semi-modern little city, the Divine Word Fathers had taken over an old mission, first established in 1893, but later left without resident priests for years on end. Father Dauphine applied himself to the study of the difficult native Ewe language. After three months of hard work, he was able to hear confessions in the strange tongue. He was given faculties for confession and assigned to Adabraka, a suburb of Accra, where most of the Ewe people lived. He used his hard-won knowledge of that dialect for only a year. In 1940 he was moved out of Accra to Koforidua, a primitive village thirty-five miles upcountry from the capital.

Before leaving, Father Dauphine wrote an article about the new S.V.D. venture, "Catholic Mission to Accra." It appeared in *St. Augustine's Messenger* in October, 1940, and gave a detailed glimpse of the mission work in West Africa. It was instrumental in stimulating interest in and enthusiasm for the foreign service on the part of seminarians back home.

The mission at Koforidua was frontier work. Father Dauphine had to devote another quarter-year to learning the Twi language before he could start out on his rounds to the thirteen mission stations assigned to his care. By bicycle, he pedaled through hills and bush country for two and three weeks at a time. His treks took him out among the semi-literate people working the huge cocoa plantations of the tropical forests. It was pioneer work, and Father Dauphine measured up to the demands made upon his strength and his missionary spirit.

In 1943 he was transferred to Nsawam as assistant to his former prefect, Father Cletus Hodapp. In charge of eighteen mission stations, Father Dauphine continued the rounds of his new assignment with such success that he was made superior of the whole district in 1945. He took a special interest in the development and extension of the mission schools, he reorganized the Sodalities and the Legion of Mary, and even found time for war work with the American and British troops stationed in the vicinity, just a score of miles from Accra.

With seven straight years of mission work to his credit, Father Dauphine in 1946 was given his first vacation. He returned to the United States and spent several months with Father Vincent Smith in his Trenton Church of Our Lady of the Divine Shepherd. He toured the East and Midwest to preach on behalf of the missions, speaking in many all-white parishes like that of Medina, New York, where he was a guest of the pastor for several days. He was well received for his talks to the children, the Sisters, and the parish societies. He collected a good supply of money and books for the missions.

By March, 1948, Father Dauphine was back at work on the Gold Coast. His new assignment was that of superior of Koforidua, to succeed Father Bowers, who was going to Rome for his canon law studies. In August, 1950, he was transferred to Kwahu Tafo, where he is still stationed at this writing.

FATHER GEORGE G. WILSON, S.V.D.

1909 –

Another New Yorker, Father George Wilson, calls St. Joseph's Orphanage of Wilmington, Delaware, his home away from home. Born of Catholic parents, he was baptized as an infant in St. Vincent Ferrer's Church in New York. He had the misfortune to lose his parents when he was still a young child. The Sisters of St. Francis welcomed him to their orphanage in Wilmington, Delaware. There he spent his grammar-school years, growing up under the spiritual tutelage of the Glen Riddle Sisters, and of the Josephite Fathers who had charge of the nearby Church of St. Joseph, one of the first built by the Mill Hill Fathers in 1891.

In company with more than a hundred lads, George spent the years of his youth in an atmosphere of piety and devotion. For seven years he was an altar boy and an assistant sacristan in St. Joseph's Church. He writes of his response to the call of God thus:

> My vocation began to bud when I was fourteen years old. I used to help Sister in Church and I served Mass almost every day. Almost at the same time I wanted to be a missionary. I felt a great desire to bring others to Christ. And so it was that while in the Home, I selected some of the boys to form a religious society with the view of influencing for good the other boys.

George had gotten the idea of his band of youthful apostles while he was reading the boys' stories of Father Finn, *Tom Playfair* and *Percy Winn*. After the model of Father Finn's "Three Hail Mary Association," George conducted his group of classmates like a good spiritual leader. The Sisters knew that he was marked out for the priestly vocation.

In 1928 Sister Gildarda wrote to Father Christman at St. Augustine's Seminary, asking for admission of the budding apostle. George entered in the fall of 1928. He satisfied the authorities in the seminary, and in 1933 entered the East Troy novitiate, took his vows in 1935, and returned to the Bay for his six years of philosophy and theology.

He was especially devoted to one of his patron saints, St. Gregory, after whom his middle name was chosen. He wrote an article in the *St. Augustine's Messenger,* "Friends of the Holy Souls" (November, 1939), in which he described the tradition of the Gregorian Masses, a series of thirty consecutive Masses offered for the repose of the Holy Souls.

On January 7, 1941, George was given the power of offering these Masses for the dead and others for the living when he was ordained by Bishop Gerow in Bay St. Louis. He returned to his "Alma Mater" in Wilmington for his homecoming and first solemn mass later in the year. "Had I known the words of Al Jolson's 'Mammy,' I would have been tempted to sing it, for I was coming home to 'Mammy,' my dear old Alma Mater, St. Joseph's Home," he wrote later of his return.[1]

September of that year witnessed his departure ceremony for the

[1] "After Thirteen Years," *St. Augustine's Messenger* 20 (1942), 30-32.

missions. Father Clarence Howard preached the sermon for his farewell to St. Augustine's on September 28. Taking the mission cross, he set out for the long journey to West Africa. Of his missionary experience he modestly writes:

> My life out here for these ten years has been uneventful—the same as thousands of other missionaries all over the world. Out here I have been in charge of mixed congregations. I experienced no difficulty. I have been Superior over my white confreres in two large central stations. I experienced no difficulty. I cannot say more because there is nothing more to add.

There is much more to add about this strong, stocky, pith-helmeted priest as he plies his trade for God under the burning sun of West Africa. As one of Bishop Bower's strongest right-hand men, Father Wilson continues in his quiet and unobtrusive way to be a worthy member of that white-cassocked corps of apostles extending the frontiers of the Kingdom of Christ everywhere throughout the world.

FATHER CURTIS WASHINGTON, S.V.D.

1 9 1 7 –

Of the days of his youth, Father Curtis Washington, now a busy missionary in Bishop Bower's cadre on the Gold Coast, wrote as follows:

> We were called the five Washington brothers—Albert, Jake, Curtis, Alex, and Tom. We acted like the five Sullivan brothers who went down on that navy ship in the movie. We scrapped and "rocked it out" with the kids in the neighborhood, shot marbles, flew kites, and Dad tanned our hides plenty of times. Back in Coconut Grove, Florida, our class in school had lots of life. As normal American boys and girls, we sang, joked, and winked at each other. Our grammar school teachers liked us. But they saw to it that we got some useful knowledge into our heads.

It was one of these lay teachers in the public school who set Curtis' feet upon the paths that led to the altar. Mrs. Ethel Dunn, a convert to Catholicism, suggested to Curtis that he enroll in St. Emma's Military Academy, in Rock Castle, Virginia, when he finished grammar school in 1931.

She took him to Coral Gables to get a letter of recommendation from Father Thomas Comber, the Irish priest in charge of the mission there. It impressed Curtis that busy Father Comber devoted a whole hour to the task of finding out about his ambitions, his background, and his character, so as to make the letter a ticket of admission to St. Emma's.

So it turned out. In the fall of 1932 Curtis was welcomed to the military academy by the Benedictine Fathers, whose home monastery was at Latrobe, Pennsylvania. Curtis came to like the friendly priests and the congenial companionship of the Catholic lads. He drilled with them in the brown and gray uniforms of the cadet battalion. He went to Mass with them, sang their Catholic hymns and prayed their Catholic prayers too. He developed the habit of prayer. "There was one thing I used to like to do," he wrote later. "I liked to stay in church and pray one minute more after the Catholic boys left the Church after the five-minute noon visit. Father Banno, one of our teachers, once told us boys: 'Pray, my boys; don't forget Jesus so soon after you leave Church.'"

Curtis was not far from the kingdom of God. He was brought even closer when he met Mrs. Louise Drexell Morrell, the co-founder of St. Emma's. She came to the academy often, dressed in unostentatious and humble clothes. Curtis wrote of her:

> In her dress and way of action you could not tell that she was rich, for she looked very ordinary. She prayed much in our school chapel like a saint, and sometimes talked to us boys like a mother would. She gave us the lesson of being kind to other people, and she gave us an example of how to help people find God.

In 1933 Curtis asked to be admitted to the Catholic Church. He was baptized in St. Edward's Chapel in Rock Castle, and made his first Communion the same year. But his ambitions did not stop there. He secretly felt a desire to become a priest. His father had died in 1926. But when he wrote his mother about his new hopes, he received no encouragement from her or from his brothers.

In his anxiety, he confided in a schoolmate, Harold Woods, who was a native of Columbus, Ohio. Harold invited him to come home to Columbus for his vacations, and to talk to the kindly and spiritual pastor of St. Cyprian's Church, Monsignor Patrick J. Kilgallen.

Once his case was laid before the vigorous Monsignor, the bright-eyed youngster's difficulties vanished. Monsignor Kilgallen was happy at the prospect of having a seminarian which his parish could claim as its own and could support through his years of studies. He arranged for Curtis to enter second year high in St. Augustine's Seminary in September, 1936. Monsignor personally drove him to the station and put him on the train for Bay St. Louis.

By 1941 Curtis was ready for the novitiate. He entered St. Mary's Seminary in Techny, Illinois, just outside of Chicago, and took his vows there on June 23, 1943.

By 1949, when he was ordained on February 24, Father Washington had the happiness of seeing one of his brothers become a Catholic. Not long after his ordination, he personally baptized his mother and received her into the Church.

For his first solemn High Mass, he returned to Monsignor Kilgallen's Church in Columbus in July, 1949. As an expression of gratitude to the parish that had sponsored him, he sang a beautiful Mass, gave Communion and his blessing to the hundreds who crowded the little church on Hawthorne Avenue.

Soon afterward, he set out for the Gold Coast mission. He has spent himself in his study of the African languages and the culture of the people. His progress was so rapid that by 1951 he was made superior of the Koforidua Mission. Working among the natives of the Krobo tribe, he has the major responsibility for the thirty mission stations that he and his assistants visit and administer. For some of them, Father Washington is on trek for six or more hours, walking on foot to reach the inaccessible villages up in the mountains and deep in the tropical jungles.

He writes of his mission work:

Our present efforts in this West African Coast consist of pioneer missionary work. Our personnel is international. In fun-
damental undertakings, we are one in charity for God's
Kingdom. One can gain solid and deep knowledge about the
African, his language and his customs, should he put his heart
into the work and rely upon grace and prayer. . . . Presently,
one cannot gain this information from books, but he must
penetrate into the interior and see and learn the language.
Also, one must endeavor to Christianize some pagan customs.
The harvest is vast. There is no rest here for the missionary.
This missionary field is full of adventure and a great challenge
to young energetic American missionaries.

FATHER RICHARD WINTERS, S.V.D.

1911 –

Ranking before Father Washington in years of priestly service, but
after him in terms of foreign mission service, Father Richard Winters
departed for his work in Africa in the fall of 1952. He was assigned to
a newly opened mission area in the Belgian Congo, becoming the
second colored American priest after Father Adrian Esnard to venture
into that tropical harvest field.

Father Richard Winters and his brother, Father Arthur C. Winters,
S.V.D., are both products of the long and enduring influence of the
Catholic culture of eastern Maryland, where Catholic incorporation
of colored communicants into the churches dates back three centuries
to the colonial era of our country. This influence descended to young
Richard Winters through his mother, an ardent Catholic from Queen
Anne County, Maud Robinson Winters. His father, James Winters, did
not become a Catholic until a year before Richard's ordination.

However, James Winters did not interfere with his wife's efforts to
educate their children as Catholics. He allowed her to take Richard
out of the public school in their native Pleasantville, New Jersey, in the
fifth grade and send him to the Catholic School of the Holy Spirit in

nearby Atlantic City. There Richard completed his grammar school in 1925 and his high school in 1929.

Richard's desire to become a priest led him first to apply to the Josephite Fathers in 1929. He failed to meet their entrance requirements and so turned to St. Augustine's Seminary in Bay St. Louis, where he was welcomed in the fall of that year.

From then on his course was in the well-disciplined routine of the minor seminary and junior college at the Bay, the novitiate at East Troy (1933-35), and the major seminary work at Bay St. Louis (1935-41). He was ordained on January 6, 1941, and he returned to say his first Mass in St. Peter's Church in Pleasantville in June of that year. Father William Leroy Lane was deacon of the Mass, and Father Arthur Winters, then a seminarian, served as master of ceremonies.

The young priest returned to Bay St. Louis to teach in the minor seminary for a year after his ordination. He did some parish work in New Orleans and in Bay St. Louis, and found that his talents and desires lay in the direction of the active apostolate of direct contact with souls.

In August, 1942, Father Richard Winters was assigned as assistant to Father Rousseve in St. Martinville. For four years he took care of St. Anthony Church at Cade, and helped with the catechism and confessions and regular parish duties in the Evangeline City. In 1946 he continued this round of pastoral work at the Immaculate Heart of Mary Church in Lafayette under Father Bourges.

Finally, in 1950, he was established as pastor in his own right at Duson. For two years he guided the rural parish of more than a thousand souls, and its satellite mission of Scott, with its eleven hundred parishioners. He conducted the regular services in both places, teaching catechism both in his own school at Duson and in the all-Catholic public school in Scott, where he received excellent co-operation from the public school teachers and administrators.

Having proved his missionary capabilities in this rural area, Father Richard Winters was selected to inaugurate the new Divine Word mission in the Congo in 1952. He sailed overseas to follow in the jungle paths hewn out by Father Adrian Esnard in his forty-year apostolate in the Belgian tropics.

CHAPTER XXI

In the Pastor's Role

FATHER CHARLES CHESTER EVERETT BALL, S.S.J.

FATHER LEANDER JOSEPH MARTIN, S.V.D.

FATHER MAXIM ANDREW WILLIAMS, S.V.D.

FATHER ALEXANDER J. LEEDIE, S.V.D.

FATHER JOHN MARCELLUS FAUSTINA

FATHER HAROLD R. PERRY, S.V.D.

Vital to the discussion of the colored priesthood is the record that these men have made in their role as pastors of fully constituted parish churches. This core area of priestly activity is of central importance both to the Universal Church and to the local parishes. The problem of selecting the men to head up these life centers of Catholicism is the gravest one that faces a bishop in his diocese, or a superior of a religious order.

Many bishops and order superiors have had the courage to intrust the life of parishes to colored priests. We have seen how eminently successful two of the three Healy brothers were as full and independent pastors in Boston. We have also analyzed the reasons why Father Tolton's pioneer missionary parishes in Quincy and Chicago were not noteworthy as institutions in the frontier towns in which he had to work. Fathers Dorsey and Joseph John also had mixed experiences as pastors, their difficulties being traceable to the kind of personality differences among staff that could arise in any typical parish. Fathers Theobald and DuKette managed missionary parishes in slum areas that did not afford them much opportunity for spectacular plant-building or church development, such as Father Esnard was able to achieve in his parishes in the foreign mission field.

The record of the other priests to whom parishes have been committed is well worth examining. We will look briefly into the career of those who, up to 1953, had functioned as fully constituted pastors.

FATHER CHARLES CHESTER BALL, S.S.J.

1 9 1 3 –

Known as "Father Chet" to all of his friends in and about the national capital, Father Chester Ball is the first colored priest to be made a full pastor of a Catholic church in Washington. In 1952 he was appointed head of the Epiphany Church on the eastern side of Georgetown. Archbishop Curley had erected the edifice and intrusted it to the Josephite Fathers in 1925. They cared for the spiritual needs of the many hundreds of Catholic Negroes who lived in the old dilapidated sections of the Potomac River town that antedated the founding of the capital and was incorporated into Washington in 1895.

In the course of the past twenty years, with the rehabilitation of the historic neighborhoods of Georgetown, the colored population of eastern Georgetown has largely moved away. Epiphany parish church is attended by almost as many white Catholics as colored. Father Ball has thus been placed at the head of an interracial parish with full responsibility for the welfare of the souls of all his parishioners.

For this responsible task, Father Ball has had admirable preparation. He knows the racial folkways of Washington, having been born in the District of Columbia on October 11, 1913. His father, Joseph A. Ball, was a non-Catholic from Annapolis who had married a devout Catholic from the southern Maryland town of Upper Marlboro. Mary Katherine Ball carried her baby boy to the parish church of St. Augustine's in Washington to be baptized in the same month in which he was born.

Young Chester grew up in the shadow of St. Augustine's, making his first Communion there in 1921 and being confirmed in 1923. He finished his grammar school education under the colored Sisters, Oblates of Providence, in 1927. He then enrolled in the Dunbar Public High School, which he attended until 1931. For two years, in the depths of the depression, he enrolled for classes at Miner Teachers' College in Washington.

All during these years, ever since he had been a faithful server at the altar in St. Augustine's, Chet had secretly hoped to be a priest. He studied Greek under Father George Rankin, who, together with his pastor, Monsignor Alonzo J. Olds, encouraged the young lad in his ambition. The colored Sisters at St. Augustine's also kept alive the spark of desire for the priesthood.

In the early thirties, Chester applied for admission to the ranks of seminarians studying for the archdiocese of Baltimore. Father Rankin interceded for him. But the church authorities rejected his application. Chester accordingly sent off his application to six other neighboring dioceses, all with the same negative result. He finally applied to Father Pastorelli, the superior of the Josephite Fathers, and was accepted for admission to their seminary in Baltimore in September, 1933.

At the end of his first year in the seminary, he returned to Washington in time to participate in the celebration of the first solemn High Mass by Father Francis Wade, S.V.D. Chester was master of ceremonies for the occasion. The fervent reception of their own priest by the happy parishioners gave new impetus to Chet's determination to proceed to the altar for ordination.

In July, 1934, the new novitiate of Mary Immaculate was opened in Newburgh, New York, not far from Poughkeepsie. Chester was with the first class that entered the new house of studies. Next year, on July 16, he made his profession as a Josephite.

For the six following years, Chet was a secluded seminarian at St. Joseph's Seminary in Washington, pursuing the sacred studies along with the other seminarians in their own college and in Catholic University nearby. He was enrolled as a student in Catholic University a full year before the new administration "officially" reopened the university to colored students. They had been tacitly excluded since 1922.

On June 10, 1941, the twenty-eight-year-old seminarian was ordained to the priesthood by Bishop McNamara at the National Shrine of the Immaculate Conception on the grounds of Catholic University. The following Sunday, his first Mass was solemnly offered in St. Augustine's Church. Father DuKette was deacon, Father Terry Evans, a white priest, was subdeacon.

All through his seminary years, Father Ball had aspired to a career as a pulpit orator and platform speaker. Toward this end, he enrolled for the summer's institute in preaching at Catholic University, and for other courses in the speech department. His Josephite superiors facilitated the development of his native talent both before and after ordination.

His first assignment as a new priest was to the post of assistant pastor in St. Joseph's Church in Wilmington, Delaware. Given a cordial reception by the bishop, Rt. Rev. Edmond J. Fitzmaurice, Father Ball served for three years under the benign and paternal guidance of the veteran pastor, Father John Neifert (who was to meet a tragic death at the hands of a demented slayer in New Orleans ten years later).

In St. Joseph's, Father Chet was prefect of the school and taught classes there in religion. He said Mass often in the white churches of St. Mary's and St. Ann's, heard as many whites' confessions as colored, and generally achieved a genial acceptance in a city that was noted for its southern exposure.

With St. Joseph's as his base of operations, Father Chet ranged far afield on his speaking engagements. He gave days of recollection in Philadelphia. He preached for special occasions at St. Mark's in New York. He gave a series of sermons in the environs of Boston, at Mattapan and Peabody, Massachusetts. He delivered the oration for the first Mass of white priest friends of his on Long Island and at McKees Rock, near Pittsburgh. He gave a mission to a mixed congregation at St. Bridget's in Indianapolis.

In 1943 Father Ball was assigned to a mission church of his own at Glen Arden, Maryland, about four miles from the District of Columbia line. Formerly attended by a Catholic University Scripture teacher, the modest little church had been frequented by the rural colored Catholics since 1922. Glen Arden itself was an all-colored town, incorporated in 1939, and numbering about 1,500 citizens, of whom more than a third were Catholics.

Father Ball, during this period as pastor of St. Joseph's Church in Glen Arden, signed up for graduate courses at Catholic University. He secured his master's degree in speech in 1949, with a minor in psychology. He taught speech in the Josephite Seminary, along with his parish duties, and found time for numerous excursions to lecture and preach up and down the Atlantic seaboard.

As he became integrated into the clerical life of the archdiocese of Washington, Father Ball came to be accepted on equal terms with the other priests. He maintained cordial relations with Archbishop Patrick A. O'Boyle, being selected as one of his personal chaplains for the archdiocesan pilgrimage to Rome in the Holy Year of 1950. In Europe, Father Ball accompanied the Washington delegation wherever it went. Oftentimes he offered Mass for the entire party of 242 pilgrims. He participated in the archbishop's official procession when the pilgrimage made its formal entry into St. Peter's in Rome. At the audience with the Holy Father, Father Ball was personally presented to the Pope, Pius XII.

In Washington, Father Ball's church was considered one of the regular stations on the archbishop's confirmation tour. In 1950, a typical year, forty-five fellow priests attended the confirmation ceremonies at St. Joseph's. For the Forty Hours' Devotions, another thirty-five priests returned. At the silver jubilee in 1947, sixty of the clergy were on hand, Bishop Sheehan of Baltimore pontificating, and four purple-gowned monsignori adding color to the ceremony.

All in all, Father "Chet's" uneventful reception at the hands of the Washington clergy has been a running commentary on what may have been over-caution on the part of the former archbishop's advisors who refused to consider Chet's candidacy for the diocesan priesthood in the ranks of the Washington-Baltimore clergy.

Father Ball has not been intimidated by those who warned him against venturing into the South for preaching and mission work. He has given retreats, missions, and sermons below the Mason-Dixon Line as well as above it. He has preached in Memphis; South Union, Kentucky; Richmond; Bay St. Louis; San Antonio; and St. Augustine,

Florida, where he filled the pulpit in the Cathedral for a sermon before the Federated Colored Catholics Convention.

This wide experience made him the logical choice when there was question of appointing a new pastor for the Josephite Church of the Epiphany in Georgetown in 1952. Able, self-possessed, unafraid, Father Ball pursued in Epiphany the same duties as before, shuttling back and forth across Washington to teach at Catholic University and at the Josephite Seminary. He makes weekly trips to Baltimore to teach psychology and catechetics to the colored Sisters, the Oblates of Providence, at St. Francis Academy. He is currently planning and writing a *Manual of Homiletics* in conjunction with Father Thomas O'Donnell, C.S.C., of the Holy Cross Seminary at Catholic University.

Nor does he sidestep the frank and open discussion of the race question in the midst of the tense situation in the riot-marred capital city. He has lectured the Catholic University seminarians (as at Holy Cross College) on the problem, and has been a featured speaker at Friendship House several times, helping them toward a more constructive program in the promotion of better interracial understanding.

There was nothing strident or off-key in his approach to the problems we discussed in Washington. Father Ball has seen great progress in the Church's race relations in the span of his lifetime in Washington. Under the forceful and vigorous leadership of Archbishop O'Boyle, he has seen the opening of the formerly exclusive white parochial schools to the colored students of the neighborhoods. He has seen the white colleges and universities of the District let down the bars against colored Catholic collegians. He has witnessed the integration of colored Catholic children into the child-care institutions, and colored patients into the general facilities for formerly segregated hospitals.

Finally, his adjustment to the clerical life of Washington has encouraged the archbishop to open the ranks of the diocesan clergy to colored candidates. At this writing, at least one native colored Washingtonian is studying for the diocesan priesthood in one of the nearby seminaries.

It is a tribute to the expansive good will of Father Chester Ball that this last move has been taken in an area where the move was unthinkable in his own case just twenty years ago.

FATHER LEANDER JOSEPH MARTIN, S.V.D.

1 9 0 5 –

Another successful pastor of a thriving colored parish in southern Louisiana, Father Leander Martin has emerged from a background of more than a century of colored Catholicism in the Evangeline country.

As far back as 1821, Grand Coteau was the site of a well-established Catholic center—the Convent of the Sacred Heart nuns, founded by the intrepid French religious who followed in the footsteps of Blessed Philippine Duchesne. In line with her traditional concern for the spiritual welfare of the colored children in the rural areas, the Ladies of the Sacred Heart maintained a school for these youngsters in conjunction with the Academy for the daughters of the planters in the area.

It was to this vicinity that the Jesuit missionaries were also attracted more than a hundred years ago. In 1837 they laid the groundwork for St. Charles College and set the stage for what would later become the novitiate for the Southern Province of the Society of Jesus.

In this milieu of a thoroughly Catholic culture, Leander Martin was born, April 8, 1905, in a sharecropper's cabin down in the bottom land below Grand Coteau (the great Hill). Prairie Bas, as the rural community was called, was a part of the Catholic parish of Grand Coteau. Thither Leander was brought for baptism next month by his Catholic parents. They raised their family of ten children as Catholics. One of Leander's sisters entered the novitiate of the Holy Family in New Orleans, as did many of the colored girls raised in the Sacred Heart School.

In 1911 Leander joined his sisters and brothers in the little grammar school, making the two-mile trip over the rolling hills each day for classes. Just as the devout girls were encouraged by the Sacred Heart nuns to become Sisters of the Holy Family, the devout boys were urged to enroll in St. Augustine's Seminary after it was established in Bay St. Louis. In 1924 a small group of Grand Coteau boys joined the class at the Divine Word minor seminary. Next year, Leander Martin sent in his name to the institution and signed up to study for the priesthood.

Like many another minor seminarian, Leander found the course of studies, especially Latin, to be rugged. He nevertheless persevered through the discouraging grades and the overstrictness of some of the professors. His innate goodness of soul and his love of the religious atmosphere of the seminary revealed to the seminary teachers that he was chosen by God to be a priest.

In 1933, after completing his course at Bay St. Louis, he journeyed to East Troy, Wisconsin, for his novitiate, and two years later pronounced his vows as a Divine Word religious. The next six years were spent at Bay St. Louis, knuckling down to the abstruse difficulties of philosophy and theology. Leander endured it all for the sake of the priesthood, though, like other hopefuls whose hearts were set on saving souls, he often wondered what on earth the technicalities of some of the theological theses could possibly contribute to the love of God and the good of souls.

In 1941 Bishop Gerow ordained him to the priesthood. He returned to St. Peter Claver Church in Grand Coteau for his homecoming as a priest. His old pastor, Father Weckx, was his deacon, and other Jesuits from the novitiate filled the sanctuary for the first Mass of their first colored priest from their parish in Grand Coteau.

His apprenticeship as an assistant lasted seven years. In 1941 he served a few months at Duson, Louisiana. From 1942 to 1948, he was an assistant to Father Rousseve in St. Martinville. Finally, in 1948 he was made pastor at Duson, and in 1950 moved to Immaculate Heart of Mary Church in Lafayette as full pastor.

It was there on the semi-rural outskirts of Lafayette that I met Father Martin in 1951. I was his house guest during the time that I did a survey of the south Louisiana missions and interviewed all of the colored priests laboring there. Father Martin was a cheerful, obliging, and generous host. He motored me around the area, introduced me to all of the other priests, and went out of his way to be of service.

In thus traveling around with him, I came to understand how well accepted he was as a priest, in a Catholic region. We drove into filling stations manned by white attendants. Invariably, they tipped their hats to "Father" Martin, before asking for his order. At another garage, the mechanics (all whites) were having an argument about a marriage case. When Father Martin came in to see about his car, they turned to him for the answer, just as they would have to any other priest.

About the parish, he is revered as *"le bon père,"* and is greeted by his white and colored parishioners with the "Mawnin', Father," and the *"Bon jour, mon père,"* that alternate in the neighborhood.

Both clergy and laity in the diocese recognize him as the man of God that his years of piety and prayer have made him. He possesses that indefinable something which characterizes the true priest of God. His parishioners view him as a sincere and dedicated apostle who doesn't know what a clerical vacation is, and whose idea of a rest is an eight-day retreat in silence and prayer.

Father Leander Martin holds his own among the clergy of the diocese. He has given papers at the clergy conferences both in New Iberia and in Grand Coteau. At the diocese-wide celebration on the feast of Christ the King each year, when more than 25,000 of the faithful gather at Grand Coteau, Father Martin has been subdeacon to the bishop at the altar for the main services. Along with the other clergy, he has been invited to dinner in the Jesuit novitiate in Grand Coteau.

With the sisters of the diocese, Father Martin has likewise achieved a notable acceptance. He is of course welcome thrice over at the Holy Family Sisters' high school at Grand Coteau. He has often given talks there and in Breaux Bridge. The white Sisters of the Blessed Sacrament in Lafayette have often invited him for Mass, as have the cloistered Carmelites in their modest chapel.

The measure of his success, and of that of the other colored pastors of the diocese, has been the bishop's move to accept other priests of color into the ranks of the diocesan clergy. Already one has been admitted (Father Chachere), and in December, 1952, the first diocesan seminarian was ordained as a priest for the diocese of Lafayette—Father Louis LeDoux.

Through it all, Father Martin remained the humble, reticent, and unostentatious religious, reluctant to receive even this much recognition for his faithful cleaving to his round of duties as a priest. But I for one was a stronger and more determined priest after contact with these genuine men of God, of whom Father Martin, in all of his simplicity, is a typical example.

He was also typical in the simple obedience he manifested when in the summer of 1954 his superiors decided to transfer him to Father Wade's place as pastor of St. Joseph's Church in Maurice, Louisiana. There he continues the same round of parish work that had been his daily chore at the big Lafayette parish.

FATHER MAXIM ANDREW WILLIAMS, S.V.D.

1 9 1 1 –

Ordained in the same class with Father Leander Martin, Father Max Williams is the first native colored Mississippian to be raised to the priesthood, as well as the first Divine Word Father of the United States from a Divine Word parish.

St. Rose of Lima parish in Bay St. Louis claims Father Max as its own. He was born within its confines in 1911, but at that time the Divine Word Fathers had not yet taken over the mission. Max was baptized in the big church of Our Lady of the Gulf. He attended school in the small mission school erected by the pastor of that church, and also in the Valena Jones Public School.

In 1923 his family moved to New Orleans. There Max completed his grammar grades at Bienville School, and matriculated at Craig School for his first-year high.

In 1925, deciding to become a priest, he returned to Bay St. Louis and finished his high school at St. Rose of Lima, taught by the Sisters of St. Joseph from New Orleans. In 1928, with the encouragement of his pastor, Father Baltes, S.V.D., he entered the seminary of St. Augustine. His course was a routine one for the seminarians in the now well-established patterns: novitiate at East Troy, philosophy and theology at the Bay, ordination finally in 1941.

During his seminary years, he took an interest in writing for *St. Augustine's Messenger*. At least one of his poems was published before ordination. He continued his writing after embarking on the active ministry. Completing his first assignment as assistant in St. Peter Claver Church in Brooklyn, he returned to Lafayette to serve as one of the staff at Immaculate Heart of Mary Church. For four years he kept close to the parish routine, organizing the Catholic Boy Scouts, establishing the parish credit union, serving as assistant editor for the *Colored Man's Friend*.

He wrote of the mission work in south Louisiana in the *St. Augustine's Messenger,* for which he also contributed articles on a variety of topics such as "Barthe, the Sculptor."[1]

In 1945 he journeyed to Rochester, New York, with Father Ford, to work among the neglected colored residents of the city with a view to initiating a new parish for them. A survey of the situation convinced the missionaries that there was a good prospect for a parish if a church could be built at a convenient point between the two large colored neighborhoods. But funds were withheld from the Society for the Progagation of the Faith on the assumption that there were not enough Negro Catholics to justify the expense; there was also danger of being charged with perpetuating a practice of segregation in the other churches of the area.

Father Williams shuttled back to the South for another tour of duty, this time as assistant in St. Martinville, 1946-48. A sudden vacancy, occurring in the Trenton diocese because of Father Leedie's illness, brought Father Max back to the North for a seven-month stand at Asbury Park, New Jersey. He finished out the school year of 1948-49 in the half-Negro, half-Italian parish, and then returned to the seminary at Bay St. Louis for a year of work as a teacher in the minor division.

For the term 1949-50, Father Max taught high-school Latin, Greek, mathematics, history, and geography. It looked as though he had become indispensable to the school, with classes in all of the four years

[1] *St. Augustine's Messenger,* 20 (September, 1942), pp. 175-77.

of high school. But next year again, he was given a different assignment.

Where Father Leander Martin had been given charge of a fully constituted parish, Father Williams was appointed pastor of a non-extant one in Washington, Louisiana, a small town in St. Landry parish, some five miles north of Opelousas. Father Max was authorized to found a parish for the colored Catholics of the town and the surrounding rural area. It proved to be a challenging task.

Washington is on the upper fringe of French Louisiana, a "Yankee" town settled mainly by the westward migrants from the Protestant areas of the South. Mingled with the Protestants are a great many French Acadian-Americans who have spread out from the coastal area and the Bayou country.

An estimated five hundred colored Catholics lived within the boundaries of the parish assigned to Father Max, almost 150 square miles. Of these, less than fifty had been attending Catholic services at the predominantly white church. Neither the white nor the colored children had the advantage of a local parochial school.

Father Williams assumed the task of rounding up the stray Catholics. He soon recruited between 250 and 300 parishioners. He conducted a special Mass for them in the big church at 9:00 A.M. on Sundays. The convenient hour attracted some white parishioners as well. Father Williams accommodated both in his ministrations.

His first three months were a period of real hardship. He resided with a poor family on the colored side of town, not at the white priest's rectory even when saying Mass in his church.

For nine months, the dual Mass arrangement persisted at the Immaculate Conception Church. Finally, after erecting a combination church and rectory building on the colored side of town, Father Williams was able to open the doors of his own parish church and set himself up as a pastor in his own right.

Since that time (June, 1951), Father Max has continued the slow task of building the living stones of the parish. He has to contend with the strong influence of the colored Baptists, who in the course of the last few generations have weaned hundreds of families away from their allegiance to French culture and Catholic antecedents. The fact that the Catholics represent less than 10 per cent of the colored population of the town adds to the difficulty. The prejudice of the majority is a hindrance to the work of conversion as well as to the return of those who would lose face with the community for their "relapse" into Catholicism.

But as of this writing, Father Max is well on his way toward duplicating the work of restoration that is quietly going on throughout French Louisiana. As a priest among his own, his chances of success are immeasurably greater than those of the outsider and the representative of the majority group.

FATHER ALEXANDER J. LEEDIE, S.V.D.

1 9 1 2 –

Another capable and efficient priest who gave great promise of a long career as a responsible pastor was tall, genial Father Alexander Leedie.

A New Yorker, born and raised in Mount Vernon, New York, Alexander Leedie applied for admission to the archdiocese of New York upon the completion of his high-school education in 1929. Though he had attended Catholic grammar school at St. Peter's in Yonkers, he had been obliged to do his secondary school work at the public high schools. He made a brilliant record at the Nathaniel Hawthorne Junior High, at Yonkers High, and at Haaren High School.

The story goes that he applied for the privilege of taking the entrance examination for the archdiocesan seminary in New York, and was allowed to take the test along with the rest of the candidates. Leedie scored a higher grade than any of the others, according to the report, but was refused by the seminary authorities in 1930. He accordingly enrolled in St. Augustine's minor seminary in Bay St. Louis.

In the regular program of seminary training, Frater Leedie often outdistanced his fellow students. He made his vows in 1936 and was advanced to holy orders in October, 1941.

At the time of the National Eucharistic Congress in St. Paul, Minnesota, in June, 1941, Frater Leedie was chosen to represent the Divine Word seminarians in the mission booth in the exhibition hall. He made a fine impression on the swarms of visitors who stood to listen while he explained the work of the S.V.D. missions. He returned to St. Augustine's to write a glowing account of the Negro apostolate in Minnesota, which was published in the *St. Augustine's Messenger* during the same month in which he was ordained.

Next year, he again showed his talent as a journalist by writing a research paper on the centennial of the Sisters of the Holy Family, founded in 1842 by Josephine Alicot in gratitude to God for her rescue from the waters of the Mississippi by a colored man.

As a young priest, Father Leedie served for two years as assistant in the Immaculate Heart of Mary parish in Lafayette. In 1944 he was transferred to Asbury Park, New Jersey, in a like capacity. While serving in St. Peter Claver Church, he became interested in the amelioration of the conditions of youth in the city. He was a member of the Juvenile Delinquency Board and helped straighten out many young people whose adventurousness had enmeshed them in the toils of the law.

In the heat of the summer of 1948, Father Leedie overworked himself in caring for his charges in Asbury Park, and suffered a partial stroke that hospitalized him for more than six months.

Upon his recovery, he was transferred to Trenton to be administrator and later pastor of Our Lady of the Divine Shepherd Mission, a seven-nationality parish in the slums, just four blocks from the Trenton Cathedral. He was officially appointed pastor of the church on September 1, 1949. His assistant was a white priest, Father John Kist, S.V.D., who as a seminarian had studied at St. Augustine in Bay St. Louis and had been ordained there along with the colored candidates for the priesthood.

Father Leedie proved himself an able and energetic pastor during his years in Trenton. He maintained his membership in the Catholic Interracial Council of New York, and constantly accepted invitations to speak at special functions designed to improve race relations in the New Jersey metropolis.

Overwork again brought on a stroke in late 1952. Father Leedie was obliged to take an extended sick leave in order to recover his health.

But he is still remembered as an impressive orator and a fine leader. The Negro picture magazine, *Ebony,* chose him as a typical (and photogenic) representative of the fast-growing body of colored priests who were stepping up the Catholic Church's appeal to the intelligent colored leadership in the country. His friends in New Jersey look forward to his return to active duty there.

FATHER JOHN MARCELLUS FAUSTINA

1 9 2 0 –

Father "Ted" Faustina is one of those priests that you like right from the first. At least, that was my experience when I first met him in Mobile, Alabama, in 1947. He had just been ordained by Bishop Scully in the Cathedral of Burlington, Vermont, and had hurried down to his birthplace for his first solemn High Mass. At the time, I was teaching at the then all-white college at Spring Hill, which has since admitted a dozen Negro students. I attended his first Mass with a group of college boys who were active in the interracial club.

We could not help sense that the parish of the Heart of Mary was proud of this their first priest. The church was crowded beyond capacity for the long ceremony. The choir sang as I had never heard them sing before. Father Howard's eloquent sermon pointed up the deep significance of the day. And Father "Ted," a picture of serenity and at-homeness on the altar, sang the Mass with a pure, clear, and exultant voice.

After the Mass and the almost endless new-priestly blessings, we met him in the circle of his family. He struck me as the kind of colored priest that more of us southerners should know: a devout, gentle, deeply good priest, with the face of a perennial altar boy and the unabashed sincerity of a dedicated soul. I was impressed with his gentle, quiet, and cultured manner, his patently shadowless faith, and his level and untroubled gaze. He had a broad sympathy and an understanding of human nature, both of which contributed to the fact that he did not go into any racist tantrums upon his return to the Deep South.

Father Faustina understood both the white clergy's predicaments and his own. He accepted the status quo with the all too patient forebearance with which the long-Catholic colored minority tolerates the overly racist respect for the color line on the part of some white Catholics.

I called upon him and his family at their home in the colored neighborhood of Mobile. It was a modest frame building located on an unpaved side street and fenced in with the typical wooden picket fence to keep stray dogs out of the flower garden. On the porch was sitting his aging mother, a benign matriarch whose eyes still twinkled with the satisfaction of seeing her son at last a priest of God. Her one regret was that her husband, Gilbert Faustina, had not lived to see the day. He had died in 1941, after forty years of married life in which they had raised to adulthood nine of the ten children that had blessed their home.

Gilbert Faustina had come originally from New Orleans. His ancestors were of many nationalities, all European. But because of these latter, he was considered a Creole, and segregated along with others of his class and caste. He was proud of being an American, first, last, and always. Once a filling station attendant sought to Jim-Crow him, with the querulous question, "What are you, anyway?" Gilbert answered, "I am an American, just like you are."

He had an American ambition to make good in life. Paid off one day for his work as a youngster in a cigar factory with a couple of hands of tobacco leaves (the cigar-maker did not have any cash on hand), Gilbert made some cigars, sold them, bought some more tobacco and out of that small beginning built up an independent and prosperous business as a cigar-maker.

In 1900 he had met and married Susie Ritter Kirkland, a Mobile Creole Catholic, of mixed ancestry. On the white side, she was related to the old southern Scotch-Irish family of the Kirklands. Her mother had been of mixed Negro and Creek Indian provenience.

In the forty years of their married life they had six boys and four girls. The first girl died at the age of three years. But all of the other children survived and are still living in various parts of the country. One of the girls, Irene, married a brother of the Fathers Chachere. Another, Frances, after finishing her college work at Xavier in New Orleans, was assistant librarian at Spring Hill College in Mobile, and later at Loyola University in Los Angeles and at the veterans' hospital medical library at Long Beach, California.

The Faustinas named their last son John Marcellus when he was born in Mobile on August 29, 1920. During the years when he was growing up and attending the parochial school in the Heart of Mary colored Catholic parish on Davis Avenue, his father was achieving national prominence among colored Catholics as one of the founders of the Knights of Peter Claver. Together with Father Conrad Rebescher, S.S.J., and Father Thomas Daly, S.S.J., Gilbert worked out the details for a Catholic fraternal order designed along the lines of the Knights of Columbus. The segregation laws of the South prevented colored Catholic laymen from joining or participating in meetings and socials with the white Knights of Columbus. Gilbert traveled all over the South and East to recruit members for the new organization. As a token of their esteem for his leadership, his fellow colored Catholics elected him as their first Supreme Knight, an office he fulfilled with dignity and courage for many years.

Along with his fellow colored Catholics, Gilbert realized the need for colored priests. But he also recognized that a vocation to the priesthood was the work of the Holy Spirit. He therefore did not try to dictate to any of his sons what they should do with their lives. But when his youngest son responded eagerly to the religious influences of home, church, and school, and began to show signs of a genuine vocation, Gilbert was more than pleased.

When he was in his second year of high school, Ted asked for and received his parents' permission to go to the St. Augustine's Seminary at Bay St. Louis. In the fall of 1935 he began the strict classical course that the Divine Word Fathers taught with German precision and discipline. In his four years with the Divine Word priests, Ted secured a solid foundation in the Church's own language and in the rudiments of seminary life. However, he did not feel called to the foreign missions. Upon the announcement in 1939 that all of the Divine Word sem-

inarians would be expected to hold themselves in readiness for overseas duty, Ted began to seek a seminary that would train him for the
much-needed home missions of the South.

The Society of St. Edmund, popularly known as the Edmundites,
accepted his application for admission to their seminary at St. Michael's
College, Winooski Park, Vermont, in the fall of 1939. A career with
this religious order of French origin seemed to offer promise of mission
work among the colored of the South. The Edmundite Fathers have
more than fifteen missions in Alabama, some of them, like their mission on Mon Luis Island, ministering to the colored people and Creoles
of the area.

Ted was in his second year of college when he transferred. In an-
other few years he had secured his bachelor's degree *cum laude* at St.
Michael's. He pronounced his first vows in the Edmundite order on
August 15, 1941. Six years later he was ordained, on April 12, 1947,
by the Coadjutor Bishop of Albany, pontificating in the Cathedral of
Burlington.

After his ordination, Father Ted returned to St. Michael's College to
teach. As an accomplished musician with years of experience in the
organist's position, Father Ted was assigned to train the college musi-
cians, along with his other classes. He faithfully fulfilled his duties for
three years, all the while hoping for a parish assignment or some mission work. When it became apparent that the Edmundites did not intend to appoint him to any parochial duties in the South, Father Ted
requested exclaustration papers.

He took leave of the Edmundites in early 1951, being accepted as a
parish priest in Winslow, Arizona, by the Bishop of the Diocese of
Gallup in New Mexico. He was later assigned to the parish of St.
Joseph in Williams, Arizona, where he is still laboring among the
Mexican-Americans at the present writing.

He still retains his convictions as to the need of a well-trained colored
clergy in the country to offset, among the Negroes, the common impression that the Catholic Church is mainly a white man's church, unable
effectively to cross the color line.

In discussing the lack of appeal of the Catholic Church to educated
Negroes, Father Ted once wrote that the main reason was that

the Church has never been represented in an appealing way to this group. In fact, the Church has not been represented to them at all, only misrepresented. . . . A great deal of this is due to the continued lack of a native clergy. The ultimate goal of the (white) missioner is to make himself unnecessary, to develop a native clergy in the place he converts. This goal has been pursued with great zeal in all foreign missions, and though there may be added complications, it should not suffer exceptions in the colored missions of this country . . . The upshot of the whole thing, is, of course, not to cast any aspersions on the white missioner in the South, for the most part zealous and holy, but to plead, day in and day out, for a bolder policy on the part of the American hierarchy toward the obtaining of a Negro clergy. This is something that can be neglected no longer. Too much depends on it.

FATHER HAROLD R. PERRY, S.V.D.

1 9 1 6 –

Another colored priest recently appointed (1952) to the responsibility of an independent and newly established parish is Father Harold R. Perry, pastor of St. Joseph's Church in Broussard, Louisiana, with the mission of St. Anthony's parish in Cade, not far from St. Martinville. He is one more priest whose vocation was grown in the Catholic gardens of south Louisiana and who has now returned to cultivate those spiritual acres anew.

His home in Lake Charles was providentially located just across the street from the Sacred Heart Church. The Holy Ghost Fathers had founded a separate parish for the colored members of the Immaculate Conception Church shortly after the first World War. Harold had been baptized in the former church, but his youth was woven around the newer church and school.

To the zealous pastor, Father A. J. Hackett, C.S.Sp., young Harold owed the earliest inspiration toward the life of the priesthood. Father

Hackett, as pastor of Sacred Heart Church, taught catechism to the school children during the early 1920's. He distributed among the boys the vocational pamphlets put out by St. Augustine's Seminary. He opened up for their minds the whole realm of hitherto unexplored possibilities for pursuing a vocation in God's service.

Harold grew up as the oldest of a family of six children. His parents, Frank and Josephine Petrie Perry, carefully nurtured his desire for the priesthood. But when he finished grammar school in the depression of 1930, they could not see their way toward financing his seminary years. In this impasse, Father Bernard Hannigan, C.S.Sp., came to Harold's rescue. He agreed to pay the tuition for the first four years. His application was sent off to the seminary. He was welcomed in the fall of 1930.

The Blessed Sacrament Sisters also helped their prize pupil in his preparation for the seminary. Sister Camilla, who had taken a special interest in his vocation, bought him the clothes he needed, packed his trunk, and even added a dozen superfluous pairs of long brown stockings. The seminarians, even those in short pants like young Harold, had scant use for long stockings because they constantly fell down while the boys were at play.

Harold was good in sports. He played basketball, baseball, and volleyball along with the best in the seminary. He sped serenely through his years of preparation both in the Bay, at East Troy, and at Techny, where he took his vows in 1938.

In the early forties, while studying theology, Harold also assisted Father Howard with the writing and editing of *St. Augustine's Messenger*. He contributed a number of historical articles dealing with some of the early African saints, like St. Moses the Hermit, and with the canonized Martyrs of Uganda.

On January 6, 1944, he received priestly orders at the hands of Bishop Gerow. He was assigned as an assistant in Lafayette during the following summer, later served in a similar capacity at St. Peter's Church in Pine Bluff, and in Notre Dame Church, St. Martinville. Before being given his present position, he had assisted Father Bowman at Mound Bayou for almost two years.

Father Perry has been active in giving retreats and missions in the

South and Midwest. When I encountered him in St. Louis in 1952, as he was on his way to give a mission in Omaha, I was very favorably impressed with his quiet self-assurance, his clerical *savoir-faire,* and his unalloyed and clear-eyed sincerity. In smiling he lighted up with an inner glow that manifested the unruffled charity of his interior life. I could not help wondering how men, when confronted with the obvious priestly holiness of deeply religious souls like Father Perry, could ever give any credence to the widespread and oft-repeated notion that colored lads could not become good priests.

Father Perry and his confreres, in their capacity as pastors of souls, have demonstrated their competence. Their parishioners' undisguised happiness at having their own competent priests is further rebuff to the baseless supposition that Negro people do not want their own priests.

CHAPTER XXII

Abbot Alcuin's Alumni

FATHER BARTHOLOMEW SAYLES, O.S.B.
FATHER HARVEY (WALTER) SHEPHERD, O.S.B.
FATHER PROSPER (EDWARD) MEYER, O.S.B.

The role of Abbot Alcuin Deutsch in the development of colored priests in the United States is a significant one. Head of St. John's Abbey and St. John's University in Collegeville, Minnesota, the abbot had been forthright in verbalizing the sane stand that seminary rectors and religious order superiors should take.

"The color of a man's skin," Abbot Alcuin said in 1945, "has nothing to do with the quality of his mind or his special bent. If a Negro priest of the Benedictine Order is the best man to teach some subject in our seminary, our college of arts and sciences, or our preparatory school, he shall become a member of the faculty. If he is suited to our administrative work, there he shall be. If he is qualified, he shall become a retreat master, or give retreats and missions in parishes. He might be sent as a missionary among Indians or other Negroes. But his spiritual and intellectual qualities, not his color, shall determine what he is to do, or where he is to go."

The men of God whom Abbot Alcuin turned out at St. John's bear testimony to the effectiveness of this ennobling and inspiring forthrightness in facing the issue on which so many others weakened and compromised.

FATHER BARTHOLOMEW (JOHN B. LETORY) SAYLES, O.S.B.

1 9 1 8 -

Outstanding among the graduates of St. John's Benedictine Seminary in Collegeville is Father Bartholomew Sayles, a priest since June, 1948. An accomplished musician in the best Benedictine tradition, Father Bartholomew has secured recognition in Catholic circles as an exponent of church music and its place in the liturgy. He has studied and taught at the famous Pius X School of Liturgical Music, at the Loras Liturgical Institute, at the University of Notre Dame, and at other colleges and universities besides St. John's.

His rise to fame is closely bound up with that of the renowned Xavier University Choir of New Orleans, whose accompanist he was during his years as a student at Xavier. He was student director of the Xavier Glee Club from 1937 to 1939. He also participated in concerts by the Male Octets at Xavier. During the 1938 National Eucharistic Congress in New Orleans, the Xavier student had much to do with the musical aspects of the program.

A native of New Orleans, he was born in Corpus Christi parish on April 24, 1918, the son of George Sayles and Evangeline Letory. His parents took him to the Holy Ghost parish for baptism on May 12, and he was given the name of John Bruno Letory Sayles. John grew up in Corpus Christi parish, at the time the largest Negro Catholic parish in the world, boasting of more than 20,000 members. He attended Corpus Christi Grammar School on St. Bernard Avenue and made his first Communion in the somber, devotional, Spanish-Mission style church.

Like Father Rousseve, John matriculated at Xavier Preparatory School on Magazine Street in uptown New Orleans, and daily made the hour-long crosstown trip for classes, being excluded from at least three closer Catholic high schools that did not admit colored boys.

In 1935 John entered Xavier University and embarked on the musical career that was to open up into a lifework for him. He had become a musician on a challenge. There was a young girl in his neighborhood who began taking music lessons and putting on airs of superiority over the other youngsters. John did not like the idea of letting a mere girl get ahead of him, so he decided to become a musician himself, and mastered the intricacies of piano, violin, cello, and organ within a few years.

Working for his bachelor of arts degree, John steadily registered excellent grades. His teachers regarded him as one of the most talented and outstanding music students in a school that had a high proportion of musical geniuses.

He was graduated with honors in June, 1939, winning the gold key of the Alpha Epsilon fraternity.

That summer, while still under the influence of the magnificent pageantry of the National Eucharistic Congress of the previous fall, John enrolled in the ranks of the aspirants for the priesthood at St. Augustine's Seminary in Bay St. Louis. He carried on his work as a musician. He was made director of the choir, organist for the seminary, and leader of the glee club. He became the favorite entertainer for the seminarians, giving two- and three-hour piano concerts in which he displayed an amazing repertoire of classical and liturgical music, as well as modern forms.

There was not too much prospect that his musical talents would be utilized to the full in the missionary work of the Divine Word priests. In 1941, consequently, when he was advised to leave the novitiate at Techny after spending some time there, he sought admission to the ranks of the religious order which was the faithful promoter and custodian of the treasures of church music and liturgy.

Abbot Alcuin Deutsch readily accepted John's application for admission to St. John's College in Minnesota. He entered the novitiate at St. John's Abbey in July, 1943, and four years later pronounced his solemn vows on July 11, 1947. By October he had received clerical tonsure and minor orders, and by December the subdiaconate.

In the meantime, he had become a member of the faculty, teaching music both in the Abbey and in St. John's University.

The following summer, June, 1948, he was ordained to the priesthood.

He returned to New Orleans for his first solemn High Mass in Corpus Christi Church on June 13, 1948.

In the years since that time, Father Bartholomew (the new name John took upon becoming a Benedictine) has remained at St. John's Abbey in Collegeville, filling the post of organist for the Abbey and the college students, teaching music and heading up the department of music there, and participating in the monastic *schola* and in the majestic chanting of the divine liturgy that has made St. John's famous all over the world.

Summers usually take Father Bartholomew away for special sessions in church music and liturgical life. He is in demand as an authority on Gregorian chants and other ecclesiastical forms. He is an interesting, if subdued, teacher, winning his students more by the quiet power of his talent as a musician than by any pyrotechnics.

As a member of the Music Teachers' National Association and of the Catholic Choirmasters' organization, Father Bartholomew smoothly carries out Abbot Alcuin's well-reasoned directives. An accomplished priest-musician, the young Benedictine is freely functioning in the realm of sacred music without any reference to color bars or racial distinctions. He has moved at ease in the society of his professional equals. His achievements have been an inspiration to the many other colored students and seminarians at St. John's and elsewhere. Shunning publicity (even to the extent of not wishing to be included in this series of sketches), Father Bartholomew continues to live the life of a Benedictine monk, retired from the world, dedicated to the cultivation of the things of the spirit, and participating in the grand Work of God that is the fully enacted liturgical life.

FATHER PROSPER (EDWARD) MEYER, O.S.B.

1 9 1 2 –

The first of Abbot Alcuin's colored seminarians to be ordained as a priest was Father Prosper (Edward) Meyer, who reached the sacred goal in the summer of 1947. I met him down in Mobile, Alabama, shortly before his ordination. He had made the journey from College-ville to be subdeacon for the first solemn High Mass of his former schoolmate, Father John Faustina.

Frater Prosper, on the eve of his ordination, was a gaunt ascetic-looking monk, deeply serious and religious, patently devout at the altar during Mass, and quiet and modest in his social dealings with the clergy and the parishioners. Like Father Faustina, Frater Prosper as a young boy had entered St. Augustine's Seminary in Bay St. Louis for his high-school work.

Some four years before, young Edward (Prosper's baptismal name) had mentioned to his father that he desired to be a priest. The father objected so strongly that he took Edward out of school altogether, though he was only in the fourth grade. His father was a Catholic. But his objection was based on the fact that he was the only boy left in the family, his other brothers having died. Edward was obliged, the father reasoned, to stay home, learn his bricklayer's craft as an apprentice and help support the family.

Edward complied with his father's demands for three years. Finally, with the help of Monsignor Joseph Shorter, pastor of Holy Epiphany parish in Leavenworth, Kansas, Edward was able to re-enter the parish school. His father warned him that he would disown him completely if he abandoned his trade and resumed his schooling. Nevertheless, Edward, feeling himself called to the priesthood, went ahead. The re-sult was a complete estrangement between father and son. This per-sisted up to a short time before his father's death in 1938.

Notwithstanding his three-year absence, Edward was soon able to catch up with his fellow classmates in school. This progess was pos-sible because of the extra help that was given him every day during the noon recess period by Sister Cyrilla, an Oblate Sister of Providence. She sacrificed her free time every day for months in order to assist Edward to catch up in his back work.

Meanwhile, because of the grave disagreement with his father, no money was forthcoming from home for his expenses. Edward went to work to earn his keep and to pay his school expenses. Each day before and after school, and all day Saturday, he worked for a local grocery store in Leavenworth. Summers, he worked during the harvesting of the wheat, riding the binder and shocking wheat. He also picked up a few dollars here and there by cutting grass and cleaning house for people. He wanted to be a priest and he knew he had to work hard if he was going to stay in school long enough for that.

The ambition had come to him when he was just a ten-year-old in the fourth grade. He was working one day for a non-Catholic woman at the time. One day she asked him what he intended to do when he grew up. Without hesitation, he answered, "I want to be a priest." The good Protestant woman was extremely shocked at the statement. So was Edward. He had never given a thought to the priesthood up to that time. To this day, he does not know why he blurted out that answer to a question that should have evoked the response, "I want to be a brick-layer like my father."

Nevertheless, that was the turning point in his life. His new desire was nurtured and kept alive by his daily attendance at Mass. He used to serve Mass for Father Kalina at 6:30 A.M. in Holy Epiphany Church. As assistant to Monsignor Shorter (who said Mass in the orphange for colored boys five miles out in the country), Father Kalina aided the pastor in encouraging Edward's holy ambition.

In 1935, hearing of the ordination of the first colored graduates of St. Augustine's Seminary, Edward prevailed upon Monsignor Shorter to open the way for his admission to the ranks of the seminarians. The good pastor wrote a high testimonial to Edward's fine moral character, his piety, common sense, and personal conduct. Edward was readily admitted to the seminary. He stayed until the issue of the foreign missions in Africa led many of his companions to seek admission to other seminaries. Like them, Edward wanted to labor in the United States.

In the interim, Edward stayed at home to help support the family. His father had been seriously injured in a fall from a scaffold in the early spring of 1937. He lingered on until June 14, 1938, when he died, fortified by the last Sacraments. During all this time Edward worked to pay the bills. After his father's death, his mother had a nervous break-down and had to move to Houston, Texas, to live with her oldest sister. When she returned to Leavenworth in the spring of 1939, Edward began negotiations for matriculating at St. John's University in College-ville, Minnesota.

His attention had been called to this possible opening by Sister Baptista, one of the Sisters of Charity of Leavenworth. She read about Abbot Alcuin's policy in regard to the race question; she knew that Edward was having difficulty in finding a seminary; so she gave him Abbot Alcuin's name and address. A letter soon brought a promise of welcome. On June 21, 1939, Edward entered St. John's. He was the first colored lad to enter the university for the purpose of studying for the Order.

It is a credit to Edward's quiet and unassuming ways that the tone of unruffled acceptance of other colored students was set once and for all on the college campus. He turned down a chance to pass for white when he entered. The doctor giving him his physical examination entered "white" in the space on his card that designated race. Edward told him to write "Negro" instead. Without being a rabid "race" man, Edward was determined to face the facts of life and master them.

His years as a student at St. John's were uneventful. Edward was the key man in the induction of the other colored students who matriculated at the college. Some came with the preconceived notion that prejudice must be expected. Edward soon set them right. There was no prejudice among the students at St. John's, and Edward would not permit either himself or others to interpret as racial prejudice what was just the normal interplay of personalities on a college campus. Even when the abbot vigorously corrected him during the public reading in the dining room (as he corrected other students), Edward learned to take it in good measure.

In time, Edward applied for and was admitted to the novitiate, was given the religious name of Frater Prosper, took his vows, and was advanced to sacred orders. In June, 1947, he was ordained to the priesthood, and he returned to Holy Epiphany Church in Leavenworth for his first solemn High Mass. One of the Benedictines from St. John's came down to preach for the occasion. The colored parishioners redecorated the church, painting it anew for the first Mass of their first priest. Father Prosper had the happiness of giving his blessing to his mother and his two sisters.

Father Prosper gave his blessing also to the mixed congregation (about half white, and half Negro), and after the Mass spoke glowingly of his gratitude to God for the grace of ordination, and his appreciation of the help his parents and his other relatives had given him. One couple in the parish had postponed their baby's baptism for more than half a year so that Father Prosper could baptize it for them.

After ordination, Father Prosper did not long enjoy the equable peace of St. John's Abbey. There was a need for more priests in the Benedictine missions of the Bahamas. Father Abbot called in Father Prosper one day and asked him if he would like to go to the British West Indies. "Well, Father Abbot," he said, "I'll go if you send me, but I don't want to stay!" Though he had his heart set on playing a part in the founding of a new interracial monastery at South Union, Kentucky, Father Prosper went where he was missioned: to Nassau, in the Bahamas.

As of this writing, Father Prosper is serving as assistant in St. Francis Xavier's Church in Nassau, and as chaplain of the Nassau Prison. He is living at the Benedictine Priory, which is a dependency of the larger Monastery of St. Augustine in Nassau. The quiet and productive work of the Benedictines in the Bahamas was given great publicity a few years ago when "The Great Heart of Cat Island" was written up in one of the nation's leading magazines. This biography of Monsignor John C. Hawes, the famous architect, caught a good glimpse of the possibilities of the missionary apostolate in the islands. While his career as a missionary is just beginning, Father Prosper can look forward to a fruitful ministry among people whose culture still bears the imprint of Catholic Europe.

FATHER HARVEY (WALTER) SHEPHERD, O.S.B.

1 9 1 4 –

More than any of his other alumni, Father Harvey Shepherd has carried Abbot Alcuin's ideal of co-racial unity into the region which most needs it—the South. Under Abbot Alcuin, the monks of St. John's

Abbey in Collegeville had developed a greater mission-mindedness than ever before. They had opened missions in the Bahamas, in Puerto Rico, Mexico, and Japan. In 1948, at Abbot Alcuin's instigation, a new foundation was opened in western Kentucky in the diocese of Owensboro. After a preliminary foundation at St. Denis near Fancy Farm in the westernmost extremity of the state, the little group of monks moved to South Union to open St. Maur's interracial priory.

It was here in the land of Jim Crow that Father Harvey Shepherd and his fellow Benedictines began to put into practice Abbot Alcuin's indomitable stand against all schisms in the Mystical Body because of color or race.

By a strange coincidence, St. Maur's occupies buildings that were formerly a Shaker-Quaker community, founded in the early part of the nineteenth century by the Society of Friends' offshoot. The property still goes by the name of Shakertown, but it is a different society of friends which occupies the land. The Shaker's "Center House" has been converted into the Benedictine Priory, housing the white and colored monks and the seminarian candidates for the monastery. In this two-story structure, the large rambling layout affords ample room for the small community, its chapel, chapter room, monastic cells, and refectory.

Off to itself is a larger, three-story building that is destined to house retreatants or major seminarians in the future. There is also a spacious guest house where traditional Benedictine hospitality is practiced.

But the central idea of St. Maur's is to create a replica of the Christian religious family bound together in the unity of Christ's Mystical Body, without regard for racial divisiveness.

In creating this example of Christian harmony in a land torn by race hatreds, Father Harvey Shepherd has had a significant part. As a member of the faculty and principal of the minor seminary, Father Harvey contributes to the practice of the ideal of co-racial unity. He joins the other monks on a basis of full equality for divine services and for the administration of the house and school. He does his best to duplicate for the young candidates the same experience of prejudice-free pursuit of priestly ideals which he enjoyed during his years of training. Like Fathers Bartholomew and Prosper, Father Harvey began his training in the South at St. Augustine's Seminary, from which he was graduated in 1938. He too had been born in New Orleans (January 31, 1914), and had been baptized as a cradle Catholic in St. Francis de Sales Church, receiving the name of Walter Augusta.

After the opening of the Holy Ghost School on Louisiana Avenue, Walter attended class there for eight years, from 1921 to 1929. Chicago was the scene of his secondary studies, pursued in a public high school while he worked at odd jobs to support himself. He gained a livelihood by working in a five-and-ten store in Chicago for fifteen dollars a week, and in a restaurant for even less. One of his public school teachers wrote of him as a "reliable, industrious, and honest boy, who will take any obligations seriously."

All through these years, the desire to become a priest had been in the back of his head. He wrote of his vocation:

> As far back as I can remember, I always wanted to be a priest. My mother seemed happy at this choice. And throughout my youth she never permitted me to forget my first choice. Whenever I mentioned another vocation, she would always say, "I thought you wanted to be a priest." Perhaps, it was her good prayers that led me to St. Augustine's in Mississippi and to St. John's in Minnesota.

In 1936 Walter returned to the South from Chicago to enter St. Augustine's high-school department for his last two years of high school. He continued his education at Xavier University upon graduating from St. Augustine's in 1938. His father (a convert) had meanwhile died, and Walter went to work in New Orleans to help support himself, his mother, and the other three children in the family.

It was during this period that he worked as a janitor in the main building at Loyola University, Marquette Hall. Here he talked over his vocation problems with the Jesuit Fathers. Thanks to the encouragement and direction he received from Fathers Hatrel, Butt, Harty, and O'Brien, he applied for admission to the St. John's Abbey in Collegeville, whither they had directed him. In the fall of 1939 his acceptance came through. He entered the sophomore class at St. John's University. The next year he became a Benedictine novice, receiving the religious name of Harvey. Six years later he pronounced his solemn vows.

Together with Father Bartholomew, he was ordained to the priesthood on June 6, 1948. His first Mass was celebrated three weeks later in the Church of St. Alphonsus in Fresno, California. His mother had gone to live with his younger sister in the Far West, and she welcomed him to this second home for the climax of all of her aspirations. She had only one more prayer to be answered—that her son would offer the requiem Mass for the repose of her soul when she went to God. Three years later that prayer was granted. In September, 1951, God called to Himself this saintly mother of a good priest. Father Harvey reached her deathbed two days before the end. He gave her the last Sacraments, said the prayers for the dying, and fulfilled her wish by offering the Mass of the Dead for her soul.

In the interim, Father Harvey, after a year at the Abbey, had been missioned to Kentucky to join Father Alexander Korte, O.S.B., in the foundation of St. Maur's Priory, a pioneer foundation which Father Alexander planned as an example of the fullness of the life of the Mystical Body. In laying the solid groundwork for the institution, Father Alexander often said, "We don't want to do anything outstanding—we only want to do what is right."

One commentator wrote that St. Maur's was urgently needed because of the "rancid facts" that white priests outnumber colored priests by a thousand to one; that forty-seven diocesan seminaries, 285 religious seminaries, and 209 congregations of nuns cannot make up their minds whether or not they should admit Negro candidates.

By 1950 the foundation had prospered to the extent of attracting two novices, five new candidates, one professed lay brother, one oblate, one brother novice, and two brother candidates.

The impact of St. Maur's on the surrounding neighborhood was reported thus: "In a quiet way, we have already, through our small beginning, changed the attitude of many Catholics and non-Catholics in our neighborhood on the race question. We hope to expand our influence and to penetrate more deeply into areas which have an even greater need of some powerful force to leaven the whole mass."

While the Trappist Monastery at Gethsemani, Kentucky, through its admission of Father Vincent Smith, S.V.D., in 1948, followed close upon St. Maur's pioneering, the credit for being the first interracial school in Catholic Kentucky goes to the latter. Other Catholic schools soon followed its example. Two Catholic girls' colleges in Louisville opened their doors to colored students within a year. Schools of nursing and even high schools are also beginning to incorporate colored Catholics into the hitherto all-white institutions in Kentucky.

Father Harvey's writing of this project of biographical sketches, gave me an insight into the spirit in which St. Maur's has approached the problem:

> My suggestion is to take a positive approach, indicating in every way the absolute normalcy on the part of superiors as regards Negro youth studying for the priesthood, stressing the notion that the Negro candidate is accepted in communities and seminaries in the same manner as any other priesthood candidate. By writing in this light, we avoid antagonizing those of our Faith for whom the Mystical Body is not a living thing. This in only my opinion—based on a few years' experience with white southern Catholics who are won over more by a positive teaching than by explicit pointing out of unchristian traditions.

CHAPTER XXIII

College and Seminary Teachers

FATHER HERMAN (MARTIN) PORTER, S.C.J.

FATHER WILLIAM ADAMS, S.V.D.

FATHER ARTHUR C. WINTERS, S.V.D.

FATHER JOSEPH ABEL FRANCIS, S.V.D.

In line with the erudite tradition begun by Father Sherwood Healy as vice-rector and professor in the Troy Seminary during and after the Civil War, a number of other colored priests have served and are serving in the useful capacity of college and seminary professors. At the same time that Father Sherwood Healy was teaching diocesan seminarians in Troy, his brother, Father Patrick Healy, was also conducting philosophy classes for the Jesuit seminarians and the lay students at Georgetown.

A generation later, Father Uncles spent his active years as a teacher in the Josephites' minor seminary, and Father Burgess also tutored the minor seminarians in the Holy Ghost College in Cornwells Heights, Pennsylvania.

Father Christman envisioned a three-year period of teaching as a regular part of the seminary training for his colored protégés in the Divine Word Society, just as it is a part of the formation of the Jesuit seminarians elsewhere. In accordance with this plan, Fathers Smith and Rousseve both taught the minor seminarians at Bay St. Louis for one year before beginning their major seminary work in 1928. Others of the colored clergy have also taught in college and seminaries: Father Earl Chachere in the Trinitarian Seminary in Holy Trinity, Alabama, and Father Sayles in Collegeville. A group of the younger colored priests is at present engaged in this important work. We will briefly review their life and work in this present section.

FATHER HERMAN A. (MARTIN) PORTER, S.C.J.

1 9 1 4 –

The first thing that impressed me when I encountered Father Porter at his temporary post of assistant in St. Joseph's parish in Saginaw, Michigan, was the marked contrast between the man and his pictures. From his published photographs, I had gotten the impression that he must be a rather stern and stiff personality, a bit on the somber side, with a cheerless and depressed attitude toward life. I had seen this often enough in people who have suffered the stunning and numbing blows that racial prejudice delivers.

But Father Porter turned out to be a genial host. He smiled easily, and his eyes lighted up with a whimsicality that lent a mellow and pleasant tone to his countenance. Far from being stern, he was frank, matter-of-fact, and open-faced in his approach to the problems that I presented to him. He talked intelligently and with a smooth flow of English, the mark of his graduate training at the University of Notre Dame. He struck me as being a secure, self-possessed, and deeply religious person, awake to the social issues that confront the Church in present-day America, but still able to keep a level head and make a balanced judgment in areas where overemotional extremists often lose their sense of proportion.

His was the story of a convert who felt ineluctably drawn to the priesthood, and who followed his vocation notwithstanding the many barriers artificially thrown in his way.

Strangely enough, his good mother was the first obstacle both to his entry into the Church and to his following of his vocation to the priesthood. He was an only child of Shirley Porter and Ellen Moreland Porter, born February 8, 1914, in Winterville, Mississippi. His mother was a strongly religious Baptist. She trained her only son carefully and scrupulously during his childhood in nearby Greenville, and in Toledo, Ohio, whither his family moved in 1920.

It was in Toledo that Herman first became interested in the Catholic Church. He attended a Catholic school there. His contact with the Sisters engendered within his soul a desire to become a Catholic. Upon asking his mother's leave, she urged him to postpone his decision until he was grown up.

In 1928, when the family moved back to Greenville, Herman made a mission in the Divine Word Father's Sacred Heart Church. It was conducted by Father Joseph Eckert, S.V.D., famed as an apostle to the Negroes. He made an indelible impression on Herman. The youngster became more determined than ever to become a Catholic. He read many Catholic books, starting with one on the Negro Dominican, Blessed Martin de Porres.

From 1929 to 1933 Herman attended high school in Greenville, keeping alive his desire to become a Catholic. It was only upon completion of his secondary education that his mother allowed him to follow his desire. He approached Father Charles Wolfe, S.V.D., and began to take instructions. He had the happiness of being received into the Church in 1935.

Even before his baptism, he had felt a further desire to become a priest. At another mission, this desire crystallized into a resolution. In 1937 Fathers Vincent Smith and Francis Wade gave a stirring week's revival at St. Elizabeth's Church in Chicago, whither Herman had moved in 1935. Father Smith's glowing oratory penetrated to the deeper reaches of Herman's soul. From then on, he wanted nothing so much as to be a holy priest like Father Vincent Smith. He continued a life of prayer and good works in St. Elizabeth's, teaching catechism to the school children and helping around the parish to deepen his determination to become a priest.

At the time it seemed impossible. His mother's frail health blocked the way. She depended on her only son to support her in her widowhood. Herman loved her too much to leave her alone at home. He stayed faithfully with her for two years after his baptism. She died peacefully on November 2, 1937, a victim of a brain hemorrhage.

After her funeral, Herman finally felt free to pursue his vocation. But obstacles of another kind began to block his way. He sent off his application to St. Augustine's Seminary late in 1937, backed by his pastor, Father Thilges of St. Elizabeth's Church in Chicago. Father Thilges wrote of him: "Now a long time since he has been longing to begin his studies for the priesthood, but could not do so because of several obstacles. With God's help he has overcome these and then began to take private lessons in Latin. . . . His progress was so remarkable that he will be qualified to enter third year Latin at St. Augustine's. In the parish he has proven himself to be a young man of good character and solid piety."

Herman returned to his native state to enter the seminary at Bay St. Louis in September, 1939. By this time, he had completed a year's work in normal college, and was much more advanced than the others in the minor seminary. He had been given to understand that St. Augustine's made special provision for belated vocations. Unfortunately, he found that he would have to follow the regular high-school courses in Latin all over again. He therefore stayed only a few months.

Returning to Chicago, he entered Loyola University in September, 1940, upon advice of Father Arnold Garvy, S.J., a well-known figure in the colored apostolate in Chicago. While at Loyola, Herman decided he would like to join the Jesuit order. His spiritual father, now President William Hussey, S.J., encouraged him to apply for admission. Father Egan, the socius to the Father Provincial, espoused his cause. But his application was turned down. Father Egan even tried to secure entry into the New England Province of the Jesuit order, which had admitted a number of Jamaican Negroes. But Herman's plea was not heeded in Boston, though possibly his rejection was owing mainly to the extremely high educational requirements both in Boston and in Chicago, and not exclusively to color prejudice.

Upon the accession of Archbishop (now Cardinal) Stritch to the episcopal throne in the archdiocese of Chicago, Herman made a personal application to him for admission to his seminary. The archbishop received him in a kindly manner, but told him that nothing could be done for him until he had received his college degree. This was but the final shutting of the door that had been closing on him in 1937 when he first asked the rector of Quigley Seminary for admission there, and had been rejected because he was considered too old to attend the high-school classes with the minor seminarians.

Similar disappointments faced him as he sent more than two dozen petitions to as many seminaries and religious orders. Often the answer bluntly stated that the only reason for his rejection was his race. But Herman persevered. He told himself that this was *not* the Catholic way, this was *not* the Catholic Church, but was only the manifestation of the vagaries of certain clergymen. Others of the clergy braced him with assurances. A Franciscan Father of Corpus Christi Church in Chicago buoyed up his spirit by telling him solemnly, "Herman, if Almighty God does want you to be a priest, no power on earth can keep you from it. If not, not even the Pope in Rome can make you one!"

Herman felt convinced that Almighty God did want him to be a priest. Even after thirty-five refusals, he continued to apply to dioceses in the Midwest and the South. Father Donohue, pastor of St. James Church in Chicago, an old priest who remembered Father Tolton and the loneliness of his life as a diocesan priest, urged Herman to join any religious order that would take him. He suggested the Fathers of the Sacred Heart, a small, hundred-man congregation that had its seminary at Hales Corner, Wisconsin. Herman wrote out another routine application and sent it off.

As he found out later, the petition caused quite a stir in the ranks of the Sacred Heart Fathers. Other applications by colored boys had been turned down for one reason or another. But when Herman's application was laid on the provincial's desk in 1941, the superior faced the issue. He called a meeting of the council and pushed through a decision to admit colored students and novices.

In June, 1941, after the provincial had paved the way with a timely instruction to the various communities of the order, Herman was placidly admitted to the secluded novitiate in the little French Catholic town of St. Marie, in central Illinois, near the thoroughly Catholic rural settlements of Teutopolis and Effingham.

There, in the quietly devotional atmosphere of the Sacred Heart Mission House, Herman was trained in the ways of the religious life. There too he made the thirty-day retreat, given by a venerable Jesuit, Father Patrick J. Phillips, of St. Louis. There he imbibed the central spirit of the devotion to the Sacred Heart which permeates the lives of the consecrated priests with a tone of reparation.

On October 2, 1942, Herman pronounced his first vows and was given the religious name of Brother Martin. He journeyed to Milwaukee to enter the major seminary in suburban Hales Corner. After five years of study, he was ordained to the priesthood on June 7, 1947, in the Milwaukee Cathedral by Archbishop Moses E. Kiley.

Both St. Elizabeth's in Chicago and Sacred Heart Church in Greenville claimed him as their own. In each of these churches, Father Martin celebrated one of his "first" High Masses. The celebration in Chicago was climaxed by a testimonial dinner given in his honor by the Knights and Ladies of Peter Claver at Sheil House. Two Sundays later, June 29, a gala procession, with a dozen white-garbed flower girls and an equal number of colorfully vested altar boys, ushered him into the home of his soul in Greenville, the Sacred Heart Church, alongside which the seminary had been started during his years as a young boy in the town. Scores of southern white Catholics also turned out for the Mass, many later kneeling on the ground and asking for the new priest's blessing.

After another year of studies, Father Porter was assigned to teach English and history in the Sacred Heart minor seminary, at Donaldson, Indiana. Along with this, he continued his higher studies by taking graduate courses in English at the nearby University of Notre Dame in South Bend. This led to the acquiring of a degree of Master of Arts within the next few years.

All the while, Father Porter nurtured the desire to labor among the Negroes of the large cities of the North or the wide spaces of the South. He hoped for the day when he might have a small mission in the South, perferably in some place where people had not been tainted with the "deadly poison of materialism." He had spoken of this to his superiors quite often, but they had decided that he should use his talents as a teacher. He persevered in the humble tasks of the classroom, teaching the white students as capably and efficiently as any other seminary professor. He was appointed one of the prefects of discipline upon his arrival. He continued to fulfill these duties, as well as those of confessor and spiritual director to the hundreds of boys whom he handled during his years in the seminary. Some of the other members of the religious order, especially the Brothers, came to him for confession and spiritual guidance as well.

Besides his apostolate within the seminary, Father Porter had some outside opportunities to exercise his zeal. His first weekend assignment was, strangely enough, to assist in the Catholic parish of Plymouth, Indiana, a town which forbids Negroes to live within its confines. Father Porter was somewhat skeptical as to how the parishioners of St. Michael's Church would react to his appearance. Unannounced, he walked out into the sanctuary, began Mass, and ascended the pulpit for the sermon. They gave rapt attention to the little homily he had carefully prepared and had written in clear concise language. As he delivered it with impeccable diction, his fears and their prejudices vanished. The faithful came to the communion rail by the dozens and received the Bread of Life without pause, from the hands of a priest who was unmistakably colored.

Father Porter became popular with the members of the Plymouth parish. He returned there more than twenty times. He addressed the Holy Name Society, and was even invited by the men to hear their confessions before their important communion Sundays.

In Chicago, in New York, and elsewhere in the North, Father Porter has addressed dozens of white audiences and scores of white congregations. In addition, he has given weekend retreats to white groups of St. Vincent de Paul men, has conducted days of recollection for groups of Catholic ladies, among them a group of "faculty wives" of Notre Dame University lay professors.

As a speaker, Father Porter creates a definite impression of deep intelligence, broad, unemotional common sense, and secure self-mastery that gives his utterings an accent of sincerity. Standing tall in the pulpit (he is slightly under six feet in height), he looks through his glasses with keen, pensive eyes, and he talks directly to his hearers without the pretentiousness of the studied orator. Invitations have continued to flood his desk in numbers far beyond his limits of time and strength. His superiors have never objected to his acceptance of the numerous offers that have carried him around the Great Lakes region and into New York for these engagements. He has had a wide field for the exercise of the apostolate of the pulpit.

Moreover, Father Porter has reached an even wider audience through his apostolate of the pen. A talented and creative writer, the young priest has for years contributed articles to the Sacred Heart magazine *Cor,* and has won a large following among their readers. Writing with a deeply spiritual insight into the devotion to the Sacred Heart, Father Martin has been instrumental in communicating a share of the great love of the Sacred Heart that is manifest in his own life. In more than a dozen and a half articles, he treated the different aspects of devotion to the Sacred Heart, and wrote with the view to stirring up a deeper love of God in his readers' hearts.

His pen has also been put to good use in the cause of interracial justice and understanding. The Catholic *Herald Citizen* of Milwaukee carried a well-thought-out analysis by Father Porter of the present position of the Negro Catholic in the Church, under the title "Color Line in Catholic Churches?" It summed up his impressions after five years of ministry in 1952, during which, he averred, he had found "little evidence" of the color line in the northern churches.

In the fall of 1952, after having completed his work for his degree at Notre Dame, Father Porter was given a temporary assignment as assistant pastor in St. Joseph's Church in Saginaw, Michigan. There in a "cross-the-tracks" parish with about one-third Mexican and one-third Negro population in the area, Father Porter pursues the daily duties of a busy priest in a working class neighborhood. He teaches two courses in the parish high school, takes his turn at the parish duties in church and on door duty, and goes out on sick calls to the hospitals of the city. Living as a priest and ministering to all of the souls that come without regard to color, Father Porter is the complete refutation of the old complaint that the colored priest is wanted neither by the whites nor by the colored.

Father Porter is frank enough to recognize that there are three groups of Negroes who do seem to prefer white priests to colored, especially in the South: 1) those who need a socially acceptable leader-priest to intercede for them in the political and economic order; 2) some social climbers who feel that their status is improved if they go to a church administered by a high-prestige white pastor; and 3) some mulattoes, in certain parts of the South, who wish to become white and prefer to have white priests rather than visibly colored ones.

His experience, however, has been that the average Negro Catholic welcomes a priest of his own race. He has found that every return visit to Chicago, where his grandparents are still living, is like a home-coming for another first Mass. Staying at Holy Angels' Rectory with the white diocesan priests who manage the large parish there, Father Porter had found that the prestige of the Church is enhanced when the neighborhood folks witness this interracial fellowship among priests. And in Saginaw, where the same mixed staff arrangement pre-vails, he has also learned that the cause of the Church among the colored is advanced considerably when even the non-Catholic Negroes are enabled to see priests publicly practicing what they preach, and what they actually practice unobserved in their private clerical gath-erings.

FATHER WILLIAM HENRY ADAMS, S.V.D.

1913 –

The newly appointed (1952) prefect of the students in the minor seminary of St. Augustine in Bay St. Louis is a spiritual protégé of Boston's great mission-minded prelate, Archbishop Richard J. Cushing. As archdiocesan director of the Society for the Propagation of the Faith, Bishop Cushing promoted the development of the colored clergy in the United States to the limit of his resources. At one time, through his stimulation and encouragement, more than ten seminarians at St. Augustine's were being supported by the Boston section of the Society.

During the early years of the war, Bishop Cushing wrote a vigorous pamphlet, *Native Clergy Are the Pillars of the Church,* in which he devoted a special section to the Catholic Negro clergy in the United States. He ended his glowing tribute to the work of the pioneer sem-inaries by stating:

All men feel the need and desire for priests of their own race, color and nationality. The idea of satisfying this desire and of raising up such a priesthood began back in the early days of the Church. St. Peter and St. Paul were the first advocates of "native" clergy, and we read in history how they chose deacons, priests, and later bishops from among their converts.

All the Popes since the time of St. Peter have seen the wisdom of this practice and have followed his example by encouraging and fostering vocations among those people and races newly converted to the Faith. The present Pontiff (Pius XII) demonstrated his desire for such a clergy when he recently consecrated twelve missionary bishops of all races, among them two Negroes.

In no way is the sincerity of the Church in her pronouncements against Racism better illustrated than in her traditional policy of encouraging native clergy. For no people does she relax the high intellectual and moral standards demanded of her priests. Her encouragement of a Negro clergy in the United States therefore gives the lie to those who would justify the Negro's inferior economic and social position by the accusation of inferiority in intelligence and character.

Father Cushing, while Boston director of the Propagation of the Faith, was approached in 1935 by a young clerk who had been trying to realize his desire to study for the priesthood for the past two years. Young William Adams had found that the tedious routine of a billing clerk in a motor transportation company was not his life's vocation. He had been back to his Alma Mater, Boston College High School, to talk to some of his old teachers and friends among the New England Jesuits. Father Thomas Feeney, later to become a missionary bishop, arrranged for an interview with the Jesuit superiors in Boston. The secretary of the Father Provincial persuaded the young clerk to seek admission to the Josephite Fathers.

It all seemed discouraging until Bill went to see Father Cushing. "I'll get you a way to the priesthood," Father Cushing promised. Though he had no power to change policy at the archdiocesan seminary in Brighton, Father Cushing used his influence to secure admission for the young aspirant to St. Augustine's in Bay St. Louis.

Bill left his native New England in 1936 to matriculate at the Bay. He had been born in Cambridge, Massachusetts, on September 18, 1913. For his Catholic education, William had gone to elementary school at St. Mary of the Annunciation School in Cambridgeport, and to high school with the Jesuits across town in the South End of Boston.

In the depression years, Bill earned his way through high school by working as a newsboy. He did odd jobs after graduating from Boston College High School in 1931, and he attended Fisher Business College in Somerville for almost two years after that.

The "Come Follow Me!" drew him away from Boston's counting houses in 1936. He advanced through the normal course of studies in St. Augustine's, and by June, 1940, had made his religious profession at St. Mary's Mission House in Techny, Illinois.

Like other seminarians at the Bay, Frater William did his share of writing for *St. Augustine's Messenger* during his student days. He wrote inspirational and biographical pieces, as well as short stories and news stories. One of his articles appeared in the *Shield* magazine, "Gold Coast Calling: Mississippi Crusaders Go to Africa" (March, 1942). It told the story of the missionary venture staffed mainly by graduates from St. Augustine's in the West African colony.

On September 29, 1945, Bishop Gerow ordained Father William Adams in the seminary chapel at the Bay. His first Mass was offered in his home parish of St. Mary's Annunciation in Cambridge.

For two years after his ordination, Father Adams served as assistant in St. Martinville under Father Rousseve. Finally, in September, 1948, he took up his work as a teacher of boys in Holy Rosary Institute in Lafayette. Prior to that time, Holy Rosary had been mainly a girls' school, conducted by the Holy Family Sisters. But Bishop Jeanmard expanded it into a central Catholic high school, accommodating upward of three hundred pupils, over half of whom boarded at the Institute.

Father Adams was head prefect in charge of the boys' division. He taught English and Latin, supervised the carpentry and other trade classes, and shepherded the youngsters in their leisure hours. He coached them in basketball and baseball. During his prefecture the carpentry class built the school gymnasium and the dormitory buildings. Father Adams helped the Institute in making the extensive adjustments necessary for the separate section designed for inclusion of the boys in a hitherto all-girl institution.

Father "Bill" is in his element as a full-time educator, thoroughly dedicated to the welfare of his charges. He has a genial smile that inspires confidence in the boys and makes him easy to get along with. He is alert athletically, of a muscular build though short of stature, and has a virile, robust approach to people.

In 1952, after four years in Lafayette, he was chosen for the key position as head prefect of the minor seminary at Bay St. Louis. In that position he continues, as of this writing, the fine work as teacher and builder of boys that he began so capably in Lafayette.

FATHER ARTHUR C. WINTERS, S.V.D.

1 9 1 6 –

Like his older brother, Father Richard Winters, the younger Father Arthur taught in the seminary after his ordination at Bay St. Louis in 1945. He held the teaching position for four years, 1945-49, and then, after a three-year tour of duty in Lafayette, returned to resume his work as a seminary prefect and professor.

His ordination in 1945 placed the Winters family first after the Healy family in the list of those having more than one priest. Father Chachere was not ordained until a month after Father Arthur Winters, on January 6, 1945. The Negro press at the time gave considerable attention to the event. *Ebony* magazine gave a three-page spread to the Fathers Winters in its first issue in 1945. It played up the fact that four of the Winters brothers were in the armed services: another was organist at St. Peter's Church in Pleasantville, New Jersey, where they were all raised.

Young Arthur followed in his brother Richard's footsteps by attending Holy Spirit High School in Atlantic City, from which he was graduated in 1933. After working a year as janitor in St. Peter's Church in Pleasantville, Arthur decided to follow Richard to St. Augustine's Seminary in Bay St. Louis. He entered in September, 1934.

During his seminary years the musical and poetical talents of Father Arthur Winters began to blossom. He had mastered the piano and other string instruments before entering, and during his seminary years he played wind instruments in the seminary orchestra. He became proficient enough to teach music, direct the polyphonic choir, and conduct the band and orchestra in later years.

His name became well known in Catholic literary circles even before ordination. As assistant editor of St. Augustine's Messenger during his seminary years and after ordination, Father Winters wrote dozens of sensitive poems. Many of them were published in the Messenger. But in 1942 and 1943 no less than three were accepted and published in Spirit magazine, the organ of the Catholic Poetry Society of America. He became recognized as a genuine poet and was admitted to membership in the select circle of the Society.

After reading his poetry and meeting Father Winters, one realizes that the deeply religious inspiration evident in his poetry is an overflow of the spiritual fervor of his inner life. Bearing his priesthood with easy dignity, the young priest still manifests in his smiling, modest, and kindly countenance, the glow of his deep spirituality. He veils much of his wistful and pensive soul with a whimsical and good-natured humor that is quick at innocent repartees, witty with well-turned expressions, and outgoing in its charity.

Short of reproducing his poems, quoting extensively from his popular retreats to seminarians and laymen, laywomen, and high-school children, and excerpting from his well-composed sermons, one could not easily take the intellectual measure of Father Arthur Winters. Without any fanfare, and in the quiet of parish and seminary life, he has fulfilled the best requirements of the priesthood, and gives promise of many more years as a good, holy man of God.

FATHER JOSEPH ABEL FRANCIS, S.V.D.

1 9 2 3 –

Up until his recent transfer to the position of prefect of students at Holy Rosary Institute in his home city of Lafayette, Father Joseph Francis had been teaching and prefecting in the minor seminary at

Bay St. Louis. As assistant editor of *St. Augustine's Messenger,* and as an occasional speaker in New Orleans, Father Francis had carried into a wider field the educational influence he exerted at St. Augustine's and continues to exert at Holy Rosary.

One of his speeches that caught my eye was an address given before the New Orleans Commission on Human Rights of the Catholic Committee of the South. It was an able discussion of the "History of the Negro Clergy in the South." While he covered much of the same ground that this book has touched upon, he made several points that are quite significant in the light of his own vocation and lifework.

For instance, in speaking of the failure of the premature efforts of the Josephites in starting St. Joseph's College for Colored Catechists in Montgomery, he stated:

> The venture did not work and was abandoned. I do not think that the failure was due to the men who attempted the undertaking; rather it was due to circumstances beyond their control. Priests are the products of *settled Catholic homes.* At the time that this attempt was made, the Negro as a whole had neither *settled* nor *Catholic* homes. The quest for a living, the struggle against disease, poverty, prejudice and apathy, the lack of education and the attitude of the majority of the Catholics in the South towards the Negro, left little room in the heart and mind of the Negro to want to become Catholics, let alone Catholic priests.

Fortunately for his own future vocation, Father Joseph Francis was born into a settled Catholic home on September 30, 1923. Among his great-grandparents was a Reynaud who had come over from France in the early days of Louisiana. The family tradition had been thoroughly Catholic, and his parents were devout, pious, and prayerful folks. They had their family shrine just like the Breton fisherfolk of the old country. Before the little statuettes of the Sacred Heart and the Blessed Virgin, his faithful father would kneel for a momentary prayer before he left the house for work each morning at the local hotel.

His mother gathered the children before the shrine in the evening for family Rosary, especially during the month of October. Once when a flood threatened their section of Lafayette after a torrential twenty-two-inch rain within the span of twenty-four hours, all of the family gathered together to pray. The flood stopped two blocks away at the railroad embankment.

In this settled Catholic home, young Joe grew up normally. At the age of six he started in the parish grammar school at St. Paul's. While he was still in primer grade, one of the colored Sisters of the Holy Family who taught school asked how many of the boys wanted to be priests. Joe put his hand up. The Sister from then on made it a point to encourage and guide him toward his goal. As an adjunct to his home training, his Catholic schooling supplemented the careful spiritual nurture that the young boy received from his parents.

In 1934, when he was still an altar boy, the parish celebrated the homecoming of the first priest raised within its ranks, Father Anthony Bourges. There were so many adults who wanted to attend the first Mass that children were not allowed in the church. Joe was kept at home with his grandmother. But when he heard the bell ring at the end of Mass, he begged his grandma to let him go to see the crowd. He ran to the church in time to witness the procession as it filed out into the churchyard.

Father Bourges caught sight of the eager little youngster who wanted to be a priest. He came through the crowd toward him, gave him a special blessing, and shook hands with him.

Two years later, after finishing first high, Joe emulated Father Bourges by entering St. Augustine's Seminary in Bay St. Louis. He returned home for his summer vacations. Father Vincent Smith kept alive the enthusiasm of the seminarians on vacation by gathering them together, taking them on the missions to teach catechism with him, and drafting them for choir duty for his High Masses. The half-dozen seminarians from around Lafayette secured valuable missionary experience by their journeys to the Long Plantation and to the other missions in the vicinity.

Joe especially liked the catechetical work. Even as a grammar school boy he had displayed a flair for preaching. He made three missions in the parish during those years and went back to his neighborhood to deliver the sermons over again to his Protestant cousins. He would even memorize Father Hyland's Sunday sermons and repeat them in his piping voice to the children of the neighborhood.

The transition from his settled home life to the sacred routine of the seminary was also a normal one for Frater Joseph. He advanced through his five years of work at the Bay and his four at Techny without any variation from the normal experience of the faithful seminarian.

Back in St. Augustine's for his second year of philosophy in 1946, Joe quickly took the lead. He liked philosophy, achieved good grades in it, and matured into a well-balanced theologian as he advanced through his other sacred studies.

On October 7, 1950, Bishop Gerow laid ordaining hands on Frater Francis to raise him to the realization of his ambition. His father and his brother served his first private Mass next day, and together with his family he returned to St. Paul's in Lafayette for his first solemn High Mass. It gave him a special thrill when old Bishop Jeanmard knelt down before him to receive his blessing and to kiss his newly anointed hands.

He returned again the following summer to fill in as assistant priest in the Immaculate Heart parish, after completing his study of theology. In September, 1951, Father Francis took up the duties of teacher and prefect in the minor seminary at the Bay. There he continued to train young candidates for the priesthood as he had been trained. He taught them the reverence that they should feel toward the founder of the seminary, Father Matthew Christman, whom he called a "martyr to the cause of the Negro clergy." He told them, as he had been told by one of the first ordained graduates of the seminary, "Son, when you hear the name of Christman, bow your head!"

The great goodness and priestliness of young priests like Father Francis is a living tribute to the sagacity of Father Christman. Anyone who meets Father "Joe" is immediately struck by the cheerful holiness that radiates from his countenance as from the face of a perennial altar boy, now become an altar man. He has the typical all-enwreathing smile of a normal American youth, and in his wholesome optimism and enthusiastic zeal, there is the promise of a long serviceable career in the apostolate.

CHAPTER XXIV

University Converts

FATHER ROLLINS LAMBERT
FATHER PETER J. CARTER

Two of the newer generation of colored priests belong in a class by themselves. Both have the distinction of having become converts to the Catholic Church while attending large universities in the North. Both found their vocation to the priesthood in the secularistic atmosphere of the university campuses.

The first of the two is Father Rollins Lambert, a tall, dignified, and self-possessed priest now laboring as an assistant pastor in a large West Side Church in the archdiocese of Chicago. Father Lambert impresses one even upon first acquaintance, with his broad human sympathy, his wide erudition, and his calm appraisal of events and trends both in the Church and in the turbulent community that is Chicago.

I requested that he write up his own story. He replied with a compact autobiographical sketch that reveals the inner stature of the man as it unfolds the outer events of his life. We present it here as he wrote it:

FATHER ROLLINS LAMBERT

1 9 2 2 –

The early years of my life were spent in Chicago, where I was born in 1922, and in Kansas City, Missouri, which was my mother's home after she left her birthplace, St. Mary's, Kansas. My father died while I was an infant, and consequently I have no memories of him. The burden of supporting herself and me fell upon my mother; this she did by working in domestic service as a cook and maid. I was seldom separated from her in the years of my childhood; we lived together in the homes of her various employers. This arrangement was not wholly satisfactory, since it prevented me from having many friendships with children of my own age, and from acquiring any proficiency in the games which boys usually play. It was, however, the best provision my mother could make, and was far better than having me put into a boarding home.

Mother began my education at home. She had not had a great deal of formal education, having completed only two years of high school, but her naturally active mind had made her continue to read much and widely, so that she could hold her own in dealing with people who had much more education. When I was six years old, I entered LeMoyne Public School in Chicago. Mrs. Abigail Ellings, the principal, tested me with a second-grade reader when I applied for admission; I read it easily and was thereupon placed in second grade. Many times in later years Mother complained that, lacking kindergarten training, I was clumsy with my hands. My first teacher, Miss Catherine LeDoux, who is still a friend, took special interest in me; she gave me such a foundation and stimulated my interest so much that I graduated from elementary school when I was twelve years old. By a strange twist of Providence, I finished eighth grade at LeMoyne, although I had transferred from school to school about twelve times in the six intervening years.

Graduation came in the middle of the depression, in 1934. By this time my mother, weary of the burden a lone woman must carry, had married Mr. Leonard Harris, a Chicagoan. I liked him, but we never became real friends. As for Mother, she had only added to her burdens; in the depression, it was often easier for a woman in domestic service to obtain work than it was for a truck driver whose job depended on the building trades. At this time, too, my maternal grandmother was living with us, so there were four mouths to feed.

After graduation I wanted to attend Lake View High School, where most of my graduating class, and especially my girl friend, was entering. Mother, knowing better or relying on intuition, insisted that I go to Nicholas Senn High School. Official school districts mattered little:

addresses could be arranged with friends who actually lived in the proper district. Since I was planning to go to college, I began the curriculum of the general science course; later, as my ability and preference for languages developed, with a corresponding distaste for sciences and mathematics, I changed to the general language course. It was Mother, again, who insisted that I study Latin, and during my first year she frequently helped me with homework. She had retained a surprising amount of the language after the twenty-five years since she had studied it in high school.

In retrospect, it is difficult to find language adequate to express my esteem and gratitude for the training I received at Senn. The women who taught me, and the men who administered the school, were intellectually well qualified, were kind, generous, devoted to their work, setting an example of scholarship and personal conduct deserving of only the highest praise. I will mention by name only the two teachers who had decisive parts in my choosing of a vocation, Miss Elsa Scheerer and Miss Henrietta Hafemann.

Since childhood Mother had been urging the idea of a career in law; I had never been attracted to it. When, in second year, I added the study of Spanish to the Latin already begun, Miss Scheerer suggested that I investigate the Foreign Service of the U.S. Government as a career. She based her recommendation on my proficiency in languages. I discovered later that language ability is only a secondary requisite for the diplomatic service, but by that time I was already enthusiastic about such work and began to direct my studies toward it. Miss Scheerer was a woman of intense and deep personality; she ardently believed in the brotherhood of all men, and often said that the world's problems would only be solved when the races melted into one by intermarriage. It was a great sorrow for me when, in the summer of 1951, she took her own life, overcome by grief when her sister died.

The other major influence on me at Senn was Miss Hafemann, now Mrs. Frank Miller. She taught me ancient, medieval, and modern history, and international relations, a course she inaugurated in the curriculum of Chicago high schools. She was also studying at the University of Chicago, and it was because of her that I conceived the ambition of attending that institution. Now that I am teaching history myself, and am struggling to make my students learn a few facts from the textbooks, I am amazed at Miss Hafemann's ability to make us learn not only the elementary facts of history, but also to learn to do research involving even primary historical sources, which is characteristic of college level teaching. She developed in her students a real sense of appreciation of history and of historical method. It was a training which has stayed with me, and has been of immeasurable value since my high-school days.

During my last year, along with several other Senn students, I took scholarship examinations for various colleges. Senn did well in 1942, its silver jubilee year, gaining a number of awards. I won the choice of a full-tuition first-year scholarship to either Northwestern University or Knox College, or a half-tuition scholarship for first year at the University of Chicago. Finances were important then as always in my life, so the choice was a difficult one. Mother, upon whom much of the burden was inevitably to fall, urged the University of Chicago; since she was backed by Miss Hafemann and my own preference, I enrolled there.

I had begun to work, during my last two years in high school, as a dishwasher in a drugstore. I worked full-time in the summers, and on weekends during the school terms. This was a considerable help for Mother, who had supported me alone for so many years. In college, where expenses mounted far beyond expectation or past experience, it was indispensable that I work if I was to continue my studies. Watchful Providence took care of that. I was assigned to a National Youth Administration job in one of the university's bookkeeping offices, and there earned enough, added to Mother's larger contribution and the scholarship, to finish first year. The university then transferred me to a part-time job in the same office, on its own payroll, and kept me in this position until after I had left the university. This was, I found out later, the first time a Negro had worked in an office at the university, and before I was hired, unknown to me, a conference of high administrators was necessary. Once hired, I was treated with perfect equality, was given increases in pay regularly, and enjoyed all the privileges of employees of the university.

My course in the university was still directed toward the Foreign

Service, in the Department of Political Science. I was further encouraged in this by three new friends: Ross Netherton, Jr., who was a student of political science a year or two ahead of me, whom I met when we were both members of the university's track team; Mr. James T. Watkins, who taught international relations at the university for a few years and enthusiastically encouraged my ambitions; and Mr. Jerome G. Kerwin, a professor of political science, my faculty advisor, who provided sympathetic aid.

At this point, a retrogression is in order, since I have failed to mention the religious side of my growing up. When I was five, my mother had entered me in the Sunday school of the Second Church of Christ, Scientist, in Chicago. I was the only colored child there, but during the seven or eight years of my attendance I met always with the kindness and charity which mark every member of that sect I have known. Mother used to attend church there, too, and we had some good friends among its members. When I was twelve, I decided to become a member, and arranged to take the oral examination which is a prerequisite. I flunked; I insisted that the doctrine of Mary Baker Eddy, as expressed in the textbook of Christian Science, could be improved upon; nothing, it seemed to me, could be perfectly expressed except the inspired word of God, the Bible. This was the wrong attitude, according to the examiners, and I was advised to wait and study a few more years. I waited, but I wandered gradually away from religious study. Freed somewhat from Mother's watchful eye when I went to college, I stopped attending services. For several years I was a non-denominational, nonattending Christian.

This was my religious status when one of my fellow office employees at the university, Albert Desrosiers, invited me to attend Easter Mass with him at the Holy Name Cathedral. It was Archbishop Stritch's first Easter in Chicago, and Albert promised me good music (he knew of my growing interest in music), and interesting ceremonial. I went with him and was fascinated. It was particularly the use of Latin, which I had studied as a "dead" language, that attracted my attention. I began to attend High Masses regularly, at the Cathedral, at the parish church of St. Thomas the Apostle, and anywhere a particularly good "show," as I then regarded it, was being celebrated. My admiration for Latin, I would like to note, has not kept me from advocating the use of English in Catholic services. Being privileged by my knowledge of Latin to understand the liturgical functions, I regret that their meaning is hidden from most Catholics by the use of an unfamiliar language.

Albert also introduced me to Miss LaVerne Landon, a Catholic student at the university. LaVerne and I used to have long conversations, usually about religion, in quiet moments while she was working evenings in Ida Noyes Hall, and it was she who first invited me to a function of the Calvert Club. This club was the Catholic student organization on the campus—unofficial as far as the Archbishop of Chicago was concerned; it was entirely in the hands of the students themselves, with Mr. Kerwin as faculty adviser. Father George Dunne, S.J., was working on a doctorate degree in international relations at that time; he was a ready and willing helper on any problem which arose for the club or for its members, and was regarded as the unofficial chaplain. The membership of the club was a group of enthusiastic Catholics; they were united by personal friendship and intellectual convictions as well as by their faith; many of them tried to sanctify their lives by daily Mass and Communion, and by singing Mass and Vespers when they had weekend gatherings at Childerley, their country retreat house. These students were aggressive in their intellectual attitude toward their Catholic faith. They made no apologies to the materialists who surrounded them, but tried to convert the materialists themselves. Several vocations to the priesthood and religious life have developed from this group—Miss Landon, for one, is now in the Convent of Our Lady of the Cenacle—and those who have married have lost none of their zeal.

This was the group, then, which became my friends. My mother was worried. Her contact with Catholics in her youth had not only alienated her from the Church, but had embittered her toward its members. She was afraid that I, seeing only the best elements of Catholicism, would be deceived by them and disillusioned later. She voiced her objections many times, but I thought (and still think) that I had the answers. We argued much and bitterly, and my Catholic interests were for a long time a real strain on the family tie.

My association with the Calvert Club also brought me in contact with Miss Johanna Doniat, a teacher of art at Senn High School. At Senn I did not study art, and so never came to know Johanna there; in college she took great interest in me, as an alumnus of her school, and did much to encourage me and instruct me on the way to the Church. She could tell me the date, I know, of the summer of 1941, when I told her that I had decided to become a Catholic.

This decision had been working its way into my mind for about a year. I had studied the teaching of the Church as presented in the St. Andrew's Daily Missal, the most-used book in my library. I found nothing to complain about, nothing which seemed impossible or disagreeable to believe. On the feast of St. Peter's Chair in 1941, I had heard the celebrant at Mass sing the words of Christ: *"Tu es Petrus, et super hanc petram aedificabo Ecclesiam meam. . . ."* (Thou art Peter, and upon this rock I will build my Church.) I knew then that *this was it.*

To my surprise I found that I would have to take instructions before entering the Church. Mr. Kerwin arranged that Father Sebastian Carlson, O.P., should instruct me at the Dominican House of Studies at River Forest. Father Carlson was surprised, too, when he met me. He was expecting, I think, a University of Chicago "intellectual," full of philosophic difficulties. I had none. I remember asking him how Mary could be the Mediatrix of all graces, since I had seen her feast under that title in my missal. He explained that, and I was content.

At this time, Archbishop Stritch acceded to an old desire of Mr. Kerwin and the other Catholics at the university, a desire also of Mr. Robert Hutchins, president of the university, that a Catholic chaplain be provided for the intellectual and spiritual needs of Catholic students. The archbishop appointed Father Joseph D. Connerton, and it was to him that I went for the completion of my instructions. We finished in time for me to be baptized on Christmas Eve at the Church of St. Thomas the Apostle. While Father Connerton performed the ceremony, Father George Dunne read the prayers in English for the benefit of my Calvert Club friends who gathered around the font to welcome me into the Church. That night I received Holy Communion from Archbishop Stritch at his midnight Mass in the Cathedral.

Simultaneously with the decision to enter the Church came the ambition to be a priest. I discussed this with Mr. Kerwin, who told me about Father Charles McCoy, another priest- alumnus of the university. Father McCoy had applied for admission to the Chicago Seminary and although he had a doctorate degree in political science, he had been refused because he knew no Greek. He had then gone to Saint Paul, where Archbishop Murray had accepted him and ordained him after only four years of study. Since I, too, knew no Greek, we decided that I, too, should apply at Saint Paul. Mr. Kerwin made the trip with me, to introduce me to the archbishop and to the rector of the Saint Paul Seminary. It was there arranged that I should enter in September, 1942. Upon my return to Chicago, I began to feel that perhaps I was leaving my native city too hastily, without even giving it a chance to reject me. Through another member of the Calvert Club, Mr. Robert Heywood, I had made the acquaintance of Monsignor Reynold Hillenbrand, rector of the Chicago Seminary at Mundelein, Illinois. I wrote to Monsignor, explaining my desires, qualifications, and the hindrances. He in turn presented my application to Archbishop Stritch who granted his approval.

In September, 1942, then, I finished my course at the University of Chicago, Mother having insisted that I take the Bachelor of Arts degree —and entered the Seminary of Saint Mary of the Lake, Mother objecting in vain.

Mother approved of neither my conversion nor my seminary ambition. She knew, and I knew, too, that the day was coming when she would no longer be able to support herself; I felt, moreover, an obligation to allow her some rest after the twenty years of labor she had spent for my sake. I decided that although the time when I could help her would be postponed, at least in the seminary I would not require further financial help from her; the years of her complete self-sacrifice would be over, and she could spend her own earnings to make her life more comfortable.

After this there is not much to say. With the help of Monsignor Hillenbrand and his successor as rector, Monsignor Malachy P. Foley, and of other generous friends, my financial needs were provided. I completed the course of studies prescribed for seminarians; I satisfied my superiors as to my qualifications for the priesthood. Archbishop Stritch, now a cardinal, who had given me my first Holy Communion and confirmed me, ordained me a priest on the seventh of May, 1949, in the seminary chapel at Mundelein. It was the first time a Negro priest had been ordained for the archdiocese of Chicago. On the first day of July I began my assignment at St. Malachy's Church, on Chicago's West Side, where, at present, I am working.

Someone may wonder if I have experienced racial prejudice against myself, either before or since my ordination. The answer to that is easy, a simple "no."

In St. Mary of the Lake Seminary I was just "one of the boys." There was no special favor shown me because of my race, and no privilege was denied me. Everyone, including myself, was completely unconscious that there was anything "different" about me. The thirty-five white priests who were ordained with me in 1949 confirmed this by electing me permanent president of the class.

My first solemn Mass, at the Church of St. Thomas the Apostle, was enthusiastically attended by a capacity crowd which was really "catholic"—universal. Many non-Catholic Negroes attended, because they wanted to see the first Negro priest ordained in Chicago (who had been advertised by the daily papers). Many white Catholics who were neither friends of mine nor parishioners of St. Thomas attended to rejoice in what the preacher of the Mass, Monsignor Joseph Morrison, called the "coming of age of the church in Chicago."

The parish in which I work contains Catholics of all races and many different nationalities. It is one of those neighborhoods in Chicago where many white people have moved out as Negroes moved in, but there is still a large number of people who have refused to leave the homes where they have lived for many years. As far as I have been able to judge, everybody in the parish welcomed me. There is no discrimination in the ordinary parish activities: when it is my turn to baptize, I baptize whatever babies are brought to church. Funerals, weddings, and preaching duties are shared by all the priests of the parish, without reference to the race of the people involved.

There has been similar acceptance outside of the parish. I have given days of recollection and book reviews for groups which were either racially mixed or entirely white. Four Catholic colleges have invited me to lecture to their students: Loyola University, Mundelein and Rosary Colleges in Chicago, and Marygrove College in Detroit. Only one of these lectures was about racial issues; the other three were on literary subjects.

The priests of the archdiocese have, of course, treated me as they did when we were seminarians, with friendliness and perfect equality. Shortly after ordination I was assigned to membership in the Priests' Choir, an organization which sings the funeral services of our brother priests and performs occasionally for other functions. These duties have taken me into many churches and rectories in the archdiocese. Each occasion is a repetition of the casually friendly reception which means that I am not marked out for special honor or special humiliation.

It is the Sisters in the Catholic Church who, more than any other group, always show honor, deference, and courtesy toward the priests of the Church. Here, too, my experience has been that of the average priest—perhaps even better, since most of the Sisters I have met have been especially enthusiastic about having a colored priest in Chicago. And not only is this true in Chicago, but in Washington, Boston, and Detroit, in Union City, New Jersey, and in Bethlehem, Connecticut, where I have had the privilege of celebrating Mass for the Sisters and enjoying overnight hospitality, when I had occasion to visit them on business or during vacation.

All in all, then, Catholics—lay people, Sisters, and priests—have shown me during these three years that they are happy about the ordination and priestly work of every priest; and particularly they have shown that they rejoice in the fact that the Negro race, which has been so much oppressed in the past, is more and more coming to occupy the place in America to which the teaching of Christ and the laws of our country entitle it.

FATHER PETER J. CARTER

1920 –

The thing that struck me most of all when I first met Father Carter in Buffalo (he was downstairs in the basement of St. Nicholas School, playing games with the boys of the parish) was his facial resemblance to Bishop Healy. He has the same olive skin, broad forehead, prominent eyebrows, and benign smile that characterized the Bishop of Portland. The one distinctive difference was his great height. Where Bishop Healy stood just a few inches over five feet, Father Carter was as much over six feet, standing erect and lithe with the springy step of a former track star.

He has returned to be assistant pastor in the very parish within whose confines he was born in 1920. His grandfather was a Catholic, converted by old Monsignor McGloin. Young Peter's first contact with the Church was his attendance of Mass at St. Nicholas in the company of his grandfather, though he himself, son of a Negro doctor, Peter J. Carter, M.D., had not been baptized. This tenuous contact was broken when young Peter was eight years old. His mother and grandfather died. He went down South with his father and settled at Tuskegee, Alabama, where his father began working at the veterans' hospital. Only once did he go to Mass at the Catholic church in Tuskegee during the eight years he was to stay there, finishing his grammar school and high school.

His father wanted young Peter to follow in his path as a medical doctor. Accordingly, upon completing his high-school education at the Tuskegee Institute High, Peter applied for admission to the premedical course at Cornell, the college where all of his former friends from Buffalo had matriculated. He was not accepted at Ithaca. But he was accepted at both Howard University in Washington and at the University of Michigan in Ann Arbor.

Peter enrolled in the premedical course at Ann Arbor that fall. He took the regular college courses along with biology, zoology, and chemistry. His father had insisted that while he was in high school in Tuskegee he should study Latin in order better to be prepared for the mastery of the medical terminology he would encounter later. He continued this study at Ann Arbor. Under Dr. Meineke, Peter studied the classical language with more than passing attention. He found the Latin courses to be much more interesting than the arid precincts of science. In his junior year, he switched from premedical studies to the classical course, and signed up for all the classics he could manage to take: Roman law, Roman history, Caesar, Virgil, Cicero, Livy. He liked the direct contact with abstract values—virtue, justice, law and order. This laid the groundwork for his conversion to the Church.

During these years, Peter had been a nominal Episcopalian, attending the upper-class Anglican church on Catherine and Division streets. He lived down at the bottom of the hill on Catherine Street in the quiet colored neighborhood behind St. Joseph's Mercy Hospital.

The climb up the gentle slope on the wintry Sunday mornings to attend services with the "big wheels" of the campus at the Anglican church hardly seemed worthwhile. No other colored people attended the church. Though he was not interested in them, he was invited to the social events at the Episcopalian Student Center. But the religious services seemed hollow and empty; the minister preached in polite generalities and distributed a low church Communion with no reference to the Body and Blood of Our Lord.

Finally, on Easter Sunday, in 1939, Peter walked out in the middle of the services. The vacuous piety of the mild minister failed to hold either his interest or his allegiance.

At the time, Peter was acquainted with some of the Catholic students at the university. He had been going around with them in the routine of college life, attending football games, taking in the shows, and trying out for the track squad as well. John O'Hara and his brother Dick struck up close friendships with their fellow trackman. But though they talked religion often, they never thought of inviting him to the St. Mary's Student Chapel or to the Newman Club meetings and socials. They gave him good example at all times, showing him that piety and kindness went well with good innocent fun.

Soon after his withdrawal from the Anglican Church, Peter happened to see an ad in the Detroit newspaper, offering to send free literature to anyone interested in the Catholic Church. Peter wrote for the pamphlets. He received a small catechism among the booklets. That deeply affected him. He told of it thus:

> A penny catechism changed my life by telling me that God made the world; and that He also made me to love Him and serve Him in this world and to be with Him in the next. My professors in school had taught me that I was a direct descendant of a mythical missing link, that I was just a group of cells, tissues, and nerve ganglia. But the Catholic Church gave me confidence and dignity by telling me that I was a child of a loving God. This revelation brought everything into focus for me, as if someone had turned on a light in a dim room.

Peter made up his mind to become a Catholic. He went to the rectory in back of St. Thomas the Apostle Church and told Father Carey that he wanted to enter the Church. The pastor instructed him to go to Father Clair Barry at the St. Mary's Student Chapel. Under the kind tutelage of the Newman Club chaplain, Peter began his course of instructions then and there. He continued them when he returned to Buffalo at the close of school.

While home on vacation, he was baptized on July 14, 1939, by Father Louis Langley in St. Nicholas Church.

He was a happy senior when he returned to Ann Arbor that fall. Peter learned to serve Mass at the Student Chapel, and became a regular member of the Newman Club. He pitched in with other members to plan all of the social events, and even to paint the large clubroom in the basement of the chapel when it was decided to use that for the socials.

In November he journeyed to Detroit to receive the Sacrament of Confirmation along with the other converts and members of the adult class who had not yet received that Sacrament. The priests at the center took such a deep interest in his spiritual welfare that he began to think of what a wonderful thing it would be if he too could become a priest. "How nice it would be," he said to himself, "but how hard, too."

For the present, however, his mind turned to the study of law. In the fall of 1940 he signed up for courses in the Law Quadrangle. Along with his two good friends, John and Dick O'Hara, he plunged into a study of torts and judicial administration.

The triumvirate was broken up in 1942 when the Ann Arbor draft board tapped him for service in the Army. Down to Alabama he traveled again, this time for military training at Camp Rucker near Dothan. Peter found it quite a jolt to go from the high standards of the Newman Club and the strict concepts of legal study to the exigencies of barracks life in the Army. He stiffened his backbone against the immorality he encountered and nourished the desire of returning to become a priest. He concentrated on the milder forms of army diversions, shooting the breeze on the barracks steps, hiking about the post to the tame shows, and avoiding the off-limits spots in the town. Reading the *Keys of the Kingdom,* he became enamored of Father Chisholm's quiet heroism and pursuit of the eternal values in the priesthood.

His prayer and his priestly desires were both maintained during his tour of duty in North Africa and in the Italian campaign. Moving up from Bizerte on Christmas in 1943, he went through all of the trying anxieties of the invasion of Italy and the tedious campaign up the boot.

Finally, after the front became more stable with the taking of the central section of Italy and of Rome, he was stationed at Tarquemia, just sixty miles away from the Eternal City. At every opportunity, he joined the truckloads of GI's who sped to Rome to see the sights. Peter sought the holy ones. He saw the Supreme Pontiff twice in public audiences. He made the pilgrimages to St. Peter's, St. Mary Major, St. John Lateran, and the catacombs. The messages of the martyrs and the saints were not lost on him.

When his forty months of service were up, he was released from the Army in November, 1945. He returned to the family home in Virginia to await his father's completion of a tour of duty with the Army Medical Corps as a doctor at Fort Huachuca in Arizona, where the famous Bouncing Buffaloes of the 92nd Division had their training. Peter stayed long enough to pay his respects to his father, then took off for Buffalo in quest of a seminary.

To the bedside of old Father McGloin, then in Providence Hospital, Peter took his problem. He told the venerable pastor of St. Nicholas of his ambition to become a priest. Father McGloin encouraged him to go ahead. He sent him to apply at the little seminary that he had founded, then headed by Monsignor Hoehn. Peter was assigned to study Latin with Father Marnon, who also sponsored his vocation by making arrangements with Bishop O'Hara, the former auxiliary bishop of the armed forces, now Bishop of Buffalo.

Bishop O'Hara sent Peter to Canisius College in Buffalo to study philosophy. In the fall of 1946 he entered the seminary at Niagara University. The following year he began his study of theology. On May 19, 1951, he was ordained to the priesthood by Bishop O'Hara in St. Joseph's new Cathedral.

Next day Father Peter Carter offered his first solemn High Mass at St. Nicholas Church in Buffalo. His archpriest at the Mass was Father James McCarthy, whose father, Timothy McCarthy, had stood sponsor for Peter when he was baptized in 1939. "I will have two sons who are priests," old Tim McCarthy long before had said proudly, anticipating that day; but he saw the new priest's happy celebration from his place in heaven. He had died some time before.

To get some needed missionary experience, Father Carter was assigned for a year to the diocese of Raleigh, North Carolina. Bishop Waters gave him an appointment as assistant to Father Paytas, a Francisan Friar of the Atonement, who conducted a small mission church for colored Catholics in High Point, North Carolina.

Father Carter helped the pastor in his ministrations to the 110 souls of his flock, and in his convert work among the neighboring Negro families. In the course of the year, Father Peter also gave sermons at other churches around the diocese. He gave the series of talks at the Forty Hours' Devotion at St. Monica's in Raleigh and elsewhere.

At the end of his year, he returned to Buffalo to assume the duties of assistant at his old parish of St. Nicholas. There, in the predominantly white parish, Father Carter continues his apostolate. At ease in his interracial contacts, he is called "Father" by old whites and young, as I heard myself when I visited there.

Like Father William Grau who preceded him on the roster of the Buffalo diocese, Father Carter feels perfectly at home with both clergy and laity. There was a big banquet for the aging pastor, Monsignor McGloin, the night I was there. Father Peter accompanied his venerable pastor to the banquet and shared the limelight with him. Honored as a priest of God, he holds up capably the high ideals of his vocation, and executes the sacred functions of the altar with efficiency and dignity. His high intelligence gives him the same advantage in dealing with minds that his tall stature affords him physically. Small men find nothing in him on which they can look down. Rather, men must look up to him for the spiritual leadership that can be expected from a true priest of God.

CHAPTER XXV

Priests of the Mid-Century

The period after the second World War saw the rise of a new generation of colored priests whose careers were just burgeoning as this study was undertaken. We have noted those who fitted into the various groups that came within the scope of our study, and we wish there was room for individual and intensive treatment of all of them. However, many agreed they would have to live out their lives before they could have biographical sketches filled in.

Many intriguing stories await telling. The full drama of the life of the one who related his story anonymously under the title of "Black Priest" in a postwar issue of the *Catholic Digest* is still to be unfolded. Other diocesan priests and religious order men also will take their place in the annals of the colored priesthood at a later date.

Two diocesan priests whom I had the pleasure of meeting agreed to let me present their up-to-now stories in this collection. They would be the first to disclaim any special title to distinction at present. But their experiences are not atypical in the matter of the difficulties they experienced in pursuing their studies for the priesthood.

Archbishop Rummel of New Orleans, speaking at the Silver Jubilee celebration of St. Augustine's Seminary, pointed toward the clarification of the problem that these men faced when he stated:

> We earnestly look forward to seeing more Negro diocesan priests. For it has never been the idea of the Church that every priest should become a Religious. No doubt there are colored youths who have the urge and vocation to become priests, but do not wish or are not called to shoulder the burden of the Religious Life. Their vocation should not be frustrated, but they should be trained and eventually integrated into the ranks of the secular clergy.

FATHER ALLEN MATTHEW SIMPSON

1918 –

The story of Father Allen Simpson is another saga of persistence. Father Simpson through years of disappointment doggedly clung to his determination to be a priest. He is today, as of this writing, fulfilling his round of priestly duties as an assistant pastor in St. Patrick's Church, Kent, Ohio.

He has gone out of his father's house, out of his native state to achieve the ambition which first became his in 1933 in the small town of Lovilia, Iowa. His parents had taken young Allen to live in Lovilia when he was only a year old. William Simpson and Elsie Chancellor had brought their first child into the world in the village of Bear Creek, Wapello County, Iowa, on January 16, 1918.

It was not until after the family was settled in Lovilia for many years that Allen became interested in the Catholic Church. While in the upper grades of grammar school, he was converted by Father Lambert Heinen, pastor of St. Peter's Church, and was baptized with the other four children of the family June 29, 1930. A year later his mother was also baptized, but though his father took the same course of religious instruction, he could not see the light at that time. He nevertheless willingly allowed the children to be baptized.

Allen finally completed the eighth grade in the public school at Lovilia in 1933. He had been obliged to drop out of school for two full years in the depths of the depression. He went to work as a motorman in a mine that his father partially owned. But all through those years he kept his mind set on something higher than going down a mineshaft. He wanted to be a priest to lift people up to God. During the summer of 1935 he applied for admission to St. Augustine's Seminary in Bay St. Louis. Admitted in the fall, he passed through four years of high school and one of college. Obliged to stay out of school for the 1940-41 season, he resumed his college studies in the fall of

1941 at St. John's University, Collegeville, Minnesota. Transferring to Trinity College, Sioux City, Iowa, later, he received his Bachelor of Arts degree there in 1944.

Bishop Edwin V. O'Hara of Kansas City, Missouri, agreed temporarily to sponsor his seminary training and sent him to Conception Seminary in Missouri for his theology in 1944. In 1946 he was permanently adopted by his present diocese under Bishop James A. McFadden of Youngstown, Ohio. On February 2, 1948, he was ordained by Bishop McFadden at St. Columba's Cathedral in Youngstown.

By that time, his family had moved to Ottumwa in southeastern Iowa. In the Sacred Heart Church there, Father Allen Simpson offered his first solemn High Mass, on February 8, 1948. Father Flanagan of Boys Town, Nebraska, preached the sermon as a tribute to the young priest who had worked with him as a seminarian during the summer vacation of 1946, serving as a counselor.

In the next weeks, Father Allen returned to the scene of his baptism, Lovilia, to offer Mass at St. Peter's Church. His old spiritual father, Rev. Lambert Heinen, had by this time been made pastor of St. Mary's Church in Albia. Thither, the newly ordained priest also journeyed to pay his devoirs to the priest who had done most to develop and encourage his vocation in his early years.

Though there is one Negro parish in the diocese of Youngstown, Bishop McFadden assigned the young priest to an all-white parish, St. Patrick's Church, Kent, Ohio. There he has led the busy life of a parish priest. He has had no difficulties with any of the parishioners, a proof that a Negro priest can function equally as well as a white priest in a white parish.

When you meet Father Simpson, as I did at the Midwest Clergy Conference for Negro Welfare, you are impressed by the quiet, dignified and unobtrusive personality of the man. He is not a pushy self-glorifier but is reticent about himself. He strikes one as a deeply religious man, still imbued with the strictness of the family's Methodist background and still persevering in the habits of his seminary training under the Divine Word Fathers and the Benedictines.

Though serving in an all-white parish, Father Simpson maintains his interest in and conversance with the racial issues that are constantly brought to his attention. He has expressed himself as wishing that something could be done to counteract the legend that colored Catholics do not want priests of their own race to minister to them.

With the quiet and effective services of priests like Father Simpson, the Church could make much more progress among the more than half-million Negroes in Ohio, of whom only about 8,900 were members of the Catholic Church in 1950.

FATHER THOMAS C. JONES

1 9 1 5 –

On the ninth floor of a Nassau Street office building near Foley Square in downtown Manhattan, a young colored priest presides over the office of the American Catholic Board for Colored Missions when its director, Father Edward C. Kramer, is away on his begging tours in behalf of the missions.

As executive secretary of the Board, Father Thomas C. Jones handles the routine office work of the large mission operation, assists in the editing and publication of its organ, *Our Colored Missions,* and in the preparation of the now famous *Annual Report,* which has been a yardstick of progress of the Church's work in the colored mission field ever since it was first published in the 1880's.

A serious, capable, and intense priest, Father Jones goes about his daily task with the quiet persistence of a good executive. Two colored Sisters, Handmaids of the Pure Heart of Mary, who aid in the secretarial work, find him an affable, soft-spoken, and efficient office manager. All of his energies are concentrated on the missions' welfare. The dingy appearance of the office, still wearing a thirty-year-old paint job and still innocent of plush or chromium-plated furniture, manifests plainly that none of the mission money is spent for the comfort of the office force or its executive secretary.

Father Jones speaks with the clipped, clear, and precise pronunciation characteristic of New Yorkers. An upstater, he was born in Albany,

New York, on January 30, 1915, of the only Catholic Negro family in St. Vincent de Paul parish. His parents had all three of their children baptized in infancy at the local church. Thomas attended the parish school along with other children, and persevered through the Vincentian Institute until his graduation in 1933.

As one of the speakers at the graduation ceremony, Thomas gave a strong talk on racial prejudice which was published in the local newspapers. His remarks were not based on personal experience, for he had been singularly free from any contact with prejudice in the genuinely Catholic atmosphere of his native parish and school. But his contact with the barriers of prejudice was soon to come. Shortly before graduation he made known to his pastor, Father William H. Charles, his desire to become a priest. He had secretly nurtured since childhood the hope to follow in the footsteps of the older boys of the parish who had left to study for the diocesan priesthood.

In the summer of 1933 he applied for admission into the diocese in which Father Sherwood Healy had been director of the seminary years before. Notwithstanding the fact that a colored priest had opened the doors of its first seminary and had taught moral theology and canon law for years, the Albany seminary was closed to this young colored aspirant.

It was only through the good offices of Father Edward C. Kramer of the Catholic Board for Colored Missions that Thomas was admitted, in the fall of 1933, to the St. Augustine's Seminary in Bay St. Louis. With the ordination, next year, of the first priests of St. Augustine's, some of Thomas' disappointment was assuaged. He became a devoted friend of Father Vincent Smith and of his other confreres, and knuckled under for the years of training for the religious life. He spent his two years of novitiate at East Troy, Wisconsin, and at Techny, Illinois, pronouncing his first vows at the latter place in 1939.

Back at Bay St. Louis, Thomas pursued his philosophy and theology studies along with his class. By 1941 he had received his minor orders at the hands of Bishop Gerow.

Meanwhile, he turned to writing for *St. Augustine's Messenger*. In 1940 he composed an interesting description of the first annual conference on the Negro in American Catholic Higher Education, held at

Catholic University under the aegis of Father Paul Hanly Furfey. The young seminarian attended the conference and became a charter member of the "Iota Kappa Alpha" (whose three letters stand for Interracial Catholic Advancement), a new organization formed to promote Negro Catholic education under the motto "Unity through Diversity."

In May of the next year appeared an essay "They've Got Religion," in which Thomas discussed the misinterpretation of emotionalism as religion on the part of many colored religionists. Young Frater Jones described the role of intellect and reason, aided by divine grace, as the instruments by which Catholics should plumb the depths of religion to discover its objective foundations in truth. It was a well-reasoned, theologically sound, and gracefully written article. The devotional side of his personality was revealed in a subsequent article next year on Simon of Cyrene, who was depicted as being forced to carry the Cross behind our Lord because he was an African.

In 1943, Thomas decided to transfer from the Divine Word Seminary to a diocesan one, if he could secure a bishop to sponsor him. In company with Father Edward Kramer, he called on Bishop Griffin of Trenton. As a result of the interview, Bishop Griffin agreed to accept both Thomas Jones and Paul Butler for his diocese.

Together, the two seminarians entered the major seminary at St. Vincent's Benedictine Abbey in Latrobe, Pennsylvania. Thomas there completed work for his bachelor's degree, and with his class of nineteen others was ordained to the priesthood on March 17, 1945, by Bishop Griffin.

The young priest offered his first Mass in his native parish of St. Vincent de Paul in Albany, and was then assigned as assistant pastor at St. Thomas' Church, Old Bridge, New Jersey. After a brief interlude as aide to Father Kramer in the office of the Mission Board, he was reassigned as assistant pastor in St. John the Baptist Church in New Brunswick, New Jersey. There he took an active interest in community affairs, serving as a board member on the New Brunswick Community Welfare Council and the Middlesex County Tuberculosis and Health League. He also served in a similar capacity on the New Brunswick Urban League. The Knights of Columbus, who elsewhere have been known to be reluctant about the admission of colored Catholics, inducted him into the Fourth Degree membership in Sayreville, New Jersey.

In 1951, after the death of Bishop Griffin, Father Jones was permanently assigned to work with Father Kramer as executive secretary of the Catholic Board for Mission Work among the Colored People. The Board, headed by Cardinal Spellman, and consisting of Cardinal Stritch, Archbishop Keough of Baltimore, and Bishops Gerow of Natchez, Dearden of Pittsburgh, and Ryan of Burlington, is well served by and well satisfied in their new executive secretary. Living at one of the Harlem churches, and ministering to souls as a diocesan priest, Father Jones has achieved a realization of his early ambition. The quiet influence of his good work is being felt throughout the many missions aided by the Board. And the many readers of *Our Colored Missions* can note evidence of his superior writing skill and his feeling for the spiritually significant trends and developments in his chosen field of work.

OTHER DIOCESAN PRIESTS

In the years immediately before and after the halfway mark in the century, a number of other diocesan colored priests were admitted to the ranks of the American Catholic clergy.

Father Paul Butler was ordained for the Trenton diocese at about the same time as his classmate, Father Thomas C. Jones. A native of Washington, and a one-time student at St. Augustine's Seminary, Father Butler served in the New Jersey diocese for almost five years before his health failed in 1950. He has been on sick leave since that time.

Father James Mosley, a native of Natchez, Mississippi, survived the great disappointment of successive refusals at diocesan seminaries all around the country, until finally Archbishop Edward Howard of Portland, Oregon, accepted him for his Far Western diocese. After his ordination in the summer of 1950, Father Mosley was appointed assistant in the parish of All Saints in Portland, under the vigorous and able leadership of Father Tobin, a priest famous for his work in labor union circles.

In the upper-middle-class parish on the outskirts of Portland, Father Mosley has capably fulfilled the duties of an active assistant. Universally liked, he has functioned as any new priest would, preaching, hearing confessions, teaching catechism, directing parish activities, and mingling in the Catholic life of the parish generally. Tall, well proportioned, athletic, and self-possessed, Father Mosley is a typical young priest, ever gracious, fully secure, alert to the spiritual needs of his people, and deeply conscious of the traditional Catholic reverence for the priesthood.

In the summer of 1951, when Father Tobin was in Rome, an article appeared in one of the local papers intimating that the archbishop would now feel free to step in and remove Father Mosley from his position. Father Mosley went to see Archbishop Howard to reassure himself of his standing with the prelate. The archbishop affirmed that he put his priests where he thought they would do good, and had placed him in All Saints parish with that in mind. He refused to have his policy dictated by anonymous suggestions in the newspapers.

A group of parishioners banded together to write a reply to the insinuation that Father Mosley was not wanted. They signed their names to the reaffirmation of their confidence in the zealous assistant.

At the opposite end of the country, two other diocesan priests were also inducted into the ranks of the diocesan clergy in 1951 and 1952. Father William Rodgers of Brooklyn was ordained for his home diocese and assigned to church work in the Brooklyn area. Father Eugene Hicks, the first colored priest of the archdiocese of New York, was given an assistantship in the Church of Regina Coeli in Hyde Park, an almost exclusively white district. As of the present writing, both are functioning in the quiet routine of neophytes in the priesthood.

In the South, the winter and spring of 1952-53 marked the ordination of the first colored priests for two of the Louisiana dioceses. Father Louis LeDoux, a native of Lake Charles, Louisiana, upon completing his course of theological studies at the Grand Seminary in Montreal, was ordained by Bishop Jeanmard of Lafayette in his own parish of the Sacred Heart in Lake Charles, December 27, 1952. Father LeDoux was assigned to take over the newly constructed Church of St. Mary in Port Barré, replacing Father Austin Chachere who moved to Lawtell, Louisiana, to lay the foundations of another parish for the Catholic Negroes of that rural area.

In the archdiocese of New Orleans, Archbishop Rummell ordained Father Aubrey Osborne, a native of Algiers, Louisiana, and a graduate of Notre Dame Archdiocesan Seminary in the Crescent City. The ordination took place in the St. Louis Cathedral in New Orleans in June, 1953.

RELIGIOUS ORDER MEN

Among the priests of the mid-century years, religious order men still outnumber diocesan priests almost two to one, and the Divine Word Fathers still outdistance all other religious orders in the total number of new priests.

Besides the postwar priests already mentioned, the Divine Word Society presented for ordination, between the years 1945 and 1953, more than a half-dozen ordinands.

Father Mark Figaro, at present an assistant at St. Anselm's Church in Chicago, was the second Divine Word priest from Lafayette, Louisiana. Ordained in 1949, he capably fulfilled the duties as assistant priest in St. Martinville before being transferred to Duson, Louisiana. In 1952 he took up his work in the thriving middle-class parish in Chicago.

Others whose careers were begun at this time include Fathers John LaBauve, Father Leonard Olivier, Father Thaddeus Boucree, and Fathers Carlos and Gerald Lewis, blood brothers from the Canal Zone.

Three young priests were advanced to holy orders in the Congregation of the Holy Ghost Fathers, following in the footsteps, albeit distantly, of Father Joseph Burgess.

Father Leonard Cunningham of Charleston, South Carolina, was the first to be ordained, reaching his goal in 1950 with the June class of new priests. He has been ably serving as assistant in the Holy Ghost Church in Detroit since he finished his studies in 1951.

Father Egbert Figaro, ordained a year later, is at present teaching and prefecting in the minor seminary in Ann Arbor, Michigan, where the Holy Ghost Fathers opened their new institution in 1952.

Father Albert McKnight, the third of the Holy Ghost Fathers, ordained in 1952, was appointed assistant at St. Paul's, Lafayette, Louisiana in 1953.

Another religious order man ordained in 1952 is Father Paul Gopaul, of the Society of St. Edmund. A native of San Francisco, Father Gopaul entered the Edmundite Fathers in Vermont, just as Father Faustina had done. Father Gopaul was ordained May 10, 1952. His first Mass was celebrated in St. Mary's Cathedral in San Francisco, May 18.

The Benedictines of St. John's Abbey in Collegeville, Minnesota, added another Negro priest to their religious order with the ordination of Father Bernardine Patterson, O.S.B. Though born in Arkansas, Bernardine was raised in St. Louis, attending both St. Elizabeth's and St. Nicholas' schools, the latter in the Divine Word Fathers' parish. Some of his seminary training was received at St. Augustine's Seminary at the Bay, but he entered the Benedictine order in 1946, following in the footsteps of Abbot Alcuin's alumni.

Finally, as though completing a full cycle in the development of the colored clergy in the country, Bishop Joseph Bowers personally ordained two Divine Word candidates for the priesthood in June, 1953. Father Vance Thorne, S.V.D., a native of Bath, North Carolina, and Father Hubert Singleton, S.V.D., of Lake Charles, Louisiana, raised to thirty-one the number of priests ordained in and for the Society of the Divine Word. In the summer of 1954, Father Lawrence Thornton became the thirty-second Divine Word Father through his ordination at St. Mary's Mission House in Techny, Illinois, on August 15.

CHAPTER XXVI

The First Hundred Years[1]

In looking back over the hundred years since the ordination of Bishop Healy in Paris in 1854, we find that colored Catholic Americans can enumerate seventy-two priests as their sacred offering to God. This number does not include the dozen or more who have come to the country on visits or for studies. It includes those who were born in the United States, or who came from the islands of the Caribbean to be ordained in and for the United States, exclusive of the five Jamaicans who have been ordained as Jesuit missionaries for work in their home islands.

One question immediately arises: Why were there *only* seventy-two? The implication, often spelled out by DuBois in the *Crisis* magazine, is that this is a very small number, indicative of a policy of non-encouragement of colored vocations.

In the first place, however, the number of seventy-two priests is not abnormally low in comparison with the total number of priests emerging from the twenty-nine million Catholics of the country. Approximately forty-seven thousand priests have come from that vast number of Catholics. The emergence of sixty-eight colored priests from the ranks of less than four hundred thousand colored Catholics is not abnormally low, considering also the few high-school opportunities of the colored Catholic boy.

Nor is the number abnormally low when the statistics relating to seminarians are considered. Slightly less than four hundred colored boys have entered American seminaries. The perseverance of seventy-

[1] Portions of this chapter appeared in *America*, 89 (June 13, 1953), pp. 295-97, under title of "U. S. Colored Priests: Hundred Year Survey." This occurred *before* it was reprinted in a certain weekly newspaper of July 27, 1953, under someone else's by-line, sans permission.

two (about 18 per cent) is approximately the same ratio as with the general body of seminarians in the country. Twenty per cent perseverance of a given class is considered normal, especially when the class begins in minor seminary.

When one takes into account the social and economic condition of colored Catholics, the number is remarkably high. Victims of the anti-Negro and the anti-Catholic types of prejudice and discrimination, colored Catholics of both rural and city slum areas have had a much harder struggle than other minority groups. That this number of seminarians and priests should arise from their midst is a tribute to the strength of their faith and the perseverance of their sons.

More than half of the native American colored priests have been born in the underprivileged areas of the South. Thirty-five are from below the Mason-Dixon Line, twenty-one from the Northeast (including Maryland and the District of Columbia), seven are from the Midwest, and two from the Far West. Only seven of the seventy-two were foreign born.

Of the southern states, Louisiana has contributed the largest number, nineteen. But each of the other states of the Southeast (except Tennessee) has been represented by at least one priest. North Carolina and Virginia both lay claim to Father Clarence Howard, S.V.D., who, though born in North Carolina, was raised and brought into the Church in Norfolk, Virginia. Mississippi is credited with three (Fathers Williams, Porter, and Mosley), and Georgia with a like number (the Healys). Texas is the birthplace for two (Fathers Murphy and Theldon Jones).

New York leads the northern states with a total of nine native sons in the ranks of the colored clergy. New Jersey is next with three, Maryland follows with two. The District of Columbia was the birthplace of six who made the grade.

Washington thus leads all cities in the total number of city-born vocations. New Orleans and New York City both have five priests, Lake Charles and Lafayette three apiece.

It has been obvious from the biographical sketches that very few of the colored priests emerged from upper-class Negro families who were rich or professional people. The vast majority came from families whose struggles were mirrored in the lives of the seminarians and the priests themselves.

It has become obvious in the course of these vignettes that, notwithstanding their socio-economic backgrounds, the more than three-score colored priests could compare favorably, as far as educational achievements are concerned, with any similar clerical group of comparable size selected at random from almost any diocese or religious order.

The roll call of the Catholic colleges and non-Catholic universities which these men have attended is an impressive one. Among the Catholic institutions are: Holy Cross College, Georgetown, Fordham, Catholic University, John Carroll University, Canisius College, Xavier University of New Orleans, Loyola of Chicago, the University of Notre Dame, Loras College (Dubuque), Trinity College (Sioux City), St. John's University (Collegeville), and others in the continental United States. Overseas, they have been educated at the Gregorian University in Rome, at Louvain University, at Charles University (Prague), and at the famous Sulpician Seminary in Paris. The non-Catholic universities include Howard University (Washington), the University of Chicago, the University of Michigan, and Cambridge University in England.

To their credit are as many academic degrees as one would gather in the census of an equal number of clergymen of a diocese or order. There are at least two holders of the degree of Doctor of Divinity; two whose specialization led to degrees in canon law, one a doctorate, the other a licentiate; one with a Doctor of Philosophy degree; three with Master of Arts diplomas; and more than two dozen with regular college undergraduate degrees.

As a consequence of these academic records, a dozen of the colored priests have successfully taught in colleges and seminaries. Their work in this area, while not spectacularly productive in terms of specialists' studies published in book form, has been adequate for the demands of the field. Father Sherwood Healy and Father Uncles both wrote books, but only the former succeeded in publishing his literary efforts.

The most vital area of activity for colored priests, as for any priests, is that of their specifically pastoral work for souls. The experience of the first hundred years, as briefly reviewed in these pages, supplies some of the answers to the two main questions: Does the hierarchy of the Church want to develop the colored priesthood for pastoral work? Do the Catholic people of the country, white and colored, want to have colored priests ministering to their spiritual needs?

Policy for the hierarchy of the Church in matters such as these is set for the whole Church by the Holy Father himself. On the subject of the training of colored clergy both here and elsewhere, the Popes of the past hundred years have been most explicit. Pope Leo XIII in at least two great encyclicals, one in 1893 and the other in 1902, spelled out church policy very carefully. In 1893, writing his letter *Ad Extremas Orientis Oras,* the Supreme Pontiff said:

> If we are resolved to have regard for the salvation of the people of India (and for that matter of all peoples), and to establish a lasting foundation for the Christian name in those vast regions, it is necessary to select from among the natives those who, after careful training, will have to discharge the priestly office and functions. (*Acta Sanctae Sedis,* 25 (1893), p. 718.)

The Holy Father traced this practice back to the Apostles, and maintained that the Roman Pontiffs had everlastingly been in the habit of putting the rest of the hierarchy under the obligation of striving "with might and main to choose a native clergy from among the inhabitants wherever a Christian community was sufficiently well rooted" (*Ibid.* pp. 718-19).

Again in 1902 the same Holy Father repeated this admonition:

> Since it is proved by experience that a native clergy is most useful everywhere, the bishops must make it their care to increase the number of native priests, in such manner, however, as to form them thoroughly in piety and character, and to make sure that they are worthy to be entrusted with ecclesiastical charges. (*Acta Sanctae Sedis,* 35 (1902), p. 271.)

The same policy was reaffirmed in 1919 by Pope Benedict XV in his encyclical *Maximum Illud.* The Pontiff insists:

> The main care of those who rule missions should be to raise and train a clergy from amidst the people among whom they dwell. As the Catholic Church of God is foreign to no nation,

so should every people yield its own sacred ministers. (*Acta Apostolicae Sedis,* 11 (1919), p. 444.)

We have seen how Pope Pius XI applied this policy to the colored clergy of the United States when he wrote his apostolic letter on the occasion of the foundation of St. Augustine's Seminary in Bay St. Louis. His other encyclicals and his official acts re-emphasized the urgency and immediacy of its application. In the encyclical letter in 1926, the Pontiff enlarged upon the need for indigenous clergymen, local seminaries, and religious congregations. He stated:

> We deem it well, Venerable Brethren and Beloved sons, to make known our own mind on certain matters. Before everything else, we call to your attention the importance of building up a native clergy. If you do not work with all your might to attain this purpose, We assert that not only will your apostolate be crippled, but it will become an obstacle and an impediment to the establishment and organization of the Church in those countries. (*Acta Apostolicae Sedis,* 18 (1926), p. 73.)

Pope Pius XII inaugurated his pontificate with a reaffirmation of the same policy. In his first encyclical *Summi Pontificatus,* he maintained:

> Those who enter the Church, whatever be their origin or their speech . . . have equal rights as children in the house of the Lord, where the law of Christ and the peace of Christ prevail. (*AAS,* 31 (1939), p. 549.)

The dramatic consecration of twelve colored missionary bishops in Rome in 1939 further portrayed the papal insistence on the policy of developing the colored Catholic clergy throughout the world. The homily which Pope Pius XII gave at the time elaborated the universality of the Church and of its priesthood, made up of men of all nations. (*Acta Apostolicae Sedis,* 31 (1939), p. 548.)

The acceptance and implementation of this policy on the part of the cardinals, archbishops, and bishops of the United States has not been uniform. But the vast majority of those concerned with the question have agreed with the Holy Father in principle, but have been almost overcautious in putting it into practice. Over thirty years ago, when a seminary was being planned for colored clergy, Pope Benedict XV fended off possible opposition on the part of the hierarchy by saying to one of the founders, "If your fathers have any trouble with bishops, lay the matter before me, and we will see whether the Pope is above the bishops!"

The main evidence that the bishops of the country are in favor of ordaining colored priests is the fact that of the seventy-two ordained in the past hundred years, only twelve have been ordained overseas. Fifty-six have been ordained in the confines of continental United States, twenty-six of these by Bishop Richard O. Gerow, of Natchez, Mississippi. Cardinal Gibbons personally ordained two early Josephites, and other bishops in Minnesota, Washington, Detroit, Connecticut, New York, Trenton, New Orleans, Lafayette, and elsewhere have willingly given this token of their assent to the development of the colored clergy in the United States.

Besides, the tradition of fostering colored boys' vocations, started by Bishop Fitzpatrick of Boston, continued by his successor, Archbishop Williams, and brought down to our day in Boston by Archbishop Cushing, has spread all over the country.

Bishop Jules B. Jeanmard ranks first in the number of colored priests whom he has willingly employed for mission work in his diocese. In 1943 he summed up the results of his first ten years of experience with a mixed clergy in his diocese:

> The advent of the colored priests in the diocese marks a new step in the work for our colored people. The enthusiasm with which they were received and the splendid work they are doing in the three parishes now entirely under their direction, slay for all time the groundless and mischievous myth that colored people did not care to have priests of their own race to minister to them.[1]

Moreover, Bishop Jeanmard became the first southern bishop to admit colored priests to the ranks of the diocesan clergy. He was not, however, the first in the country. Almost a score of other dioceses have incorporated colored priests in the past century. Boston, of course, remains the first; Portland (Maine) the second. But colored priests

---

[1] Letter to Father Clarence Howard, October 19, 1943.

have also been admitted to the archdioceses and dioceses of Springfield, Chicago, Detroit, Lansing, Trenton, Buffalo, Youngstown, Brooklyn, St. Paul, Omaha, Dallas, Los Angeles, Gallup, Portland (Oregon), New York, New Orleans, and Lafayette.

As we have mentioned above, the religious orders have been the major force in the promotion of the colored priesthood in the United States. Of the seventy-two ordained since 1854, forty-six have been members of various religious orders. The first in point of time is the Jesuit order. Through their education of the Healy brothers and their admission of one of them to the ranks of the order, the Jesuits became the first order to have a colored member. Save for the five Jamaicans ordained in the New England Province of the Jesuit order since 1939, no other colored priests have followed Father Patrick Healy's example. Admission of colored novices into the Missouri and Chicago provinces points to a revival of the lapsed tradition.

Second in the point of time, the Sulpician Fathers have had a prominent part to play in the promotion of these vocations. They furnished the seminary training for two of the three Healys; they educated in the sacred sciences the two Josephites ordained by Cardinal Gibbons; and through their theological classes at Catholic University also contributed to the ecclesiastical education of Father Ball.

But by all measures the Society of the Divine Word is justly honored as the foremost promoter of the colored priesthood in the United States. Through their seminary at Bay St. Louis they have not only trained their own thirty-two Divine Word colored priests, but they have also given at least a partial education to another eighteen of the present-day colored Fathers.

Among the other religious orders that played significant roles in the earlier days of the century, we have had occasion to note the contribution of the German Franciscans of Quincy, Illinois (Father Tolton), the Immaculate Heart Fathers (Father Esnard), the old Trinitarians (Father Derricks), the Society of the African Missions (Father John), and the Holy Ghost Fathers (Father Burgess).

These last, as of the present writing, are also represented among the newer Negro clergy by their three new priests, Fathers Cunningham, E. Figaro, and McKnight. Four of the colored priests belong to the

Order of St. Benedict, which has also had a hand in the education of at least three other living colored priests. The Society of St. Edmund counts two colored priests among its adherents up to the recent past, and the Missionary Servants of the Holy Trinity had one. The Society of the Sacred Heart, as we have seen, boasts a lone representative as well.

To the other question as to whether or not the laity, white and colored, desire to secure the ministrations of colored priests, some definite answer has been given in these pages.

Starting with Bishop Healy and his brothers, we have seen that not a single colored priest was confined to an exclusive ministry, serving only one racial group. With all of the living priests the question was pressed carefully by the present writer. In all cases it was discovered that they had ministered the Sacraments alike to white and colored Catholics. In only two cases out of the thousands did it happen that a white person refused to receive the Sacraments from a colored priest. In fact, with the more recently ordained priests, the case has been just the opposite. Demands upon their time and their strength on the part of members of both racial groups have been so insistent as to burden them with too many spiritual occupations. At least one of the newly ordained men seriously jeopardized his health by exhausting himself with the meeting of these demands, especially by white congregations and organizations.

Lastly, the perennial question as to whether colored Catholics want their own priests is affirmatively answered in each of these cases we have examined. The spirit of the welcome that Catholic Aframerica has given to them is captured by the greeting that his Washington parish gave Father Burgess: "You are as welcome as the flowers in May!"

The two cases in which Negro priests were rumored to have come into their own, and their own received them not, turned out to be a baseless conjecture. Father Plantevigne, rumor to the contrary notwithstanding, was not *railroaded* out of town in south Louisiana. Father Dorsey was the victim of a homicidal maniac, himself the victim of a jailhouse brutalization that drove him to insane crime.

We have seen that the colored priest is fully capable of functioning efficiently in all areas of the sacred ministry, both in the domestic parish work and in the foreign missions. Up to the present, eleven American colored priests have been engaged in mission work overseas. Forty-five are still active in educational and pastoral work in the country. The range of their duties runs from routine parish work to mission preaching, retreat giving, and military chaplaincies; from editorial desks to labor-college work; from training other clergy in sacred studies and church music, to youth work in Father Flanagan's famous Boys Town; from executive work on the Catholic Board for Colored Missions, to similar work on the Mission Secretariat of the National Catholic Welfare Conference.

It is an impressive array of achievements. By all the tests that can be applied to the genuineness of priestly work and character, these men of God measure up to the standards of Catholic clergy life as set up by canon law and poised in expectations of the Catholic people.

It has not been our intention in this volume to do anything more than cite the positive achievements of the Catholic colored priests in the first hundred years of their service to God and the Church. We have no desire to revive dead controversies or to open old wounds. Perhaps at some later date the full story of the struggles, difficulties, and discouragements that these men have conquered will be told.

Like St. Paul they have had perils from many sources—"perils from my own nation, perils from the Gentiles, perils in the city, perils in the wilderness, perils from false brethren" (2 Cor. 11:26). They have won through them all to the goal they sought. They have fought a good fight. They have kept the faith.

The apostolate of these colored priests to the whites has been a not insignificant phase of their work. The blindly prejudiced have seen. The deaf have heard. The spiritually impoverished have had the Gospel preached to them by the silent sermons contained in the achievements of these genuine Godsmen of color.

For the furtherance of their achievements in the new century ahead, we can all join in the prayer:

> Keep them, we pray Thee, dearest Lord,
> Keep them for they are Thine—
> Thy priests whose lives burn out
> Before Thy consecrated shrine.

Keep them and comfort them in hours
Of loneliness and pain
When all their lives of sacrifice
For souls seem but in vain.
Keep them, and O remember Lord,
They have no one but Thee,
And yet have only human hearts
With human frailty.
Keep them spotless as the Host
That daily they caress.
Their every thought and word and deed
Deign, dearest Lord, to bless.

Index